SPEECHES THAT DEFINED
THE WORLD

ALAN J. WHITICKER

NEW
HOLLAND

Contents

Introduction

In making a speech one must study three points: first, the means of producing persuasion; second, the language; third the proper arrangement of the various parts of the speech.

Aristotle

Speeches that Defined the World is a collection of the greatest speeches of the 20th Century through to the present day ... speeches that not only shaped and changed the world but ultimately helped define it. The speeches in this special volume, made up of speeches from the bestselling *Speeches that Shaped the Modern World* (2005) and *Speeches that Reshaped the Modern World* (2008) as well as speeches from the new millennium, have also moved us a people – emotionally, politically and even socially.

The speeches in this book reflect the lives and achievements of history's famous and infamous – Mahatma Gandhi, Adolf Hitler, Nelson Mandela, Joseph McCarthy, the Kennedy family, Fidel Castro and Barack Obama to name but a few. Many of these speeches – FDR's 'A Day that will Live in Infamy' in 1941; Martin Luther King's 'I Have a Dream' in 1963, and Queen Elizabeth II's 'Annus Horribilis' in 1992, have become iconic signposts in time. Others, such as Bishop Romero's 'Stop the Repression' in 1980, New Zealand Prime Minister David Lange's Nuclear Disarmament' speech in 1985 and Elie Weisel's 'Perils of Indifference' in 1999 remain relatively unknown.

While many United States leaders are present – Theodore Roosevelt, Dwight D. Eisenhower, Douglas MacArthur, Robert Kennedy and Malcolm X are just some of the people featured in this volume – international leaders are also recognised. It is also heartening to see so many high profile female leaders in this book – Hilary Clinton, Indira Gandhi, Golda Meir and Aung San Suu Kyi, for example – who provide important perspectives on social issues such as equality, human rights and education.

This book is not meant to be a definitive list of the 'greatest' speeches of all time – that has been already done by other authors. This eclectic group of speeches reinforce recurring themes such as politics, war and peace, freedom and justice, civil rights and human rights and cover many of the historic events and issues of the past century. Speeches that have already resonated with the world over time and still speak to us. Included in this volume are speeches by Steve Jobs, Stephen Hawking, Julia Gillard, Malala Yousafzai, Pope Francis and out-going US President Barack Obama.

As author and editor, I have endeavoured to provide an historical context for each speech and a biographical background of each speaker. Wherever possible, however, I avoided offering my own critique of the merits of each speech. Let the words speak for themselves … they are, after all, the speeches that defined the world.

Alan Whiticker

Mary Church Terrell

'Being Colored in the Nation's Capital'

Speech to United Women's Club, Washington, DC, 10 October 1906.

T he life of Mary Church Terrell (1863-1954) bridged an expanse of history from the emancipation of the slaves in the American Civil War (1861-65) to the US Supreme Court decision to end segregation in schools (*Brown v Board of Education*, 1954).

Terrell spent her life at the forefront of the fight for civil rights. In 1884 she was the first African-American woman to earn a college degree and later studied education in Europe for two years. A high school teacher and principal, she became the first black woman in America to be appointed to an Education Board (District of Columbia).

As the first president of the National Association of Colored Women, Mary Church Terrell spoke out in support of women's suffrage and an end to racial segregation. In October 1906, Terrell addressed the United Women's Club in Washington DC about the discrimination faced by black women because of both their race and their gender. Terrell's speech is considered to be one of the most influential speeches on race in the 20th century.

❮ Washington DC has been called 'The Colored Man's Paradise'. Whether this sobriquet was given to the national capital in bitter irony by a member of the handicapped race, as he reviewed some of his own persecutions and rebuffs, or whether it was given immediately after the war by an ex-slaveholder who for the first time in his life saw colored people walking about like free men, minus the overseer and his whip, history saith not. It is certain that it would be difficult to find a worse misnomer for Washington than 'The Colored

Man's Paradise' if so prosaic a consideration as veracity is to determine the appropriateness of a name.

For fifteen years I have resided in Washington, and while it was far from being a paradise for colored people when I first touched these shores, it has been doing its level best ever since to make conditions for us intolerable. As a colored woman I might enter Washington any night, a stranger in a strange land, and walk miles without finding a place to lay my head. Unless I happened to know colored people who live here or ran across a chance acquaintance who could recommend a colored boarding-house to me, I should be obliged to spend the entire night wandering about. Indians, Chinamen, Filipinos, Japanese and representatives of any other dark race can find hotel accommodations, if they can pay for them. The colored man alone is thrust out of the hotels of the national capital like a leper...

As a colored woman I cannot visit the tomb of the Father of this Country, which owes its very existence to the love of freedom in the human heart and which stands for equal opportunity to all, without being forced to sit in the Jim Crow section of an electric car which starts from the very heart of the city—midway between the Capitol and the White House. If I refuse thus to be humiliated, I am cast into jail and forced to pay a fine for violating the Virginia laws...

As a colored woman I may enter more than one white church in Washington without receiving that welcome which as a human being I have a right to expect in the sanctuary of God. Sometimes the color blindness of the usher takes on that peculiar form which prevents a dark face from making any impression whatsoever upon his retina, so that it is impossible for him to see colored people at all. If he is not so afflicted, after keeping a colored man or woman waiting a long time, he will ungraciously show these dusky Christians who have had the temerity to thrust themselves into a temple where only the fair of face are expected to worship God to a seat in the rear, which is named in honor of a certain personage, well known in this country, and commonly called Jim Crow.

Unless I am willing to engage in a few menial occupations, in which the pay for my services would be very poor, there is no way for me to earn an honest living, if I am not a trained nurse or a dressmaker or can secure a position as a teacher in the public schools, which is exceedingly difficult to do. It matters not what my intellectual attainments may be or how great is the need of the services of a competent person, if I try to enter many of the numerous vocations in which my white sisters are allowed to engage, the door is shut in my face.

From one Washington theater I am excluded altogether ... [After explaining that] in some of the theaters colored nurses were allowed to sit with the white children for whom they cared, the ticket seller told me that in Washington it was very poor policy to employ colored nurses, for they were excluded from many places where white girls would be allowed to take children for pleasure.

If I possess artistic talent, there is not a single art school of repute which will admit me. A few years ago a colored woman who possessed great talent submitted some drawings to the Corcoran Art School, of Washington, which were accepted by the committee of awards, who sent her a ticket entitling her to a course in this school. But when the committee discovered that the young woman was colored, they declined to admit her, and told her that if they had suspected that her drawings had been made by a colored woman, they would not have examined them at all...

With the exception of the Catholic University, there is not a single white college in the national capital to which colored people are admitted, no matter how great their ability, how lofty their ambition, how unexceptionable their character or how great their thirst for knowledge may be. A few years ago the Columbian Law School [in Washington] admitted colored students, but in deference to the Southern white students the authorities have decided to exclude them altogether...

I might go on citing instance after instance to show the variety of ways in which our people are sacrificed on the altar of prejudice in the capital of the United States and how almost insurmountable are the obstacles which block our paths to success. Early in life many a colored youth is so appalled by the helplessness and the hopelessness of his situation in this country that, in a sort of stoical despair he resigns himself to his fate. 'What is the good of our trying to acquire an education? We can't all be preachers, teachers, doctors and lawyers. Besides those professions, there is almost nothing for colored people to do but engage in the most menial occupations, and we do not need an education for that.' More than once such remarks, uttered by young men and women in our public schools who possess brilliant intellects, have wrung my heart.

It is impossible for any white person in the United States, no matter how sympathetic and broadminded, to realize what life would mean to him if his incentive to effort were suddenly snatched away. To the lack of incentive to effort, which is the awful shadow under which we live, may be traced the wreck and ruin of scores of colored youth. And surely nowhere in the world do oppression and persecution based solely on the color of the skin appear more hateful and hideous than in the capital of the United States, because the chasm between the principles upon which this Government was founded, in which it still professes to believe, and those which are daily practiced under the protection of the flag, yawns so wide and deep. ’

The fact that Church Terrell's speech was delivered in the national capital— the centre of American democracy—contrasted the ideals of the country's founding fathers with the realities experienced by many of the city's minorities. Martin Luther King exposed the same paradox 57 years later when he delivered his famous 'I Have a Dream' speech on the steps of the Lincoln Memorial (see Revolution, 1960-69).

In 1953, a year before her death at 91, Mary Church Terrell led a campaign to end the segregation of public facilities in Washington, DC.

Theodore Roosevelt

'The Man with the Muck-Rake'

Laying the cornerstone of the House of Representatives, Washington DC, 1906.

Theodore 'Teddy' Roosevelt (1858-1919) became the twenty-sixth President of the United States in September 1901 upon the assassination of President William McKinley. He was re-elected for a second term in 1904.

Roosevelt was leader of the New York legislature at the age of 26, and came back from the Cuban War in 1898 as a hero after raising a volunteer army known as 'Roosevelt's Roughriders'. Elected Republican Vice-President in 1900 he was a popular, idiosyncratic public speaker. In 1900 he used a West African proverb that became the motto of his political career: 'Speak quietly but carry a big stick.'

In this famous speech delivered at the laying of the cornerstone of the House of Representatives in Washington DC in 1906, Roosevelt established a new idiom—the muck-raking journalist—when he cleverly compared the political and journalistic 'mudslinging' of his time with a character from John Bunyon's *The Pilgrim's Progress* of 1684. It was a trend that would dominate the mass media during the entire twentieth century and beyond.

❛Over a century ago Washington laid the cornerstone of the Capitol in what was then little more than a tract of wooded wilderness here beside the Potomac. We now find it necessary to provide great additional buildings for the business of the government. This growth in the need for the housing of the government is but a proof and example of the way in which the nation has grown and the sphere of action of the National Government has grown. We now administer the affairs of a nation in which the extraordinary growth of population has been outstripped by the growth of wealth and the growth in complex interests.

The material problems that face us today are not such as they were in Washington's time, but the underlying facts of human nature are the same now as they were then. Under altered external form we war with the same tendencies toward evil that were evident in Washington's time, and are helped by the same tendencies for good.

It is about some of these that I wish to say a word to-day. In Bunyan's *Pilgrim's Progress* you may recall the description of the 'man with the muck-rake', the man who could look no way but downward, with the muck-rake in his hand; who was offered a celestial crown for his muck-rake, but who would neither look up nor regard the crown he was offered, but continued to rake to himself the filth of the floor.

In *Pilgrim's Progress,* the 'man with the muck-rake' is set forth as the example of him whose vision is fixed on carnal instead of on spiritual things. Yet he also typifies the man who in this life consistently refuses to see aught that is lofty, and fixes his eyes with solemn intentness only on that which is vile and debasing. Now, it is very necessary that we should not flinch from seeing what is vile and debasing. There is filth on the floor and it must be scraped up with the muck-rake; and there are times and places where this service is the most needed of all the services that can be performed. But the man who never does anything else, who never thinks or speaks or writes, save of his feats with the muck-rake, speedily becomes, not a help to society, not an incitement to good, but one of the most potent forces for evil.

There are, in the body politic, economic and social, many and grave evils, and there is urgent necessity for the sternest war upon them. There should be relentless exposure of and attack upon every evil man whether politician or business man, every evil practice, whether in politics, in business, or in social life. I hail as a benefactor every writer or speaker, every man who, on the platform, or in book, magazine, or newspaper, with merciless severity makes such attack, provided always that he in his turn remembers that the attack is of use only if it is absolutely truthful. The liar is no whit better than the thief, and if his mendacity takes the form of slander, he may be worse than most thieves. It puts a premium upon knavery untruthfully to attack an honest man, or even with hysterical exaggeration to assail a bad man with untruth. An epidemic of indiscriminate assault upon character does not good, but very great harm. The soul of every scoundrel is gladdened whenever an honest man is assailed, or even when a scoundrel is untruthfully assailed.

Now, it is easy to twist out of shape what I have just said, easy to affect to misunderstand it, and, if it is slurred over in repetition, not difficult really to misunderstand it. Some persons are sincerely incapable of understanding that to denounce mud-slinging does not mean the endorsement of whitewashing; and both the interested individuals who need whitewashing, and those others who practice mud-slinging, like to encourage such confusion of ideas. One of the chief counts against those who make indiscriminate assault upon men in business or men in public life, is that they invite a reaction which is sure to tell powerfully in favor of the unscrupulous scoundrel who really ought to be attacked, who ought to be exposed, who ought, if possible, to be put in the penitentiary. If Aristides is praised overmuch as just, people get tired of hearing it; and over censure of the unjust finally and from similar reasons results in their favor.

Any excess is almost sure to invite a reaction; and, unfortunately, the reaction, instead of taking the form of punishment of those guilty of the excess, is very apt to take the form either of punishment of the unoffending or of giving immunity, and even strength, to offenders. The effort to make financial or political profit out of the destruction of character can only result in public calamity.

Gross and reckless assaults on character, whether on the stump or in newspaper, magazine, or book, create a morbid and vicious public sentiment, and at the same time act as a profound deterrent to able men of normal sensitiveness and tend to prevent them from entering the public service at any price.

As an instance in point, I may mention that one serious difficulty encountered in getting the right type of men to dig the Panama Canal is the certainty that they will be exposed, both without, and, I am sorry to say, sometimes within, Congress, to utterly reckless assaults on their character and capacity.

At the risk of repetition let me say again that my plea is not for immunity from the most unsparing exposure of the politician who betrays his trust, or the big business man who makes or spends his fortune in illegitimate or corrupt ways. There should be a resolute effort to hunt every such man out of the position he has disgraced. Expose the crime, and hunt down the criminal; but remember that even in the case of crime, if it is attacked in sensational, lurid, and untruthful fashion, the attack may do more damage to the public mind than the crime itself. It is because I feel that there should be no rest in the endless war against the forces of evil that I ask that the war be conducted with sanity as well as with resolution.

The men with the muck-rakes are often indispensable to the well-being of society; but only if they know when to stop raking the muck, and to look upward to the celestial crown above them, to the crown of worthy endeavor.

There are beautiful things above and roundabout them; and if they gradually grow to feel that the whole world is nothing but muck, their power of usefulness is gone. If the whole picture is painted black there remains no hue whereby to single out the rascals for distinction from their fellows. Such painting finally induces a kind of moral color-blindness; and people affected by it come to the conclusion that no man is really black, and no man is really white, but they are all gray. In other words, they neither believe in the truth of the attack, nor in the honesty of the man who is attacked; they grow as suspicious of the accusation as of the offense; it becomes well-nigh hopeless to stir them either to wrath against wrong-doing or to enthusiasm for what is right; and such a mental attitude in the public gives hope to every knave, and is the despair of honest men.

To assail the great and admitted evils of our political and industrial life with such crude and sweeping generalizations as to include decent men in the general condemnation means the searing of the public conscience. There results a general attitude either of cynical belief in and indifference to public corruption or else of a distrustful inability to discriminate between the good and the bad. Either attitude is fraught with untold damage to the country as a whole. The fool who has not sense to discriminate between what is good and what is bad is well-nigh as dangerous as the man who does discriminate and yet chooses the bad. There is nothing more distressing to every good patriot, to every good American, than the hard, scoffing spirit which treats the allegation of dishonesty in a public man as a cause for laughter.

Such laughter is worse than the crackling of thorns under a pot, for it denotes not merely the vacant mind, but the heart in which high emotions have been choked before they could grow to fruition.

There is any amount of good in the world, and there never was a time when loftier and more disinterested work for the betterment of mankind was being done than now. The forces that tend for evil are great and terrible, but the forces of truth and love and courage and honesty and generosity and sympathy are also stronger than ever before. It is a foolish and timid, no less than a wicked, thing to blink the fact that the forces of evil are strong, but it is even worse to fail to take into account the strength of the forces that tell for good.

Hysterical sensationalism is the very poorest weapon wherewith to fight for lasting righteousness. The men who with stern sobriety and truth assail the many evils of our time, whether in the public press or in magazines, or in books, are the leaders and allies of all engaged in the work for social and political betterment. But if they give good reason for distrust of what they say, if they chill the ardor of those who demand truth as a primary virtue, they thereby betray the good cause, and play into the hands of the very men against whom they are nominally at war ... ,

'Teddy' Roosevelt won the Nobel Peace prize in 1906 for helping to negotiate an end to the Russo-Japanese War (1904-05) but was not afraid to exercise an 'expansionist' foreign policy during his career. He invaded Panama in order to protect the building of the Panama Canal and intervened in the Philippines, but he was also a vigorous reformer of government social policy and introduced the 'Square Deal' reform. Roosevelt stood as a Progressive Party candidate at the 1912 presidential election but was defeated by Democratic nominee Woodrow Wilson. Roosevelt was a supporter of United States intervention in World War I long before it acted in 1917. He passed away in 1919.

Emmeline Pankhurst

'Freedom or Death'

Fundraising Speech, Hartford, Connecticut, United States, 13 November 1913.

Emmeline Pankhurst (1857-1928) is arguably the most famous representative of the struggle for Votes for Women. The English barrister drafted the first women's suffrage bill in Britain and founded the Women's Franchise League in 1899.

Pankhurst took the fight for women's suffrage to a new level. Public demonstrations and rallies often resulted in police violence and the arrest of her and her followers. Under arrest, Pankhurst and her fellow suffragettes staged hunger and thirst strikes and had to be force-fed by the police—usually through a funnel thrust down their throats. The police released the women until they were nursed back to health and re-arrested them. The cycle—known as the 'cat and mouse game'—would start all over again. The damage to the women's health was 'astounding', and Pankhurst would often speak at rallies from a stretcher.

In November 1913 Pankhurst made her third 'fundraising' tour of the United States, where her tactics had received widespread publicity since the turn of the century.

'I do not come here as an advocate, because whatever position the suffrage movement may occupy in the United States of America, in England it has passed beyond the realm of advocacy and it has entered into the sphere of practical politics. It has become the subject of revolution and civil war, and so tonight I am not here to advocate women's suffrage. American suffragists can do that very well for themselves. I am here as a soldier who has temporarily left the field of battle in order to explain—it seems strange it should have to be explained—what civil war is like when civil war is waged by women. I am not only here as a soldier temporarily absent from the field of battle; I am here—and that, I think, is the strangest part of my coming—I am here as a person who, according to the law courts of my country, it has been decided, is of no value to the community at all; and I am adjudged because of my life to be a dangerous person, under sentence of penal servitude in a convict prison. So you see there is some special interest in hearing so unusual a person address you. I dare say, in the minds of many of you—you will perhaps forgive me this personal touch—that I do not look either very like a soldier or very like a convict, and yet I am both.

It would take too long to trace the course of militant methods as adopted by women, because it is about eight years since the word militant was first used to describe what we were doing; it is about eight years since the first militant action was taken by women. It was not militant at all, except that it provoked militancy on the part of those who were opposed to it. When women asked questions in political meetings and failed to get answers, they were not doing anything militant. To ask questions at political meetings is an acknowledged right of all people who attend public meetings; certainly in my country, men have always done it, and I hope they do it in America, because it seems to me that if you allow people to enter your legislatures without asking them any questions as to what they are going to do when they get there you are not exercising your citizen rights and your citizen duties as you ought.

At any rate in Great Britain it is a custom, a time-honoured one, to ask questions of candidates for Parliament, and ask questions of members of the government. No man was ever put out of a public meeting for asking a question until Votes for Women came on to the political horizon. The first people who were put out of a political meeting for asking questions were women; they were brutally ill-used; they found themselves in jail before twenty-four hours had expired. But instead of the newspapers, which are largely inspired by the politicians, putting militancy, and the reproach of militancy, if reproach there is, on the people who had assaulted the women, they actually said it was the women who were militant and very much to blame.

It was not the speakers on the platform who would not answer them who were to blame, or the ushers at the meeting; it was the poor women who had had their bruises and their knocks and scratches, and who were put into prison for doing precisely nothing but holding a protest meeting in the street after it was all over. However, we were called militant for doing that, and we were quite willing to accept the name, because militancy for us is time-honoured; you have the church militant and in the sense of spiritual militancy we were very militant indeed. We were determined to press this question of the enfranchisement of the women to the point where we were no longer to be ignored by the politicians as had been the case for about fifty years, during which time women had patiently used every means open to them to win their political enfranchisement.

Experience will show you that if you really want to get anything done, it is not so much a matter of whether you alienate sympathy; sympathy is a very unsatisfactory thing if it is not practical sympathy. It does not matter to the practical suffragist whether she alienates sympathy that was never of any use to her. What she wants is to get something practical done, and whether it is done out of sympathy or whether it is done out of fear, or whether it is done because you want to be comfortable again and not be worried in this way, doesn't particularly matter so long as you get it. We had enough of sympathy for fifty years; it never brought us anything; and we would rather have an angry man going to the government and saying, my business is interfered with and I won't submit to its being interfered with any longer because you won't give women the vote, than to have a gentleman come on to our platforms year in and year out and talk about his ardent sympathy with woman suffrage.

'Put them in prison,' they said, 'that will stop it.' But it didn't stop it. They put women in prison for long terms of imprisonment, for making a nuisance of themselves—that was the expression when they took petitions in their hands to the door of the House of Commons; and they thought that sending them to prison, giving them a day's imprisonment, would cause them to all settle down again and there would be no further trouble. But it didn't happen so at all: instead of the women giving it up, more women did it, and more and more and more women did it until there were three hundred women at a time, who had not broken a single law, only 'made a nuisance of themselves' as the politicians say.

The whole argument with the anti-suffragists, or even the critical suffragist man, is this: that you can govern human beings without their consent. They have said to us, 'Government rests upon force; the women haven't force, so they must submit.' Well, we are showing them that government does not rest upon force at all; it rests upon consent. As long as women consent to be unjustly governed, they can be; but directly women say: 'We withhold our consent, we will not be governed any longer so long as that government is unjust,' not by the forces of civil war can you govern the very weakest woman. You can kill that woman, but she escapes you then; you cannot govern her. And that is, I think, a most valuable demonstration we have been making to the world.

Now, I want to say to you who think women cannot succeed, we have brought the government of England to this position, that it has to face this alternative; either women are to be killed or women are to have the vote. I ask American men in this meeting, what would you say if in your State you were faced with that alternative, that you must either kill them or give them their citizenship—women, many of whom you respect, women whom you know have lived useful lives, women whom you know, even if you do not know them personally, are animated with the highest motives, women who are in pursuit of liberty and the power to do useful public service? Well, there is only one answer to that alternative; there is only one way out of it, unless you are prepared to put back civilization two or three generations; you must give those women the vote. Now that is the outcome of our civil war.

You won your freedom in America when you had the Revolution, by bloodshed, by sacrificing human life. You won the Civil War by the sacrifice of human life when you decided to emancipate the negro. You have left it to the women in your land, the men of all civilised countries have left it to women, to work out their own salvation. That is the way in which we women of England are doing. Human life for us is sacrificed, but we say if any life is to be sacrificed it shall be ours; we won't do it ourselves, but we will put the enemy in the position where they will have to choose between giving us freedom or giving us death. ,

Emmeline Pankhurst was detained on Ellis Island Immigration Station, New York during this tour, which was not unusual for her. She was arrested several times during her life—for conspiracy in 1912 and for inciting violence under the 'Cat and Mouse' Act in 1913. (She was arrested twelve times during 1914.) Her call was 'freedom or death' and some took Pankhurst at her word. In June 1913, suffragette Emily Davidson threw herself in front of King George V's horse, Anmer, as it competed in the English Derby. The 40 year old Miss Davidson lingered on for six days before she died—the women's movement's first heroine and martyr.

Despite New Zealand granting women the vote in 1889 (the first country to do so) and Australian women achieving suffrage in 1902, World War I put the issue of 'Votes for Women' in England and the United States on hold for four years. In England, women over the age of thirty were finally granted the vote in 1918 with full suffrage achieved in 1928. In 1920 the Nineteenth Amendment to the US Constitution was passed giving American women the right to vote, one year after Pankhurst had returned to America and settled in Canada after remarrying.

Historians now credit the work of suffragists Millicent Fawcett (England) and Carrie Chapman Catt (USA) as the driving force which led to women achieving the right to vote in the two largest democracies in the world at the time. However, it was Emmeline Pankhurst who put the movement—through her own example and sacrifice—on the world stage.

Helen Keller

'Against the War'

Carnegie Hall, New York City, 5 January 1916

With the rest of the world engulfed in a catastrophic war in Europe, there was a concerted push within the United States of America for the elected government to reverse its isolationist stance and enter the conflict. One of the many voices calling out against American involvement in World War I (1914–1918)—and conscription of its troops—was that of author and lecturer Helen Keller (1880–1968).

After losing her sight and hearing when she contracted meningitis as an infant, Keller had been taught to speak, read and write by teacher Anne Sullivan.

Keller, who obtained her degree in 1904, had already published her autobiography, *The Story of My Life*, and had since established a career as a respected lecturer and author.

On 5 January 1916, Helen Keller addressed a gathering under the auspices of the Women's Peace Party and the Labor Forum at Carnegie Hall, New York City.

❛To begin with, I have a word to say to my good friends, the editors, and others who are moved to pity me. Some people are grieved because they imagine I am in the hands of unscrupulous persons who lead me astray and persuade me to espouse unpopular causes and make me the mouthpiece of their propaganda.

Now, let it be understood once and for all that I do not want their pity; I would not change places with one of them. I know what I am talking about. My sources of information are as good and reliable as anybody else's. I have papers and magazines from England, France, Germany and Austria that I can read myself. Not all the editors I have met can do that. Quite a number of them have to take their French and German second hand. No, I will not disparage the editors. They are an overworked, misunderstood class. Let them remember, though, that if I cannot see the fire at the end of their cigarettes, neither can they thread a needle in the dark. All I ask, gentlemen, is a fair field and no favor. I have entered the fight against preparedness and against the economic system under which we live. It is to be a fight to the finish and I ask no quarter.

The future of the world rests in the hands of America. The future of America rests on the backs of 80 million working men and women and their children. We are facing a grave crisis in our national life. The few who profit from the labor of the masses want to organize the workers into an army which will protect the interests of the capitalists. You are urged to add to the heavy burdens you already bear, the burden of a larger army and many additional warships. It is in your power to refuse to carry the artillery and the dreadnoughts and to shake off some of the burdens, too, such as limousines, steam yachts and country estates. You do not need to make a great noise about it. With the silence and dignity of creators you can end wars and the system of selfishness and exploitation that causes wars. All you need to do to bring about this stupendous revolution is to straighten up and fold your arms.

We are not preparing to defend our country. Even if we were as helpless as Congressman Gardner says we are, we have no enemies foolhardy enough to attempt to invade the United States. The talk about attack from Germany and Japan is absurd. Germany has its hands full and will be busy with its own affairs for some generations after the European war is over.

With full control of the Atlantic Ocean and the Mediterranean Sea, the allies failed to land enough men to defeat the Turks at Gallipoli; and then they failed again to land an army at Salonica in time to check the Bulgarian invasion of Serbia. The conquest of America by water is a nightmare confined exclusively to ignorant persons and members of the Navy League.

Yet, everywhere, we hear fear advanced as argument for armament. It reminds me of a fable I read. A certain man found a horseshoe. His neighbor began to weep and wail because, as he justly pointed out, the man who found the horseshoe might some day find a horse. Having found the shoe, he might shoe him. The neighbor's child might some day go so near the horse's heels as to be kicked, and die. Undoubtedly the two families would quarrel and fight and several valuable lives would be lost through the finding of the horseshoe.

You know, the last war we had we quite accidentally picked up some islands in the Pacific Ocean which may some day be the cause of a quarrel between ourselves and Japan. I'd rather drop those islands right now and forget about them than go to war to keep them. Wouldn't you?

Congress is not preparing to defend the people of the United States. It is planning to protect the capital of American speculators and investors in Mexico, South America, China and the Philippine Islands. Incidentally, this preparation will benefit the manufacturers of munitions and war machines.

Until recently there were uses in the United States for the money taken from the workers. But American labor is exploited almost to the limit now and our national resources have all been appropriated. Still the profits keep piling up new capital. Our flourishing industry in implements of murder is filling the vaults of New York's banks with gold. And a dollar that is not being used to make a slave of some human being is not fulfilling its purpose in the capitalistic scheme. That dollar must be invested in South America, Mexico, China or the Philippines...

Every modern war has had its root in exploitation. The Civil War was fought to decide whether the slave holders of the South or the capitalists of the North should exploit the West. The Spanish-American War decided that the United States should exploit Cuba and the Philippines. The South African War decided that the British should exploit the diamond mines. The Russo-Japanese War decided that Japan should exploit Korea. The present war is to decide who shall exploit the Balkans, Turkey, Persia, Egypt, India, China, Africa. And we are whetting our sword to scare the victors into sharing the spoils with us. Now, the workers are not interested in the spoils; they will not get any of them anyway.

The preparedness propagandists have still another object, and a very important one. They want to give the people something to think about besides their own unhappy condition. They know the cost of living is high, wages are low, employment is uncertain and will be much more so when the European call for munitions stops. No matter how hard and incessantly the people work, they often cannot afford the comforts of life; many cannot obtain the necessities.

Every few days we are given a new war scare to lend realism to their propaganda. They have had us on the verge of war over the *Lusitania*, the *Gulflight*, the *Ancona*, and now they want the working men to become excited over the sinking of the *Persia*. The working man has no interest in any of these ships. The Germans might sink every vessel on the Atlantic Ocean and the Mediterranean Sea and kill Americans with every one—the American working man would still have no reason to go to war.

All the machinery of the system has been set in motion. Above the complaint and din of the protest from the workers is heard the voice of authority.

"Friends," it says, "fellow workmen, patriots; your country is in danger! There are foes on all sides of us. There is nothing between us and our enemies except the Pacific Ocean and the Atlantic Ocean. Look at what has happened to Belgium. Consider the fate of Serbia. Will you murmur about low wages when your country—your very liberties—are in jeopardy? What are the miseries you endure compared to the humiliation of having a victorious German army sail up the East River? Quit your whining, get busy and prepare to defend your firesides and your flag. Get an army, get a navy; be ready to meet the invaders like the loyal-hearted free men you are."

Will the workers walk into this trap? Will they be fooled again? I am afraid so. The people have always been amenable to oratory of this sort. The workers know they have no enemies except their masters. They know that their citizenship papers are no warrant for the safety of themselves or their wives and children. They know that honest sweat, persistent toil and years of struggle bring them nothing worth holding on to, worth fighting for. Yet, deep down in their foolish hearts they believe they have a country. Oh blind vanity of slaves!

The clever ones, up in the high places, know how childish and silly the workers are. They know that if the government dresses them up in khaki and gives them a rifle and starts them off with a brass band and waving banners, they will go forth to fight valiantly for their own enemies. They are taught that brave men die for their country's honor. What a price to pay for an abstraction—the lives of millions of young men; other millions crippled and blinded for life; existence made hideous for still more millions of human beings; the achievement and inheritance of generations swept away in a moment-and nobody better off for all the misery!

This terrible sacrifice would be comprehensible if the thing you die for and call country fed, clothed, housed and warmed you, educated and cherished your children. I think the workers are the most unselfish of the children of men; they toil and live and die for other people's country, other people's sentiments, other people's liberties and other people's happiness! The workers have no liberties of their own; they are not free when they are compelled to work twelve or ten or eight hours a day. They are not free when they are ill-paid for their exhausting toil. They are not free when their children must labor in mines, mills and factories or starve and when their women may be driven by poverty to lives of shame. They are not free when they are clubbed and imprisoned because they go on strike for a raise of wages and for the elemental justice that is their right as human beings.

We are not free unless the men who frame and execute the laws represent the interests of the lives of the people and no other interest. The ballot does not make a free man out of a wage slave. There has never existed a truly free and democratic nation in the world. From time immemorial, men have followed with blind loyalty the strong men who had the power of money and of armies. Even while battlefields were piled high with their own dead, they have tilled the lands of the rulers and have been robbed of the fruits of their labor. They have built palaces and pyramids, temples and cathedrals that held no real shrine of liberty.

As civilization has grown more complex, the workers have become more and more enslaved, until today they are little more than parts of the machines they operate. Daily they face the dangers of railroad, bridge, skyscraper, freight train, stokehold, stockyard, lumber raft and mine. Panting and straining at the docks, on the railroads and underground and on the seas, they move the traffic and pass from land to land the precious commodities that make it possible for us to live. And what is their reward? A scanty wage, often poverty, rents, taxes, tributes and war indemnities.

The kind of preparedness the workers want is reorganization and reconstruction of their whole life, such as has never been attempted by statesmen or governments. The Germans found out years ago that they could not raise good soldiers in the slums, so they abolished the slums. They saw to it that all the people had at least a few of the essentials of civilization—decent lodging, clean streets, wholesome if scanty food, proper medical care and proper safeguards for the workers in their occupations. That is only a small part of what should be done, but what wonders that one step toward the right sort of preparedness has wrought for Germany! For eighteen months it has kept itself free from invasion while carrying on an extended war of conquest and its armies are still pressing on with unabated vigor. It is your business to force these reforms on the administration. Let there be no more talk about what a government can or cannot do. All these things have been done by all the belligerent nations in the hurly-burly of war. Every fundamental industry has been managed better by the governments than by private corporations.

It is your duty to insist upon still more radical measures. It is your business to see that no child is employed in an industrial establishment or mine or store and that no worker is needlessly exposed to accident or disease. It is your business to make them give you clean cities, free from smoke, dirt and congestion. It is your business to make them pay you a living wage. It is your business to see that this kind of preparedness is carried into every department of the nation, until everyone has a chance to be well born, well nourished, rightly educated, intelligent and serviceable to the country at all times.

Strike against all ordinances and laws and institutions that continue the slaughter of peace and the butcheries of war. Strike against war, for without you no battles can be fought. Strike against manufacturing shrapnel and gas bombs and all other tools of murder. Strike against preparedness that means death and misery to millions of human being. Be not dumb, obedient slaves in an army of destruction. Be heroes in an army of construction. '

Helen Keller's remarkable story was later immortalised in William Gibson's stage play, *The Miracle Worker*. The film version, which was released in 1962, won Academy Awards for Anne Bancroft (as Anne Sullivan) and teenager Patty Duke, as Helen Keller, who both reprised their Broadway roles.

Woodrow Wilson

'Fourteen-Point Peace Plan'

Washington DC, 8 January 1918

I n January 1918, US President Woodrow Wilson (1856–1924) appeared before a joint session of the US Congress and outlined possible peace terms to end the so called Great War of 1914–1918. The fourteen points outlined in this speech served as both the basis for peace and the establishment of a League of Nations aimed at promoting 'post-war understanding and peaceful relations'.

The League of Nations would rise above national governments, Wilson maintained, and be the guardian of liberty for the people of the world. 'We must concert our best judgment,' he said, 'to make the League of Nations a vital thing—not merely a formal thing, not an occasional thing, not a thing sometimes called into life to meet an exigency—but always functioning in watchful attendance upon the interests of the nations, and that its continuity should be a vital continuity.'

❛ ...It will be our wish and purpose that the processes of peace, when they are begun, shall be absolutely open and that they shall involve and permit henceforth no secret understandings of any kind. The day of conquest and aggrandizement is gone by. So is also the day of secret covenants entered into in the interest of particular governments and likely at some unlooked-for moment to upset the peace of the world. It is this happy fact, now clear to the view of every public man whose thoughts do not still linger in an age that is dead and gone, which makes it possible for every nation whose purposes are consistent with justice and the peace of the world to avow now or at any other time the objects it has in view.

We entered this war because violations of right had occurred which touched us to the quick and made the life of our own people impossible unless they were corrected and the world secured once and for all against their recurrence.

What we demand in this war, therefore, is nothing peculiar to ourselves. It is that the world be made fit and safe to live in; and particularly that it be made safe for every peace-loving nation which, like our own, wishes to live its own life, determine its own institutions, be assured of justice and fair dealing by the other peoples of the world, as against force and selfish aggression.

All the peoples of the world are in effect partners in this interest and, for our own part, we see very clearly that unless justice be done to others it will not be done to us.

The program of the world's peace, therefore, is our program; and that program, the only possible program, all we see it, is this:

1. Open covenants of peace must be arrived at, after which there will surely be no private international action or rulings of any kind, but diplomacy shall proceed always frankly and in the public view.

2. Absolute freedom of navigation upon the seas, outside territorial waters, alike in peace and in war, except as the seas may be closed in whole or in part by international action for the enforcement of international covenants.

3. The removal, so far as possible, of all economic barriers and the establishment of equality of trade conditions among all the nations consenting to the peace and associating themselves for its maintenance.

4. Adequate guarantees given and taken that national armaments will be reduced to the lowest points consistent with domestic safety.

5. A free, open-minded and absolutely impartial adjustment of all colonial claims, based upon a strict observance of the principle that in determining all such questions of sovereignty, the interests of the population concerned must have equal weight with the equitable claims of the government whose title is to be determined.

6. The evacuation of all Russian territory and such a settlement of all questions affecting Russia as will secure the best and free-est cooperation of the other nations of the world in obtaining for her an unhampered and unembarrassed opportunity for the independent determination of her own political development and national policy, and assure her of a sincere welcome into the society of free nations under institutions of her own choosing;

and, more than a welcome, assistance also of every kind that she may need and may herself desire. The treatment accorded Russia by her sister nations in the months to come will be the acid test of their good will, of their comprehension of her needs as distinguished from their own interests, and of their intelligent and unselfish sympathy.

7. Belgium, the whole world will agree, must be evacuated and restored, without any attempt to limit the sovereignty which she enjoys in common with all other free nations. No other single act will serve, as this will serve, to restore confidence among nations in the laws which they have themselves set and determined for the government of their relations with one another. Without this healing act, the whole structure and validity of international law is forever impaired.

8. All French territory should be freed and the invaded portions restored and the wrong done to France by Prussia in 1871 in the matter of Alsace-Lorraine, which has unsettled the peace of the world for nearly fifty years, should be righted, in order that peace may once more be made secure in the interest of all.

9. A readjustment of the frontiers of Italy should be effected along clearly recognizable lines of nationality.

10. The peoples of Austria-Hungary, whose place among the nations we wish to see safeguarded and assured, should be accorded the free-est opportunity of autonomous development.

11. Romania, Serbia, and Montenegro should be evacuated; occupied territories restored; Serbia accorded free and secure access to the sea; and the relations of the several Balkan states to one another determined by friendly counsel along historically established lines of allegiance and nationality; and international guarantees of the political and economic independence and territorial integrity of the several Balkan states should be entered into.

12. The Turkish portions of the present Ottoman Empire should be assured a secure sovereignty, but the other nationalities which are now under Turkish rule should be assured an undoubted security of life and an absolutely unmolested opportunity of autonomous development; and the Dardanelles should be permanently opened as a free passage to the ships and commerce of all nations under international guarantees.

13. An independent Polish state should be erected which should include the territories inhabited by indisputably Polish populations, which should be assured free and secure access to the sea; and whose political and economic independence and territorial integrity

should be guaranteed by international covenant.

14. A general association of nations must be formed under specific covenants for the purpose of affording mutual guarantees of political independence and territorial integrity to great and small states alike.

In regard to these essential rectifications of wrong and assertions of right, we feel ourselves to be intimate partners of all the governments and peoples associated together against the imperialists. We cannot be separated in interest or divided in purpose. We stand together until the end.

For such arrangements and covenants, we are willing to fight and to continue to fight until they are achieved; but only because we wish right to prevail and desire a just and stable peace such as can be secured only by removing the chief provocations to war, which this program does remove...'

We have no jealousy of German greatness and there is nothing in this program that impairs it. We grudge her no achievement or distinction of learning or of pacific enterprise such as have made her record very bright and very enviable. We do not wish to injure her or to block in any way her legitimate influence or power. We do not wish to fight her either with arms or with hostile arrangements of trade, if she is willing to associate herself with us and the other peace-loving nations of the world in covenants of justice and law and fair dealing.

We wish her only to accept a place of equality among the peoples of the world—the new world in which we now live—instead of a place of mastery.

Neither do we presume to suggest to her any alteration or modification of her institutions. But it is necessary, we must frankly say, and necessary as a preliminary to any intelligent dealings with her on our part, that we should know whom her spokesmen speak for when they speak to us, whether for the Reichstag majority or for the military party and the men whose creed is imperial domination.

We have spoken now, surely, in terms too concrete to admit of any further doubt or question. An evident principle runs through the whole program I have outlined. It is the principle of justice to all peoples and nationalities and their right to live on equal terms of liberty and safety with one another, whether they be strong or weak.

Unless this principle be made its foundation, no part of the structure of international justice can stand. The people of the United States could act upon no other principle; and to the vindication of this principle they are ready to devote their lives, their honor and everything that they possess. The moral climax of this, the culminating and final war for human liberty, has come; and they are ready to put their own strength, their own highest purpose, their own integrity and devotion to the test. **"**

The war dragged on until the end of 1918, when Germany's allies collapsed or surrendered and English, French and American troops were poised to invade Germany itself. In August, the Chancellor of Germany, Prince Max of Baden, appealed for an armistice based upon Wilson's 14 points, but by the time the war ended—at 11.00 am on 11 November 1918—nearly 40 million people had perished in the conflict.

Wilson was forced to make compromise after compromise to bring his dream of a League of Nations into reality. Despite winning the Nobel Peace Prize in 1919, the Republican-dominated US Congress rejected the Treaty of Versailles and the US President suffered a complete breakdown.

It is now clear that a President who had lost the support of his own country had outlined his personal dream of future international security based upon an idealism for which the world was not yet ready.

Woodrow Wilson died a broken man in 1924.

Margaret Sanger

'The Children's Era'

Address to The Birth Control League, New York, March 1925.

Margaret H. Sanger (1883-1966) was the founder of the American birth control movement and fought for the revision of archaic rules which prohibited the publication of facts about contraception. Sanger's mother died at the age of 49 after 18 pregnancies (seven children died). As a practising nurse in New York's impoverished lower East Side, Sanger learnt first hand about the relationship between high infant and maternal mortality rates and poverty. Of most concern was the methods used by some women to induce abortion.

Sanger resolved to seek out the 'root of the evil'—the lack of education about birth control. In 1914 she began publishing material about contraception and opened the first American birth control clinic in Brooklyn. Sanger also argued—controversially for the time—that birth control would 'fulfill a critical psychological need by enabling women to fully enjoy sexual relations free from the fear of pregnancy'. Opposition to Sanger was strong and many of her speeches were greeted with shouts of abuse. She fled to England under an alias in 1914 to escape prosecution, and spent 30 days in the workhouse in 1917 for 'maintaining a public nuisance'. Her greatest opposition came from the Catholic Church.

Sanger founded the American Birth Control League in 1921, serving as its president for seven years, and offered women an alternative that the Church could not—the ability to control their own lives. In March 1925, Sanger addressed a Birth Control League conference in New York.

❛My subject is 'The Children's Era'. The Children's Era! This makes me think of Ellen Key's book—The Century of the Child. Ellen Key hoped that this twentieth century was to be the century of the child. The twentieth century, she said, would see this old world of ours converted into a beautiful garden of children. Well, we have already lived through a quarter of this twentieth century. What steps have we taken toward making it the century of the child? So far, very, very few.

Why does the Children's Era still remain a dream of the dim and the distant future? Why has so little been accomplished? In spite of all our acknowledged love of children, all our generosity, all our good-will, all the enormous spending of millions on philanthropy and charities, all our warm-hearted sentiment, all our incessant activity and social consciousness? Why?

Before you can cultivate a garden, you must know something about gardening. You have got to give your seeds a proper soil in which to grow. You have got to give them sunlight and fresh air. You have got to give them space and the opportunity (if they are to lift their flowers to the sun), to strike their roots deep into that soil. And always—do not forget this—you have got to fight weeds. You cannot have a garden, if you let weeds overrun it. So, if we want to make this world a garden for children, we must first of all learn the lesson of the gardener.

So far we have not been gardeners. We have only been a sort of silly reception committee, a reception committee at the Grand Central Station of life. Trainload after trainload of children are coming in, day and night—nameless refugees arriving out of the Nowhere into the Here. Trainload after trainload—many unwelcome, unwanted, unprepared for, unknown, without baggage, without passports, most of them without pedigrees. These unlimited hordes of refugees arrive in such numbers that the reception committee is thrown into a panic—a panic of activity. The reception committee arouses itself heroically, establishes emergency measures: milk stations, maternity centers, settlement houses, playgrounds, orphanages, welfare leagues, and every conceivable kind of charitable effort. But still trainloads of children keep on coming—human weed crop up that spread so fast in this sinister struggle for existence, that the overworked committee becomes exhausted, inefficient, and can think of no way out.

When we protest against this immeasurable, meaningless waste of motherhood and child-life; when we protest against the ever-mounting cost to the world of asylums, prisons, homes for the feeble-minded, and such institutions for the unfit, when we protest against the disorder and chaos and tragedy of modern life, when we point out the biological corruption that is destroying the very heart of American life, we are told that we are making merely an "emotional" appeal. When we point to the one immediate practical way toward order and beauty in society, the only way to lay the foundations of a society composed of happy children, happy women, and happy men, they call this idea indecent and immoral.

It is not enough to clean up the filth and disorder of our overcrowded cities. It is not enough to stop the evil of Child Labor—even if we could! It is not enough to decrease the rate of infantile mortality. It is not enough to open playgrounds, and build more public schools in which we can standardize the mind of the young. It is not enough to throw millions upon millions of dollars into charities and philanthropies. Don't deceive ourselves that by so doing we are making the world 'Safe for Children'.

Those of you who have followed the sessions of this Conference must, I am sure, agree with me that the first real step towards the creation of a Children's Era must lie in providing the conditions of healthy life for children not only before birth but even more imperatively before conception. Human society must protect its children—yes, but prenatal care is most essential! The child-to-be, as yet not called into being, has rights no less imperative.

We have learned in the preceding sessions of this Conference that, if we wish to produce strong and sturdy children, the embryo must grow in a chemically healthy medium. The blood stream of the mother must be chemically normal. Worry, strain, shock, unhappiness, enforced maternity, may all poison the blood of the enslaved mother. This chemically poisoned blood may produce a defective baby—a child foredoomed to idiocy, or feeble-mindedness, crime, or failure.

Do I exaggerate? Am I taking a rare exception and making it a general rule? Our opponents declare that children are conceived in love, and that every new-born baby converts its parents to love and unselfishness. My answer is to point to the asylums, the hospitals, the ever-growing institutions for the unfit. Look into the family history of those who are feeble-minded; or behind the bars of jails and prisons. Trace the family histories; find out the conditions under which they were conceived and born, before you attempt to persuade us that reckless breeding has nothing to do with these grave questions.

There is only one way out. We have got to fight for the health and happiness of the Unborn Child. And to do that in a practical, tangible way, we have got to free women from enforced, enslaved maternity. There can be no hope for the future of civilization, no certainty of racial salvation, until every woman can decide for herself whether she will or will not become a mother, and when and how many children she cares to bring into the world. That is the first step.

I would like to suggest Civil Service examinations for parenthood! Prospective parents after such an examination would be given a parenthood license, proving that they are physically and mentally fit to be the fathers and mothers of the next generation.

This is an interesting idea—but then arises the questions: 'Who is to decide?', 'Would there be a jury, like a play jury?' Would a Republican administration give parenthood permits only to Republicans—or perhaps only to Democrats? The more you think of governmental interference, the less it works out. Take this plan of civil service examination for parenthood. It suggests Prohibition: there might even be bootlegging in babies!

No, I doubt the advisability of governmental sanction. The problem of bringing children into the world ought to be decided by those most seriously involved—those who run the greatest risks; in the last analysis—by the mother and the child. If there is going to be any Civil Service examination, let it be conducted by the Unborn Child, the Child-to-be.

Just try for a moment to picture the possibilities of such an examination. When you want a cook or housemaid, you go to an employment bureau. You have to answer questions. You have to exchange references. You have to persuade the talented cook that you conduct a proper well-run household. Children ought to have at least the same privilege as cooks.

Sometimes in idle moments I like to think it would be a very good scheme to have a bureau of the Child-to-be. At such a bureau of the unborn, the wise child might be able to find out a few things about its father—and its mother. Just think for a moment of this bureau where prospective parents might apply for a baby. Think of the questions they would be asked by the agent of the unborn or by the baby itself.

First: "Mr. Father, a baby is an expensive luxury. Can you really afford one?"

"Have you paid for your last baby yet?"

"How many children have you already? Six? You must have your hands full. Can you take care of so many?"

"Do you look upon children as a reward—or a penalty?"

"How are your ductless glands—well balanced?"

"Can you provide a happy home for one! A sunny nursery? Proper food?"

"What's that you say? Ten children already? Two dark rooms in the slums?"

"No, thank you! I don't care to be born at all if I cannot be well-born. Good-bye!"

And if we could organize a society for the prevention of cruelty to unborn children, we would make it a law that children should be brought into the world only when they were welcome, invited, and wanted; that they would arrive with a clean bill of health and heritage; that they would possess healthy, happy, well-mated, and mature parents.

And there would be certain conditions of circumstances which would preclude parenthood. These conditions, the presence of which would make parenthood a crime, are the following:

1. Transmissible disease
2. Temporary disease
3. Subnormal children already in the family
4. Space out between births
5. Twenty-three years as a minimum age for parents
6. Economic circumstances adequate
7. Spiritual harmony between parents.

In conclusion, let me repeat: we are not trying to establish a dictatorship over parents. We want to free women from enslavery and unwilling motherhood. We are fighting for the emancipation for the mothers of the world, of the children of the world, and the children to be. We want to create a real Century of the Child—usher in a Children's Era. We can do this by handling the terrific gift of life in bodies fit and perfect as can be fashioned. Help us to make this Conference, which has aroused so much interest, the turning point toward this era. Only so can you help in the creation of the future. ⟩

Margaret Sanger had many of her writings labelled lewd, even pornographic. She was charged with nine counts of violating the postal act regarding the distribution of 'vulgar' material and travelled to England to escape prosecution.

Lies were spread about her teachings regarding 'planned parenthood' and much was misrepresented in the press in order to discredit her.

In 1927 Margaret Sanger organised the first World Population Conference in Geneva, Switzerland, and was the first president of the International Planned Parenthood Federation. Jailed eight times during her adult life, one of the compromises she had to make was to secure her message among the upper and middle classes, thereby missing her target audience—the poor and uneducated.

In the late 1950s, with donations from her supporters, she funded the development of the birth control pill based on the research of the Worcester Foundation, at a time when the transference of birth control information was still a criminal act in some American states.

Mustafa Kemal 'Atatürk'

'Message to the Gallipoli Fallen'

Turkey, 1934

Mustafa Kemal (1881–1938)—who was given the honorary title 'Atatürk' in 1934, which means 'Father of the Turks'—was both the hero of the Dardanelles in World War I and the founder of the modern republic of Turkey.

Kemal was born in Salonica (now called Thessaloniki), which is now part of Greek Macedonia, but was part of the Ottoman Empire in the 1880s.

As a young army major he was a central figure in the coup that ousted Sultan Abdülhamid II in 1908 and he played a vital role in defending the Dardanelles in the Balkan Wars (1912–13).

Three years later, with the Ottoman Empire allied to the Central Powers (Germany and Austria-Hungary) in World War I (1914–18) Kemal used his knowledge of the region to save Turkey from invasion by British and ANZAC forces in the ill-fated Gallipoli campaign.

In January 1915, the British Naval Command approved an attack on the Dardanelles to free the narrow strait for shipping into the Black Sea. When naval attacks failed in February and March, the British approved a land invasion on the Gallipoli peninsula.

On 25 April 1915, Australian and New Zealand forces landed at Anzac Cove, British forces landed at Cape Helles to the south and French forces made a diversionary landing at Kum Kale on the Asian side of the strait.

Kemal, however, had been appointed to the command of the 19th Division and had taken position at the top of Gallipoli peninsula. The advance of the Anzac troops was severely checked by the Turkish forces—an estimated 2000 soldiers lost their lives on the first day—and very little ground was captured in the next eight months.

Finally, on 9 January 1916, the Dardanelles Campaign was abandoned and Allied troops withdrawn. The Allied forces lost more than 44,000 men during the campaign with almost 100,000 wounded. The Turks lost even more—almost 56,000 killed and 140,000 wounded—but they had won the battle.

Kemal was promoted to General, put in command of the 16th Army and posted to the Caucuses front in Southern Russia.

Following the armistice of November 1918, he was the inspector of the Third Army in Anatolia and, in opposing both the Sultan's regime in Istanbul and Allied attempts to partition the Ottoman Empire, became the leader of Turkey's national liberation struggle.

In 1920, when the Sultan signed away parts of Anatolia to the Greeks, he set up a rival government in Ankara.

Kemal effectively seized control of the country by defeating the Greeks at Sakarya (1921) and Dumlupinar (1922). On 1 November 1922, the 'Caliphate' (sultanate) was abolished and on 29 October 1923, the Republic of Turkey was declared with Kemal as President.

Within three years, Kemal had imprisoned many of his political rivals, accusing them of assassination conspiracy and established one party rule under the Republican People's Party.

In 1928, a law was imposed which resulted in Islam no longer being the state religion, education became compulsory, the country's Arabic script was abolished and the Latin alphabet was incorporated into the Turkish language. As founding father of the modern Turkish republic and President until his death in 1938, Kemal modelled many of his reforms on the Western democracies. He introduced a broad range of reforms that swept across the country's political, social, legal, economic and cultural life.

Despite his military background, Kemal became a great defender of peace at home and abroad. With the rise of Fascism and Nazism in Europe in the 1930s, Kemal established stronger relationships with World War I enemies, Britain and France.

In 1933 Kemal stated: 'I look to the world with an open heart full of pure feelings and friendship.'

In 1934, the year the Grand National Assembly bestowed the name 'Atatürk' upon him, the Father of Turkey reached out to his former Gallipoli foes with a speech that is today regarded 'among the finest words of reconciliation ever uttered'.

'Those heroes who shed their blood and lost their lives... you are now lying in the soil of a friendly country.

Therefore rest in peace.

There is no difference between the Johnnies and the Mehmets to us where they lie side by side in this country of ours...

You, the mothers who sent their sons from far away countries, wipe away your tears.

Your sons are now lying in our bosoms and are in peace.

After having lost their lives on this land they have become our sons as well.'

King Edward VIII

'Abdication Speech'

Radio broadcast, London, England, 11 December 1936.

E dward VIII (1894-1972) became King of the United Kingdom upon the death of his father, George V, on 20 January 1936. In his early forties and a bachelor, Edward was both popular and good-looking but quickly made known his desire to marry an American woman, Wallis Warfield (Spencer) Simpson, whom he had known since 1931. When King Edward sought the approval of his family, the Church of England, Prime Minister Stanley Baldwin and his government in order to marry her, he met with complete opposition. Simpson had been married twice before, her second divorce was still pending and her ability to provide an heir was questionable (Simpson was already forty, and childless).

On 10 December, King Edward VIII submitted his abdication and became the only British monarch to voluntarily resign his station. The decision was endorsed by Parliament on 11 December, and on that day Edward publicly announced his decision via radio to a breathless, worldwide audience.

‘At long last I am able to say a few words of my own. I have never wanted to withhold anything, but until now it has not been constitutionally possible for me to speak.

A few hours ago I discharged my last duty as King and Emperor, and now that I have been succeeded by my brother, the Duke of York, my first words must be to declare my allegiance to him. This I do with all my heart.

You all know the reasons which have impelled me to renounce the throne. But I want you to understand that in making up my mind I did not forget the country or the empire, which, as Prince of Wales and lately as King, I have for twenty-five years tried to serve.

But you must believe me when I tell you that I have found it impossible to carry the heavy burden of responsibility and to discharge my duties as King as I would wish to do without the help and support of the woman I love.

And I want you to know that the decision I have made has been mine and mine alone. This was a thing I had to judge entirely for myself. The other person most nearly concerned has tried up to the last to persuade me to take a different course.

I have made this, the most serious decision of my life, only upon the single thought of what would, in the end, be best for all.

This decision has been made less difficult to me by the sure knowledge that my brother, with his long training in the public affairs of this country and with his fine qualities, will be able to take my place forthwith without interruption or injury to the life and progress of the empire. And he has one matchless blessing, enjoyed by so many of you, and not bestowed on me—a happy home with his wife and children.

During these hard days I have been comforted by Her Majesty, my mother, and by my family. The ministers of the crown, and in particular, Mr Baldwin, the Prime Minister, have always treated me with full consideration. There has never been any constitutional difference between me and them, and between me and Parliament. Bred in the constitutional tradition by my father, I should never have allowed any such issue to arise.

Ever since I was Prince of Wales, and later on when I occupied the throne, I have been treated with the greatest kindness by all classes of the people wherever I have lived or journeyed throughout the empire. For that I am very grateful.

I now quit altogether public affairs and I lay down my burden. It may be some time before I return to my native land, but I shall always follow the fortunes of the British race and empire with profound interest, and if at any time in the future I can be found of service to His Majesty in a private station, I shall not fail.

And now, we all have a new King. I wish him and you, his people, happiness and prosperity with all my heart. God bless you all! God save the King! '

Edward's younger brother, George VI, took the throne and immediately gave Edward the title Duke of Windsor. The Duke and Mrs Simpson (who was given the title Duchess of Windsor) were married in France on 3 June, 1937 and lived in Paris. An apparent personal appeasement of Hitler's Nazi regime (the Windsors met the German Chancellor in 1937 and found him 'charming') made them something of an embarrassment when World War II broke out. Edward and Wallis were sent to the Commonwealth outposts of Bermuda and the Bahamas to serve out the conflict, with the former monarch serving as Governor. The family of King George VI, especially his wife Mary (the Queen Mother) and daughter Elizabeth (later Queen Elizabeth II) never forgave Edward for abdicating and exposing his brother George to the throne. They indirectly blamed Edward for the premature death of George VI—a quiet, shy man with a nervous stutter—from cancer in 1953, aged 57.

Edward died in Paris on 28 May, 1972, forever estranged from his family and former subjects. His wife, the former Mrs Simpson, died there also, on April 24, 1986, a virtual recluse. She was afforded one concession by the Royal family and was buried beside her late husband in Windsor Castle.

Almost 67 years after King Edward VIII's abdication, the British Parliament and the Church of England avoided another potential constitutional crisis and allowed Charles, Prince of Wales and heir to the throne, to marry fellow divorcee Camilla Parker-Bowles in April 2005.

Adolf Hitler

'The Jewish Question'
The Reichstag, Berlin, 30 January 1939.

In this speech marking the sixth anniversary of his ascension to power, Adolf Hitler (1889-1945) reveals the paranoia and obsession that drove him to become one of the most evil dictators of the twentieth century. The tactic of playing on people's insecurities—especially about the economy, nationalism and the shame of losing World War I, as Hitler did—was not unusual in politics, but Hitler directed this fear at one ethnic minority. Here, the German Fuehrer shows his unbridled hatred of the Jewry of Europe … a contempt that led to World War II, the death of over 50 million people and the systematic murder of an estimated 6 million people during the Holocaust. Hitler delivered this speech on the eve of Britain's entry into World War II.

❮ When on the evening of 30 January 1933, six years ago today, beneath the light of their torches the tens of thousands of National Socialist fighters passed through the Brandenberger Tor to express to me the newly nominated Chancellor of the Reich, their feelings of overflowing joy and their confession of loyalty as my followers, countless anxious eyes both here in Berlin and throughout Germany gazed at the beginning of a development the issue of which it appeared impossible to discern or to foresee. Some 13 million German voters, men and women then stood beside me. An imposing number, but yet only a little more than a third of the sum of the votes cast. It was true that the remaining twenty million were divided and split up between thirty five other parties and groups.

The one thing which united the opponents of National Socialism was their common hatred of the young movement, a hatred born of their guilty consciences and worse intentions. As is still does today in other parts of the world, this united the priests of the Centre Party and Communist atheists, the Socialist out to abolish private property and capitalists whose interests were bound up with the stock exchange, Conservatives who wished to destroy the State and Republicans whose aim was to destroy the Reich. During the long battle of National Socialism for the leadership of the country they had all come together in defense of their interests and made common cause with Jewry. The bishop politicians of the various Churches extended their hands in benediction over this union. And against this splitting up of the nation, united only in negation stood that third of German men and women, with their faith, those who had undertaken to raise anew the German people and Reich in the face of world internal and external opposition.

The whole picture of the greatness of the collapse of Germany at that time begins gradually to grow dim, but one thing even today is not forgotten. It seemed that only a miracle could save Germany at the twelfth hour. And we National Socialists believed in this miracle. Over the belief in this miracle our foes made merry. The thought that one should wish to redeem the nation from a ruin which now lasted a decade and a half simply through the force of a new idea appeared to those who were not National Socialists as the delusion of visionaries [phantasterei]; to the Jews and other enemies of the State it appeared as the last insignificant spasm of force within the national resistance, and when that was exhausted one might hope to be able finally to annihilate not only Germany but Europe.

A Germany sinking in Bolshevist chaos would at that time have hurled the whole West into a crisis of unimaginable gravity. Only the most limited of islanders could persuade themselves into believing that the Red plague would of its own accord have cried a halt before the sacredness of a democratic idea at the frontiers of States who had shown no interest in its advance. The rescue of Europe began at one end of the continent with Mussolini and Fascism. National Socialism continued this rescue in another part of Europe, and at the present moment we are witnessing in still a third country the same drama of a brave triumph over the Jewish international attempt to destroy European civilization. The six years which now lie behind us are filled with the most stupendous events in the whole of our German history. On 30 January 1933 I entered the Wilhelmstrasse filled with profound anxiety for the future of my people. Today after six years I am able to speak before the Reichstag of Greater Germany. We are indeed perhaps better able than other generations to realize the full meaning of those pious words "What a change by the grace of God" …

The German nation has no feeling of hatred towards England, America or France; all it wants is peace and quiet. But the other nations are continually being stirred up to hatred for Germany and the German people by Jewish and non-Jewish agitators. And so, should warmongers achieve what they are aiming at, our own people would be landed in a situation for which they would be psychologically quite unprepared and which they would thus fail to grasp. I therefore consider it necessary that from now on our propaganda and our press should always make a point of answering these attacks, and above all bring them to the notice of the German people. The German nation must know who the men are who want to bring about war by hook or crook. It is my conviction that these people are mistaken in their calculations, for when once National Socialist propaganda is devoted to the answering of the attacks, we shall succeed just as we succeeded inside Germany herself in overcoming, through the convincing power of our propaganda, the Jewish world-enemy. The nations will in a short time realize that National Socialist Germany wants no enmity with other nations; that all the assertions as to our intended attacks on other nations are lies, lies born of morbid hysteria, or of a mania for self-preservation on the part of certain politicians; but that in certain States these lies are being used by unscrupulous profiteers to salvage their own finances. That, above all, international Jewry may hope in this way to satisfy its thirst for revenge and gain, but that on the other hand this is the grossest defamation which can be brought to bear on a great and peace loving nation. Never, for instance, have German soldiers fought on American soil, unless it was in the cause of American independence and freedom; but American soldiers were brought to Europe to help strangle a great nation which was fighting for its freedom. Germany did not attack America, but America attacked Germany and as the Committee of Investigation of the American House of Representatives concluded: from purely capitalist motives, without any other cause. There is but one thing that everyone should realize: these attempts cannot influence Germany in the slightest as to the way in which she settles her Jewish problem. On the contrary, in connection with the Jewish question I have this to say: it is a shameful spectacle to see how the whole democratic world is oozing sympathy for the poor tormented Jewish people, but remains hard-hearted and obdurate when it comes to helping them—which is surely, in view of its attitude, an obvious duty. The arguments that are brought up as an excuse for not helping them actually speak for us Germans and Italians.

For this is what they say:

1. 'We', that is the democracies, 'are not in a position to take in the Jews'. Yet in these empires there are not 10 people to the square kilometre. While Germany, with her 135 inhabitants to the square kilometre, is supposed to have room for them!
2. They assure us: We cannot take them unless Germany is prepared to allow them a certain amount of capital to bring with them as immigrants.

For hundreds of years Germany was good enough to receive these elements, although they possessed nothing except infectious political and physical diseases. What they possess today, they have by a very large extent gained at the cost of the less astute German nation by the most reprehensible manipulations.

Today we are merely paying this people what it deserves. When the German nation was, thanks to the inflation instigated and carried through by Jews, deprived of the entire savings which it had accumulated in years of honest work, when the rest of the world took away the German nation's foreign investments, when we were divested of the whole of our colonial possessions, these philanthropic considerations evidently carried little noticeable weight with democratic statesmen.

Today I can only assure these gentlemen that, thanks to the brutal education with which the democracies favoured us for fifteen years, we are completely hardened to all attacks of sentiment. After more than 800 000 children of the nation had died of hunger and undernourishment at the close of the War, we witnessed almost one million head of milking cows being driven away from us in accordance with the cruel paragraphs of a dictate which the humane democratic apostles of the world forced upon us as a peace treaty. We witnessed over one million German prisoners of war being retained in confinement for no reason at all for a whole year after the War was ended. We witnessed over one and a half million Germans being torn away from all that they possessed in the territories lying on our frontiers, and being whipped out with practically only what they wore on their backs. We had to endure having millions of our fellow countrymen torn from us without their consent, and without their being afforded the slightest possibility of existence. I could supplement these examples with dozens of the most cruel kind. For this reason we ask to be spared all sentimental talk.

The German nation does not wish its interests to be determined and controlled by any foreign nation. France to the French, England to the English, America to the Americans, and Germany to the Germans. We are resolved to prevent the settlement in our country of a strange people which was capable of snatching for itself all the leading positions in the land, and to oust it. For it is our will to educate our own nation for these leading positions. We have hundreds of thousands of very intelligent children of peasants and of the working classes. We shall have them educated—in fact we have already begun—and we wish that one day they, and not the representatives of an alien race, may hold the leading positions in the State together with our educated classes. Above all, German culture, as its name alone shows, is German and not Jewish, and therefore its management and care will be entrusted to members of our own nation.

If the rest of the world cries out with a hypocritical mien against this barbaric expulsion from Germany of such an irreplaceable and culturally eminently valuable element, we can only be astonished at the conclusions they draw from this situation. For how thankful they must be that we are releasing these precious apostles of culture, and placing them at the disposal of the rest of the world. In accordance with their own declarations they cannot find a single reason to excuse themselves for refusing to receive this most valuable race in their own countries. Nor can I see a reason why the members of this race should be imposed upon the German nation, while in the States, which are so enthusiastic about these 'splendid people', their settlement should suddenly be refused with every imaginable excuse. I think that the sooner this problem is solved the better; for Europe cannot settle down until the Jewish question is cleared up. It may very well be possible that sooner or later an agreement on this problem may be reached in Europe, even between those nations which otherwise do not so easily come together.

The world has sufficient space for settlements, but we must once and for all get rid of the opinion that the Jewish race was only created by God for the purpose of being in a certain percentage a parasite living on the body and the productive work of other nations. The Jewish race will have to adapt itself to sound constructive activity as other nations do, or sooner or later it will succumb to a crisis of an inconceivable magnitude.

One thing I should like to say on this day which may be memorable for others as well as for us Germans. In the course of my life I have very often been a prophet, and have usually been ridiculed for it. During the time of my struggle for power it was in the first instance the Jewish race which only received my prophecies with laughter when I said that I would one day take over the leadership of the State, and with it that of the whole nation, and that I would then among many other things settle the Jewish problem. Their laughter was uproarious, but I think that for some time now they have been laughing on the other side of their face. Today I will once more be a prophet: If the international Jewish financiers in and outside Europe should succeed in plunging the nations once more into a world war, then the result will not be the Bolshevization of the earth, and thus the victory of Jewry, but the annihilation of the Jewish race in Europe!

For the time when the non-Jewish nations had no propaganda is at an end. National Socialist Germany and Fascist Italy have institutions which enable them when necessary to enlighten the world about the nature of a question of which many nations are instinctively conscious, but which then have not yet clearly thought out. At the moment the Jews in certain countries may be fomenting hatred under the protection of the press, of the film, of wireless propaganda, of the theatre, of literature, etc., all of which they control. If this nation should once more succeed in inciting the millions which compose the nations into a conflict which is utterly senseless and only serves Jewish interests, then there will be revealed the effectiveness of an enlightenment which has completely routed the Jews of Germany in the space of a few years. The nations are no longer willing to die on the battlefield so that this unstable international race may profiteer from a war or satisfy its Old Testament vengeance. The Jewish watchword 'Workers of the world unite' will be conquered by a higher realization, namely 'Workers of all classes and of all nations, recognize your common enemy! **'**

Born illegitimately in Braunau, Austria, Hitler enlisted in World War I where he achieved the modest rank of corporal. When the war ended in 1918, Hitler felt betrayed by the conditions set out in the Treaty of Versailles and found a platform for venting his anger and frustration against the federal government in one of the minor, post-war political parties—the National

Socialist German Workers' Party (abbreviated to Nazi).

Hitler was appointed Chancellor in January 1933 when President Paul von Hindenberg was wrongly advised that the 'little corporal' could be more closely controlled inside the German Parliament. Hitler's followers burned the Reichstag to the ground that year—an act he blamed on the Communist Party—and after calling a general election and seizing power, he crushed rivals inside his own party in June 1934.

When von Hindenberg died in August, Hitler was named sole ruler of Germany and opposition parties were outlawed. In 1938 he created 'Greater Germany' by annexing Austria and then engineered events to present to an appeasing Britain and Franc an excuse to reclaim the German-populated borderland (Sudetenland) of neighbouring Czechoslovakia. On 1 September 1939 German troops marched in to Poland and precipitated the start of World War II (1939–45).

After almost six years of world conflict Hitler's megalomania ended with a self-inflicted gunshot wound on 30 April, 1945 as Russian troops attacked his Berlin bunker. Surrounded by his new wife, Eva Braun, his Minister of Propaganda Joseph Goebbels and his family, and many of his closest associates who calmly followed their *Fuhrer's* lead, Hitler's death drew to a close the most cataclysmic war known to mankind with an estimated 55 millions lives lost.

Édouard Daladier

'The Nazis' Aim is Slavery'

Radio Broadcast (Paris, France), 29 January 1940

É douard Daladier (1876–1970) was the Prime Minister of France at the outbreak of World War II in 1939. Together with British Prime Minister Neville Chamberlain, Daladier signed the Munich Pact with Germany on 30 September 1938, all but abandoning Czechoslovakia to Nazi occupation, in the hope of avoiding another World War. Daladier was under no illusion as to the threat Germany now posed to his own homeland—as French War Minister he knew that his country was militarily, politically and socially unprepared for war—and he supported Britain's appeasement of Hitler rather than defending their Czech allies in an armed conflict with Germany.

A year later, Hitler's armies invaded Poland, Britain and France declared war against Germany and France itself was vulnerable to invasion. In January 1940, Daladier delivered the following radio address to the people of France in a belated recognition of Hitler's true intentions:

❛At the end of five months of war, one thing has become more and more clear. It is that Germany seeks to establish a domination over the world completely different from any known in history.

The domination at which the Nazis aim is not limited to the displacement of the balance of power and the imposition of supremacy of one nation. It seeks the systematic and total destruction of those conquered by Hitler and it does not treaty with the nations which he has subdued. He destroys them. He takes from them their whole political and economic existence and seeks even to deprive them of their history and their culture. He wishes to consider them only as vital space and a vacant territory over which he has every right.

The human beings who constitute these nations are for him only cattle. He orders their massacre or their migration. He compels them to make room for their conquerors. He does not even take the trouble to impose any war tribute on them. He just takes all their wealth and, to prevent any revolt, he wipes out their leaders and scientifically seeks the physical and moral degradation of those whose independence he has taken away.

Under this domination, in thousands of towns and villages in Europe, there are millions of human beings now living in misery which, some months ago, they could never have imagined. Austria, Bohemia, Slovakia and Poland are only lands of despair. Their whole peoples have been deprived of the means of moral and material happiness. Subdued by treachery or brutal violence, they have no other recourse than to work for their executioners who grant them scarcely enough to assure the most miserable existence.

There is being created a world of masters and slaves in the image of Germany herself. For, while Germany is crushing beneath her tyranny the men of every race and language, she is herself being crushed beneath her own servitude and her domination mania. The German worker and peasant are the slaves of their Nazi masters while the worker and peasant of Bohemia and Poland have become in turn slaves of these slaves. Before this first realization of a mad dream, the whole world might shudder.

Nazi propaganda is entirely founded on the exploitation of the weakness of the human heart. It does not address itself to the strong or the heroic. It tells the rich they are going to lose their money. It tells the worker this is a rich man's war. It tells the intellectual and the artist that all he cherished is being destroyed by war. It tells the lover of good things that soon he will have none of them. It says to the Christian believer: "How can you accept this massacre?" It tells the adventurer: "A man like you should profit by the misfortunes of your country."

It is those who speak this way who have destroyed or confiscated all the wealth they could lay their hands on, who have reduced their workers to slavery, who have ruined all intellectual liberty, who have imposed terrible privations on millions of men and women and who have made murder their law. What do contradictions matter to them if they can lower the resistance of those who wish to bar the path of their ambitions to be masters of the world?

For us, there is more to do than merely win the war. We shall win it, but we must also win a victory far greater than that of arms. In this world of masters and slaves, which those madmen who rule at Berlin are seeking to forge, we must also save liberty and human dignity. *

In March 1940, Édouard Daladier resigned as Prime Minister when France failed to defend Finland from Russian invasion in the Winter War of December 1939 – March 1940.

When France fell in June of that year, Daladier was arrested by the Vichy puppet government and, following an aborted trial in 1942, he spent the remainder of the war under German guard in Austria. Two other failed French Prime Ministers, Paul Reynaud and Leon Blum, later joined him there.

Winston Churchill

'We Shall Fight on the Beaches'
British Parliament, London, 4 June 1940

When Winston Churchill (1874–1965) replaced Neville Chamberlain as British Prime Minister on 10 May 1940, his country was in a perilous position. In the first months of World War II, Norway had fallen, Germany's neighbours were under attack and France was poised for invasion. As he stated on 13 May, Churchill only had 'blood, toil, tears and sweat' to offer his people—a quote borrowed from a speech delivered by future US President Theodore Roosevelt in 1897—but he also had other qualities he would use to maximum effect...an affinity with the historic times in which he lived, a paternal and easily recognisable voice and the ability to inspire millions with his mastery of the English language.

On 4 June, in response to the remarkable evacuation of more than 331,000 British and French troops from the beaches of Dunkirk (France) after they had been cut off by the advancing German Army, Prime Minister Churchill delivered this rousing speech in the House of Commons.

Although France would soon fall, the escape of almost all the stranded troops on British destroyers, commercial vessels and small civilian boats raised hopes that all was not lost in the face of German military aggression. Churchill's anaphoric speech—often mimicked and more often misquoted—raised the morale of the British people as they now prepared for 'The Battle of Britain'.

❛ I have, myself, full confidence that if all do their duty, if nothing is neglected and if the best arrangements are made, as they are being made, we shall prove ourselves once again able to defend our Island home, to ride out the storm of war and to outlive the menace of tyranny, if necessary for years, if necessary alone.

At any rate, that is what we are going to try to do. That is the resolve of His Majesty's Government—every man of them. That is the will of Parliament and the nation.

The British Empire and the French Republic, linked together in their cause and in their need, will defend to the death their native soil, aiding each other like good comrades to the utmost of their strength.

Even though large tracts of Europe and many old and famous States have fallen or may fall into the grip of the Gestapo and all the odious apparatus of Nazi rule, we shall not flag or fail.

We shall go on to the end, we shall fight in France, we shall fight on the seas and oceans, we shall fight with growing confidence and growing strength in the air, we shall defend our Island, whatever the cost may be, we shall fight on the beaches, we shall fight on the landing grounds, we shall fight in the fields and in the streets, we shall fight in the hills; we shall never surrender, and even if, which I do not for a moment believe, this Island or a large part of it were subjugated and starving, then our Empire beyond the seas, armed and guarded by the British Fleet, would carry on the struggle, until, in God's good time, the New World, with all its power and might, steps forth to the rescue and the liberation of the old. **'**

The Royal Air Force (RAF) maintained its air superiority over the Luftwaffe in the 'Battle of Britain' (July–October 1940) and put Germany's plans for an amphibious invasion on permanent hold. Winston Churchill worked tirelessly with allies France, the United States and later Russia, to bring a successful end to the war but, in the greatest blow of his political career, his Conservative government was voted out of office in July 1945—a month after Germany surrendered but before Japan could be defeated in the Pacific.

Winston Churchill spent the next six years as Opposition leader but in March 1946 he accepted an invitation from Westminster College, in Fulton, Missouri, to receive an honorary degree. There Churchill showed that he still had the power to influence world politics when he used the term 'Iron Curtain' in a speech entitled 'The Sinews of Peace'. Churchill had actually used the term for some decades and had included it in letters to US President Harry Truman, but ultimately it defined the way the Democratic West viewed the Communist East.

In 1951, Churchill's Conservative Party narrowly defeated the Labour Government and he was returned to power for a second time as Prime Minister. His four years in government, until his resignation in 1955 at age 80, saw him knighted in 1953 and receive the Nobel Prize for Literature (for his six-volume account, *The Second World War*) the same year. In 1963, two years before his death, the man once described as 'the greatest living Englishman' was granted honorary US citizenship by an Act of Congress.

Franklin D. Roosevelt

'A Day That Will Live In Infamy'
Washington DC, 8 December 1941

Franklin Delano Roosevelt (1882–1945) was the 32nd President of the United States of America. Born into great wealth to a prominent New York family, he married Eleanor Roosevelt—his father's fifth cousin and the niece of President Theodore Roosevelt—in 1905. Despite being stricken with polio in 1921 (which left him partially paralysed in the legs and necessitated the use of a wheelchair and a 'standing frame' to deliver public speeches), the former New York State Senator (1910–13) ran for President in 1928 and was elected governor of New York.

Popularly known as FDR, he was elected President in November 1932 at a time when America, and the world, had been paralysed by economic Depression for the past three years.

From his Inaugural Address in 1933, when he famously declared 'the only thing we have to fear is fear itself', Roosevelt outlined his plan for a 'New Deal' for the American public. But by the late 1930s, the United States faced an even greater hurdle—to retain its isolationist stance in the face of increased fascism in Europe and Japanese nationalism. During the decade, Japan's foreign policy was inexorably linked to expansion, invasion and occupation in South East Asia.

When Britain and America froze oil imports to Japan, the United States—the dominant Pacific naval power at the time—was now seen as a severe threat to Japan's plans to extend its empire.

On 26 November 1941, a Japanese fleet of 33 warships and auxiliary craft under the control of Admiral Yamamoto sailed to the northern tip of Japan under strict radio silence before travelling westward 6500 km to Hawaii.

On 30 November 1941, US State Secretary Hull telephoned President Franklin D. Roosevelt at Warm Springs and prompted the US President to return to Washington DC because of the extreme acuteness of the diplomatic situation with Japan.

When Japan attacked the following Sunday morning, the US government was still negotiating for a diplomatic solution to the impasse with Japanese ambassadors in Washington.

In the early hours of 7 December, 183 planes armed with bombs and torpedos took off from six Japanese aircraft carriers 400 km north of Hawaii. During the previous night, five midget submarines with two-man crews were launched 15 km outside Pearl Harbour from larger 'mother' submarines. They were already inside the harbour when the first wave struck.

Japanese planes reached Pearl Harbour shortly before 8.00 am and completely surprised the US naval base because a long-range attack from the north was totally unsuspected. After the first wave arrived from the northwest, a second wave of Japanese planes attacked the Naval Air Station and Pearl Harbour at 8.40 am from the northeast.

American military losses were massive—12 battleships were sunk or beached (nine were damaged), 164 aircraft destroyed (159 damaged) with approximately 2400 lives lost. Most of the 1177 crew on the USS *Arizona* were killed when the ship was sunk by a 1760 lb armour piercing bomb that cut through the deck and ignited the ship's forward ammunition magazine. The ship sank in less than nine minutes.

The USS *Oklahoma* rolled over on its side after being hit by several torpedoes, with a loss of over 400 lives. The *California*, *West Virginia*, *Utah* and the *Shaw* were also sunk. The *Nevada* was beached after making a run for the open seas and the *Maryland*, *Pennsylvania* and *Tennessee* were severely damaged. Incredibly, three American aircraft carriers based at Pearl Harbour were outside on manoeuvres when the Japanese struck and survived the attack.

At about 5.00 pm that night in Washington DC, following meetings with his military advisers, President Roosevelt dictated to his secretary, Grace Tully, a request to Congress for a declaration of war. Roosevelt then revised the typed draft and made the most significant change in the opening sentence, which originally read 'a date which will live in world history.' On 8 December, at 12.30 pm, President Roosevelt addressed a joint session of Congress and the American people via radio.

❛Yesterday, December 7 1941—a date which will live in infamy—the United States of America was suddenly and deliberately attacked by naval and air forces of the Empire of Japan.

The United States was at peace with that Nation and, at the solicitation of Japan, was still in conversation with its Government and its Emperor looking toward the maintenance of peace in the Pacific. Indeed, one hour after Japanese air squadrons had commenced bombing in Oahu, the Japanese Ambassador to the United States and his colleague delivered to the Secretary of State a form reply to a recent American message. While this reply stated that it seemed useless to continue the existing diplomatic negotiations, it contained no threat or hint of war or armed attack.

It will be recorded that the distance of Hawaii from Japan makes it obvious that the attack was deliberately planned many days or even weeks ago. During the intervening time the Japanese Government had deliberately sought to deceive the United States by false statements and expressions of hope for continued peace.

The attack yesterday on the Hawaiian Islands has caused severe damage to American naval and military forces. Very many American lives have been lost. In addition, American ships have been reported torpedoed on the high seas between San Francisco and Honolulu.

Yesterday the Japanese Government also launched an attack against Malaya.

Last night Japanese forces attacked Hong Kong.

Last night Japanese forces attacked Guam.

Last night Japanese forces attacked the Philippine Islands.

Last night the Japanese attacked Midway Island.

Japan has, therefore, undertaken a surprise offensive extending throughout the Pacific area. The facts of yesterday speak for themselves. The people of the United States have already formed their opinions and well understand the implications to the very life and safety of our Nation.

As Commander-in-Chief of the Army and Navy, I have directed that all measures be taken for our defense.

Always will we remember the character of the onslaught against us.

No matter how long it may take us to overcome this premeditated invasion, the American people in their righteous might will win through to absolute victory.

I believe I interpret the will of the Congress and of the people when I assert that we will not only defend ourselves to the uttermost but will make very certain that this form of treachery shall never endanger us again.

Hostilities exist. There is no blinking at the fact that our people, our territory and our interests are in grave danger.

With confidence in our armed forces—with the unbounded determination of our people—we will gain the inevitable triumph—so help us God.

I ask that the Congress declare that since the unprovoked and dastardly attack by Japan on Sunday, December 7, a state of war has existed between the United States and the Japanese Empire. **'**

The US Senate responded with a unanimous vote in support of war (Montana pacifist Jeanette Rankin abstained from voting in the House of Representatives). At 4.00 pm that afternoon, President Roosevelt signed the declaration of war. Several days later, Germany and Italy declared war on the United States.

A new theatre had been opened in the Second World War—the Pacific. Franklin D. Roosevelt served an unprecedented four consecutive terms as President (1933–45)—a record no longer allowable due to a constitutional amendment—but died in office, aged 63, on 12 April 1945, before the war ended.

Mohandas K Gandhi

'Quit India'

Address to All India Congress Committee, Bombay, 8 August 1942.

Mohandas Gandhi proved in his lifetime that non-violent defiance of unjust laws could change the world. He used this effectively both against the British and in an attempt to broker peace between Muslim and Hindu factions in his own country. It was a message as old as the time of Jesus and one subsequently used in protest movements throughout the world.

'Mahatma' (which means 'Great Soul') Gandhi's belief in the injustice of British colonialism in India saw him imprisoned several times, where he used fasting as an act of defiance and protest. In 1931 Gandhi was released from prison and, after brokering a truce between the National Congress and the British, travelled to London to attend the Round Table Conference on Indian constitutional reform. Returning to India, his pattern of civil disobedience and arrest continued but he also threatened to fast 'unto death' to placate warring religious factions. Finally Britain allowed Indian Congress ministers to hold office in provincial legislatures in 1937.

After the outbreak of World War II in September 1939, Gandhi stepped up his campaign for Indian home rule, arguing that an independent India could best serve Britain in her fight against fascism. In August 1942 Gandhi outlined his plan of action to the All India Congress Committee in Bombay, which was the formal vehicle being used to communicate with Britain. The following extract is part of the concluding portion of Gandhi's speech which was delivered in English.

❛ I have taken such an inordinately long time over pouring out what was agitating my soul, to those whom I had just now the privilege of serving. I have been called their leader or, in the military language, their commander. But I do not look at my position in that light. I have no weapon but love to wield my authority over anyone. I do sport a stick which you can break into bits without the slightest exertion. It is simply my staff with the help of which I walk. Such a cripple is not elated, when he has been called upon to bear the greatest burden. You can share that burden only when I appear before you not as your commander but as a humble servant. And he who serves best is the chief among equals.

I want to declare to the world. Although I may forfeit the regard of many friends in the West and I must bow my head low; but even for their friendship or love I must not suppress the voice of conscience—promoting my inner basic nature today. There is something within me impelling me to cry out my agony. I have known humanity. I have studied something of psychology. Such a man knows exactly what it is. I do not mind how you describe it. That voice within tells me, ʻYou have to stand against the whole world although you may have to stand alone. You have to stare in the face the whole world although the world may look at you with bloodshot eyes. Do not fear. Trust the little voice residing within your heart. It says : "Forsake friends, wife and all; but testify to that for which you have lived and for which you have to die. I want to live my full span of life. And for me I put my span of life at 120 years. By that time India will be free, the world will be free."

Let me tell you that I do not regard England or for that matter America as free countries. They are free after their own fashion, free to hold in bondage coloured races of the earth. Are England and America fighting for the liberty of these races today? If not, do not ask me to wait until after the war. You shall not limit my concept of freedom.

Unconsciously from its very foundations long ago, this Congress has been building on non-violence known as constitutional methods. I trust the whole of India today to launch upon a non-violent struggle. I trust, because of my nature to rely upon the innate goodness of human nature which perceives the truth and prevails during the crisis as if by instinct. But even if I am deceived in this I shall not swerve. I shall not flinch. From its very inception the Congress based its policy on peaceful methods, included Swaraj and the subsequent generations added non-violence. When Dadabhai entered the British Parliament, Salisbury dubbed him as a black man; but the English people defeated Salisbury and Dadabhai went to the Parliament by their vote. India was delirious with joy. These things however India has outgrown.

It is, however, with all these things as the background that I want Englishmen, Europeans and all the United Nations to examine in their hearts what crime has India committed in demanding Independence. I ask, is it right for you to distrust such an organization with all its background, tradition and record of over half a century and misrepresent its endeavours before all the world by every means at your command? Is it right that by hook or by crook, aided by the foreign press, aided by the President of the USA, or even by the Generalissimo of China [Chiang Kai-shek] who has yet to win his laurels, you should present India's struggle in shocking caricature? I have met the Generalissimo. I have known him through Madame Shek who was my interpreter; and though he seemed inscrutable to me, not so Madame Shek; and he allowed me to read his mind through her. There is a chorus of disapproval and righteous protest all over the world against us. They say we are erring, the move is inopportune. I used to have great regard for British diplomacy which has enabled them to hold the Empire so long. Now it stinks in my nostrils, and others have studied that diplomacy and are putting it into practice. They may succeed in getting, through these methods, world opinion on their side for a time; but India will speak against that world opinion. She will raise her voice against all the organized propaganda. I will speak against it. Even if all the United Nations opposed me, even if the whole of India forsakes me, I will say, "You are wrong. India will wrench with non-violence her liberty from unwilling hands."

I will go ahead not for India's sake alone, but for the sake of the world. Even if my eyes close before there is freedom, non-violence will not end. They will be dealing a mortal blow to China and to Russia if they oppose the freedom of non-violent India which is pleading with bended knees for the fulfilment of debt along overdue. Does a creditor ever go to debtor like that? And even when India is met with such angry opposition, she says, "We won't hit below the belt, we have learnt sufficient gentlemanliness. We are pledged to non-violence." I have been the author of the non-embarrassment policy of the Congress and yet today you find me talking this strong language. I say it is consistent with our honour. If a man holds me by the neck and wants to drawn me, may I not struggle to free myself directly? There is no inconsistency in our position today.

There are representatives of the foreign press assembled here today. Through them I wish to say to the world that the United Powers who somehow or other say that they have need for India, have the opportunity now to declare India free and prove their bona fides. If they miss it, they will be missing the opportunity of their lifetime, and history will record that they did not discharge their obligations to India in time, and lost the battle. I want the blessings of the whole world so that I may succeed with them. I do not want the United Powers to go beyond their obvious limitations. I do not want them to accept non-violence and disarm today. There is a fundamental difference between fascism and this imperialism which I am fighting. Do the British get from India which they hold in bondage? Think what difference it would make if India was to participate as a free ally. That freedom, if it is to come, must come today. It will have no taste left in it today if you who have the power to help cannot exercise it. If you can exercise it, under the glow of freedom what seems impossible, today, will become possible tomorrow.

If India feels that freedom, she will command that freedom for China. The road for running to Russia's help will be open. The Englishmen did not die in Malaya or on Burma soil. What shall enable us to retrieve the situation? Where shall I go, and where shall I take the forty crores of India? How is this vast mass of humanity to be aglow in the cause of world deliverance, unless and until it has touched and felt freedom. Today they have no touch of life left. It has been crushed out of them. It lustre is to be put into their eyes, freedom has to come not tomorrow, but today. '

Mohandas Karamchand Gandhi was born in 1869 in Poorbandar, West India. The son of the chief minister of the province and his fourth wife, a deeply religious Hindu, Gandhi was unable to find suitable work as a barrister and so accepted a contract to work in Natal, South Africa. There he came face to face with institutionalised racial discrimination and for the next 20 years opposed legislation that sought to deprive Indians and other minorities of their rights. Gandhi's non-violent defiance of unfair laws focused attention on his civil activities for the first time and his establishment of a volunteer Ambulance Corps during the Boer War (1899-1902) won him the English War Medal.

Returning to India in 1914, Gandhi became an advocate for 'home rule'—the complete withdrawal of English Imperial interests. He became the dominant figure of the National Congress movement but never wavered from his policies of non-violent, non co-operation in achieving Indian independence despite the threat of arrest and jail.

In the 1920s, with Hindu and Muslim members of the National Congress unable to find common ground, warring factions aligned to the two religious groups led to bloodshed. Unable to reason with either side Gandhi undertook a three-week fast that not only restored the non-violent aims of the 'home rule' campaign but also promoted his personal act of spiritual cleansing.

Gandhi famously described a British proposal for a new constitution after the war as 'a post-dated cheque on a crashing bank.' In 1942 he was jailed for civil disobedience designed to 'obstruct the war effort' and was not released until 1944. Gandhi then negotiated with the British Cabinet Mission in India which ultimately recommended a new constitutional structure for home rule in India.

However, divisions between Muslim and Hindu factions within the National Congress ultimately led to the formation of separate nations, India and Pakistan, and the dream of a country united in its freedom was lost. Britain effectively relinquished 163 years of empirial rule in India on 15 August, 1947—an act Gandhi described as 'the noblest act of the British nation.'

The final months of Gandhi's life were spent shaming the instigators of community and religious violence by fasting. Just as his fasting looked set to avert the country from plummeting into complete anarchy, Mohandas Gandhi was assassinated in Delhi on 30 January, 1948 by Hindu fanatic Nathuram Godse while walking in a garden with his grandchildren.

Golda Meir

'The Struggle for a Jewish State'

Council of Jewish Federations, Chicago, 2 January 1948.

Israel's third Prime Minister, Golda Meir (1898-1978) was born in Kiev in Russia and emigrated with her family to Milwaukee, Wisconsin, US in 1906. In 1915 she joined the Labor Zionist Organization (Poalei Zion) and moved to Palestine with her husband Morris Myerson. A leading socialist Zionist during the 1930s, she was also an International Zionist representative and spent 1932 working in the United States. After the end of World War II, Golda adopted the Hebrew name 'Meir' (which means 'to burn brightly') and became president of the political bureau of the Jewish Agency as thousands of Palestinian Jews and European refugees agitated for the formation of an official Jewish State in the traditional Holy Land region.

In February 1947 Britain ceded control of occupied Palestine to the United Nations which passed the seemingly impossible resolution to partition Palestine into Jewish and Arab states. Britain was ordered to leave Palestine by August 1948 but could do little to prepare either Jewish or Arab communities for independence. By the end of 1947, Palestinian and resettled Jewry were fighting both Arab terrorist and British peace-keeping forces.

In January 1948, Golda Meir flew to the United States to raise funds for weapons that were urgently needed to defend the 700 000 Jews in Palestine being threatened by Arab attacks. She made an unscheduled appearance before the Council of Jewish Federations and gave this heartfelt speech that moved thousands of people to give moral and financial support to the fledgling nation of Israel.

‘I have had the privilege of representing Palestine Jewry in this country and in other countries when the problems that we faced were those of building more kibbutzim, of bringing in more Jews in spite of political obstacles and Arab riots.

We always had faith that in the end we would win, that everything we were doing in the country led to the independence of the Jewish people and to a Jewish state.

Long before we had dared pronounce that word, we knew what was in store for us.

Today we have reached a point when the nations of the world have given us their decision—the establishment of a Jewish state in a part of Palestine. Now in Palestine we are fighting to make this resolution of the United Nations a reality, not because we wanted to fight. If we had the choice, we would have chosen peace to build in peace.

We have no alternative.

Friends, we have no alternative in Palestine. The Mufti and his men have declared war upon us. We have to fight for our lives, for our safety, and for what we have accomplished in Palestine, and perhaps above all, we must fight for Jewish honour and Jewish independence. Without exaggeration, I can tell you that the Jewish community in Palestine is doing this well. Many of you have visited Palestine; all of you have read about our young people and have a notion as to what our youth is like. I have known this generation for the last twenty-seven years. I thought I knew them. I realize now that even I did not.

These young boys and girls, many in their teens, are bearing the burden of what is happening in the country with a spirit that no words can describe. You see these youngsters in open cars—not armoured cars—in convoys going from Tel Aviv to Jerusalem, knowing that every time they start out from Tel Aviv or from Jerusalem there are probably Arabs behind the orange groves or the hills, waiting to ambush the convoy.

These boys and girls have accepted the task of bringing Jews over these roads in safety as naturally as though they were going out to their daily work or to their classes in the university.

We must ask the Jews the world over to see us as the front line.

All we ask of Jews the world over, and mainly of the Jews in the United States, is to give us the possibility of going on with the struggle.

When trouble started, we asked young people from the age of seventeen to twenty-five who were not members of Haganah, to volunteer. Up to the day that I left home on

Thursday morning, when the registration of this age group was still going on, over 20 000 young men and women had signed up. As of now we have about 9 000 people mobilized in the various parts of the country. We must triple this number within the next few days.

We have to maintain these men. No government sends its soldiers to the front and expects them to take along from their homes the most elementary requirements—blankets, bedding, clothing.

A people that is fighting for its very life knows how to supply the men they send to the front lines. We too must do the same.

Thirty-five of our boys, unable to go by car on the road to besieged Kfar Etzion to bring help, set out by foot through the hills; they knew the road, the Arab villages on that road, and the danger they would have to face. Some of the finest youngsters we have in the country were in that group, and they were all killed, every one of them. We have a description from an Arab of how they fought to the end for over seven hours against hundreds of Arabs. According to this Arab, the last boy killed, with no more ammunition left, died with a stone in his hand.

I want to say to you, friends, that the Jewish community in Palestine is going to fight to the very end. If we have arms to fight with, we will fight with those, and if not, we will fight with stones in our hands.

I want you to believe me when I say that I came on this special mission to the United States today not to save 700 000 Jews. During the last few years the Jewish people lost 6 million Jews, and it would be audacity on our part to worry the Jewish people throughout the world because a few hundred thousand more Jews were in danger. That is not the issue.

The issue is that if these 700 000 Jews in Palestine can remain alive, then the Jewish people as such is alive and Jewish independence is assured. If these 700 000 people are killed off, then for many centuries, we are through with this dream of a Jewish people and a Jewish homeland.

My friends, we are at war. There is no Jew in Palestine who does not believe that finally we will be victorious. That is the spirit of the country. And every Jew in the country also knows that within a few months a Jewish state in Palestine will be established.

We knew that the price we would have to pay would be the best of our people. There are over 300 killed by now. There will be more. There is no doubt that there will be more. But there is also no doubt that the spirit of our young people is such that no matter how many Arabs invade the country, their spirit will not falter. However, this valiant spirit alone cannot face rifles and machine guns. Rifles and machine guns without spirit are not worth very much, but spirit without arms can in time be broken with the body.

I have come to the United States, and I hope you will understand me if I say that it is not an easy matter for any of us to leave home at present—to my sorrow I am not in the front line. I am not with my daughter in the Negev or with other sons and daughters in the trenches. But I have a job to do.

I have come here to try to impress Jews in the United States with the fact that within a very short period, a couple of weeks, we must have in cash between 25 and 30 million dollars. In the next two or three weeks we can establish ourselves. Of that we are convinced, and you must have faith; we are sure that we can carry on.

I said before that the Yishuv will give, is giving of its means. But please remember that even while shooting is going on, we must carry on so that our economy remains intact. Our factories must go on. Our settlements must not be broken up.

We know that this battle is being waged for those not yet in the country.

There are 30 000 Jews detained right next door to Palestine in Cyprus. I believe that within a very short period, within the next two or three months at most, these 30 000 will be with us, among them thousands of infants and young children. We must now think of preparing means of absorbing them. We know that within the very near future, hundreds of thousands more will be coming in. We must see that our economy is intact.

I want you to understand that there is no despair in the Yishuv. When you go to Tel Aviv now, you will find the city full of life; only the shooting that you hear on the outskirts of Tel Aviv and Jaffa reminds one that the situation in the country is not normal. But it would be a crime on my part not to describe the situation to you exactly as it is.

Merely with our ten fingers and merely with spirit and sacrifice, we cannot carry on this battle, and the only hinterland that we have is you. The Mufti has the Arab states—not all so enthusiastic about helping him but states with government budgets. The Egyptian government can vote a budget to aid our antagonists. The Syrian government can do the same.

We have no government. But we have millions of Jews in the Diaspora, and exactly as we have faith in our youngsters in Palestine I have faith in Jews in the United States; I believe that they will realize the peril of our situation and will do what they have to do.

I know that we are not asking for something easy. I myself have sometimes been active in various campaigns and fund collections, and I know that collecting at once a sum such as I ask is not simple.

But I have seen our people at home. I have seen them come from the offices to the clinics when we called the community to give their blood for a blood bank to treat the wounded. I have seen them lined up for hours, waiting so that some of their blood can be added to this bank.

It is blood plus money that is being given in Palestine.

We are not a better breed; we are not the best Jews of the Jewish people. It so happened that we are there and you are here. I am certain that if you were in Palestine and we were in the United States, you would be doing what we are doing there, and you would ask us here to do what you will have to do.

I want to close with paraphrasing one of the greatest speeches that was made during the Second World War—the words of Churchill. I am not exaggerating when I say that the Yishuv in Palestine will fight in the Negev and will fight in Galilee and will fight on the outskirts of Jerusalem until the very end.

You cannot decide whether we should fight or not. We will. The Jewish community in Palestine will raise no white flag for the Mufti. That decision is taken. Nobody can change it. You can only decide one thing: whether we shall be victorious in this fight or whether the Mufti will be victorious. That decision American Jews can make. It has to be made quickly within hours, within days.

And I beg of you—don't be too late. Don't be bitterly sorry three months from now for what you failed to do today. The time is now.

I have spoken to you without a grain of exaggeration. I have not tried to paint the picture in false colours. It consists of spirit and certainty of our victory on the one hand, and dire necessity for carrying on the battle on the other.

I want to thank you again for having given me the opportunity at a conference that I am certain has a full agenda to say these few words to you. I leave the platform without any doubt in my mind or my heart that the decision that will be taken by American Jewry will be the same as that which was taken by the Jewish community in Palestine, so that within a few months from now we will all be able to participate not only in the joy of resolving to establish a Jewish state, but in the joy of laying the cornerstone of the Jewish state. ,

The State of Israel was proclaimed on 14 May 1948 but the fight against Egypt, Transjordan, Iraq, Syria and Lebanon for ultimate survival began the next day. Thousands of Israeli and Arab soldiers died in the ensuing fighting with 600 000 Palestinian refugees fleeing their homeland—a problem that continues today. Foundation Prime Minister, David Ben-Gurion, later stated: 'Someday, when history will be written, it will be said that there was a Jewish woman who got the money which made the state possible.'

In 1966 Golda Meir became secretary general of the Israeli Workers Party (Mapai) and following its incorporation into the Israeli Labor Party, she was chosen as its secretary. Upon the death of Levi Eshkol in 1969 the respective party factions chose Meir as Prime Minister. Her first challenge as Israeli leader was during the victorious Six-Day War in June 1967 in which neighbouring Arab States of Egypt, Syria and Jordan attempted to exact revenge for territories lost in disputes in 1948 and 1956.

In 1972 Palestinian terrorists killed 11 Israeli athletes competing in the Munich Olympics. The following year, Israel was involved in another conflict—the 'Yom Kippur War'—in which Egyptian leader Anwar el-Sadat attempted to enforce the United Nations 'Resolution 242'—Israel's total withdrawal from territories taken in 1967. Although Meir was able to form a government following the end of the conflict in the December 1973 elections, she had lost the control of her cabinet and resigned as Prime Minister in April 1974.

Golda Meir died in Jerusalem on 8 December, 1978, aged 80.

Margaret Chase Smith

'Declaration of Conscience'

Speech to the US Senate, 1 June 1950.

Margaret Madeline Chase (1897-1995) was the only woman elected to serve both houses of the United States Congress. After establishing the Maine chapter of the Business and Professional Women's Club in 1922 she married newspaper publisher Clyde Smith, who was elected to Congress in 1936. When Smith died suddenly, she succeeded him in the House of Representatives and began 33 years of Congressional service.

Although a Republican, she often opposed her party and voted with her conscience in the best interests of the people of Maine.

In 1948 Mrs Chase Smith was elected to the US Senate without the support of her party with the greatest majority total vote in the history of Maine—70 per cent—which she maintained in election victories in 1954, 1960 and 1966. In June 1950 she was one of the first elected representatives to speak out against Joseph McCarthy—a fellow Republican—and denounce the smear and bullying tactics used by the Senator in his anti-communist campaign.

❬Mr. President. I would like to speak briefly and simply about a serious national condition. It is a national feeling of fear and frustration that could result in national suicide and the end of everything that we Americans hold dear. It is a condition that comes from the lack of effective leadership in either the Legislative Branch or the Executive Branch of our Government.

That leadership is so lacking that serious and responsible proposals are being made that national advisory commissions be appointed to provide such critically needed leadership.

I speak as briefly as possible because too much harm has already been done with irresponsible words of bitterness and selfish political opportunism. I speak as briefly as possible because the issue is too great to be obscured by eloquence. I speak simply and briefly in the hope that my words will be taken to heart.

I speak as a Republican. I speak as a woman. I speak as a United States Senator. I speak as an American.

The United States Senate has long enjoyed worldwide respect as the greatest deliberative body in the world. But recently that deliberative character has too often been debased to the level of a forum of hate and character assassination sheltered by the shield of congressional immunity.

It is ironical that we Senators can in debate in the Senate directly or indirectly, by any form of words, impute to any American who is not a Senator any conduct or motive unworthy or unbecoming an American—and without that non-Senator American having any legal redress against us—yet if we say the same thing in the Senate about our colleagues we can be stopped on the grounds of being out of order.

It is strange that we can verbally attack anyone else without restraint and with full protection and yet we hold ourselves above the same type of criticism here on the Senate Floor. Surely the United States Senate is big enough to take self-criticism and self-appraisal. Surely we should be able to take the same kind of character attacks that we "dish out" to outsiders.

I think that it is high time for the United States Senate and its members to do some soul-searching—for us to weigh our consciences—on the manner in which we are performing our duty to the people of America—on the manner in which we are using or abusing our individual powers and privileges.

I think that it is high time that we remembered that we have sworn to uphold and defend the Constitution. I think that it is high time that we remembered that the Constitution, as amended, speaks not only of the freedom of speech but also of trial by jury instead of trial by accusation.

Whether it be a criminal prosecution in court or a character prosecution in the Senate, there is little practical distinction when the life of a person has been ruined.

Those of us who shout the loudest about Americanism in making character assassinations are all too frequently those who, by our own words and acts, ignore some of the basic principles of Americanism:

The right to criticize;
The right to hold unpopular beliefs;
The right to protest;
The right of independent thought.

The exercise of these rights should not cost one single American citizen his reputation or his right to a livelihood nor should he be in danger of losing his reputation or livelihood merely because he happens to know someone who holds unpopular beliefs. Who of us doesn't? Otherwise none of us could call our souls our own. Otherwise thought control would have set in. The American people are sick and tired of being afraid to speak their minds lest they be politically smeared as "communists" or "fascists" by their opponents. Freedom of speech is not what it used to be in America. It has been so abused by some that it is not exercised by others.

The American people are sick and tired of seeing innocent people smeared and guilty people whitewashed. But there have been enough proved cases, such as the 'Amerasia' case, the Hiss case, the Coplon case, the Gold case, to cause the nationwide distrust and strong suspicion that there may be something to the unproved, sensational accusations.

As a Republican, I say to my colleagues on this side of the aisle that the Republican Party faces a challenge today that is not unlike the challenge that it faced back in Lincoln's day. The Republican Party so successfully met that challenge that it emerged from the Civil War as the champion of a united nation—in addition to being a Party that unrelentingly fought loose spending and loose programs.

Today our country is being psychologically divided by the confusion and the suspicions that are bred in the United States Senate to spread like cancerous tentacles of "know nothing, suspect everything" attitudes. Today we have a Democratic Administration that has developed a mania for loose spending and loose programs. History is repeating itself—and the Republican Party again has the opportunity to emerge as the champion of unity and prudence.

The record of the present Democratic Administration has provided us with sufficient campaign issues without the necessity of resorting to political smears. America is rapidly losing its position as leader of the world simply because the Democratic Administration has pitifully failed to provide effective leadership.

The Democratic Administration has completely confused the American people by its daily contradictory grave warnings and optimistic assurances—that show the people that our Democratic Administration has no idea of where it is going.

The Democratic Administration has greatly lost the confidence of the American people by its complacency to the threat of communism here at home and the leak of vital secrets to Russia though key officials of the Democratic Administration. There are enough proved cases to make this point without diluting our criticism with unproved charges.

Surely these are sufficient reasons to make it clear to the American people that it is time for a change and that a Republican victory is necessary to the security of this country. Surely it is clear that this nation will continue to suffer as long as it is governed by the present ineffective Democratic Administration.

Yet to displace it with a Republican regime embracing a philosophy that lacks political integrity or intellectual honesty would prove equally disastrous to this nation. The nation sorely needs a Republican victory. But I don't want to see the Republican Party ride to political victory on the Four Horsemen of Calumny—Fear, Ignorance, Bigotry, and Smear.

I doubt if the Republican Party could—simply because I don't believe the American people will uphold any political party that puts political exploitation above national interest. Surely we Republicans aren't that desperate for victory.

I don't want to see the Republican Party win that way. While it might be a fleeting victory for the Republican Party, it would be a more lasting defeat for the American people. Surely it would ultimately be suicide for the Republican Party and the two-party system that has protected our American liberties from the dictatorship of a one party system.

As members of the Minority Party, we do not have the primary authority to formulate the policy of our Government. But we do have the responsibility of rendering constructive criticism, of clarifying issues, of allaying fears by acting as responsible citizens.

As a woman, I wonder how the mothers, wives, sisters, and daughters feel about the way in which members of their families have been politically mangled in the Senate debate -- and I use the word "debate" advisedly.

As a United States Senator, I am not proud of the way in which the Senate has been made a publicity platform for irresponsible sensationalism. I am not proud of the reckless abandon in which unproved charges have been hurled from the side of the aisle. I am not proud of the obviously staged, undignified counter-charges that have been attempted in retaliation from the other side of the aisle.

I don't like the way the Senate has been made a rendezvous for vilification, for selfish political gain at the sacrifice of individual reputations and national unity. I am not proud of the way we smear outsiders from the Floor of the Senate and hide behind the cloak of congressional immunity and still place ourselves beyond criticism on the Floor of the Senate.

As an American, I am shocked at the way Republicans and Democrats alike are playing directly into the Communist design of "confuse, divide, and conquer." As an American, I don't want a Democratic Administration "whitewash" or "cover-up" any more than I want a Republican smear or witch hunt.

As an American, I condemn a Republican "Fascist" just as much I condemn a Democratic "Communist." I condemn a Democrat "Fascist" just as much as I condemn a Republican "Communist." They are equally dangerous to you and me and to our country. As an American, I want to see our nation recapture the strength and unity it once had when we fought the enemy instead of ourselves.

It is with these thoughts that I have drafted what I call a "Declaration of Conscience." I am gratified that Senator Tobey, Senator Aiken, Senator Morse, Senator Ives, Senator Thye, and Senator Hendrickson have concurred in that declaration and have authorized me to announce their concurrence. **'**

Although she didn't mention her Republican colleague by name, Smith's 15-minute speech earned McCarthy's ire—and the admiration of her president, Harry S Truman. McCarthy removed Mrs Chase Smith as a member of the Permanent Subcommittee on Investigations, and gave her place to the junior senator from California—Richard M Nixon.

In 1964 Margaret Chase Smith became the first woman to be nominated by a major party as a Presidential candidate and received 27 nominating votes at the Republican National Convention. In 1973, after serving in the Senate for 24 years, Chase Smith lost her seat. After leaving the Senate, Smith lectured at colleges and conducted public policy seminars. She wrote for newspapers and magazines and authored *Gallant Women* (biographies of twelve American women) and *Declaration of Conscience*, about her time serving the American people.

Chase Smith continued to champion women's rights and oppose bigotry and injustice long after she left office. She received innumerable awards during her lifetime and was one of the original inductees of the National Women's Hall of Fame (1973). She received more than 85 honorary degrees and was named 'Woman of the Year' by the Associated Press in 1948, 1949, 1950 and 1957. In 1989 she received the Presidential Medal of Freedom from President Bill Clinton. Margaret Chase Smith died in Skowhegan, Maine in 1995.

Harry S. Truman

'MacArthur and Korea'

Washington DC, 11 April 1951

F ollowing the end of World War II in 1945, US President Harry S. Truman (1884–1972) proposed the 'Fair Deal' program but battled a 'do-nothing' Republican-dominated Congress which blocked most of his domestic reforms.

In March 1947, he committed America's economic, political and military support to countries threatened by 'outside pressures'—Communism. The Truman Doctrine, as it became known, hastened the advent of the Cold War and was directly responsible for portraying the United States as the democratic sheriff of the free world.

After winning a narrow victory over the Republican candidate, Thomas E. Dewey, in 1948 (newspapers actually reported that Dewey had won) Truman approved a post-war loan to Britain and sent US troops to South Korea for the police-action that eventually escalated into the Korean War (1950–53).

Under the command of General Douglas MacArthur, United Nations troops pushed the North Korean army back beyond the 38th Parallel in September 1950 and then pressed on to the northern capital, Pyongyang.

MacArthur was sure Russian and Chinese troops would not support the North Koreans, but he was wrong—many of the prisoners captured near the Yula River which bordered Manchuria were Chinese regulars. MacArthur bombed bridges on the Yula but this did not stop Chairman Mao sending 300,000 troops to support the North Koreans. United Nations forces, with MacArthur at the helm, were forced to retreat back below the 38th Parallel.

By early 1951, General MacArthur was openly critical of his President, his own military superiors and America's allies, for their lack of support in the face of Chinese aggression. When he made his intentions clear in the press—to blockade the Chinese mainland, use atomic weapons to suppress the enemy and invade both China and Korea with the help of Chiang Kai-shek's Chinese Nationalist forces—and then invited the Chinese Communist leadership to meet with him, Truman removed MacArthur from his command.

In this speech to the American people, relying heavily on the facts at hand, President Truman explained the reasons why he took this action:

❟In the simplest terms, what we are doing in Korea is this: We are trying to prevent a third world war.

I think most people in this country recognized that fact last June. And they warmly supported the decision of the Government to help the Republic of Korea against the Communist aggressors. Now, many persons, even some who applauded our decision to defend Korea, have forgotten the basic reason for our action.

It is right for us to be in Korea. It was right last June. It is right today.

I want to remind you why this is true. The Communists in the Kremlin are engaged in a monstrous conspiracy to stamp out freedom all over the world. If they were to succeed, the United States would be numbered among their principal victims. It must be clear to everyone that the United States cannotand will not sit idly by and await foreign conquest.

The only question is: When is the best time to meet the threat and how?

The best time to meet the threat is in the beginning. It is easier to put out a fire in the beginning when it is small than after it has become a roaring blaze.

And the best way to meet the threat of aggression is for the peace-loving nations to act together. If they don't act together, they are likely to be picked off, one by one.

If they had followed the right policies in the 1930's—if the free countries had acted together, to crush the aggression of the dictators, and if they had acted in the beginning, when the aggression was small, there probably would have been no World War II.

If history has taught us anything, it is that aggression anywhere in the world is a threat to peace everywhere in the world. When that aggression is supported by cruel and selfish rulers of a powerful nation who are bent on conquest, it becomes a clear and present danger to the security and independence of every free nation.

This is a lesson that most people in this country have learned thoroughly. This is the basic reason why we joined in creating the United Nations. And since the end of World War II, we have been putting that lesson into practice—we have been working with other free nations to check the aggressive designs of the Soviet Union before they can result in a third world war.

That is what we did in Greece, when that nation was threatened by the aggression of internationalCommunism. The attack against Greece could have led to general war. But this country came to the aid of Greece. The United Nations supported Greek resistance. With our help, the determination and efforts of the Greek people defeated the attack on the spot. Another big communist threat to peace was the Berlin blockade. That too could have led to war. But again it was settled because free men would not back down in an emergency. The aggression against Korea is the boldest and most dangerous move the communists have yet made. The attack on Korea was part of a greater plan for conquering all of Asia....

They want to control all Asia from the Kremlin....

The whole communist imperialism is back of the attack on peace in the Far East. It was the Soviet Union that trained and equipped the North Koreans for aggression. The Chinese communists massed 44 well-trained and well-equipped divisions on the Korean frontier. These were the troops they threw into battle when the North Korean Ccommunists were beaten....

So far, by fighting a limited war in Korea, we have prevented aggression from succeeding and bringing on a general war. And the ability of the whole free world to resist Communist aggression has been greatly improved.

We have taught the enemy a lesson. He has found out that aggression is not cheap or easy. Moreover, men all over the world who want to remain free have been given new courage and new hope. They know now that the champions of freedom can stand up and fight and that they will stand up and fight. Our resolute stand in Korea is helping the forces of freedom now fighting in Indochina and other countries in that part of the world. It has already slowed down the timetable of conquest....

But you may ask: Why can't we take other steps to punish the aggressor? Why don't we bomb Manchuria and China itself? Why don't we assist Chinese Nationalist troops to land on the mainland of China?

If we were to do these things, we would be running a very grave risk of starting a general war. If that were to happen, we would have brought about the exact situation we are trying to prevent.

If we were to do these things, we would become entangled in a vast conflict on the continent of Asia and our task would become immeasurably more difficult all over the world.

What would suit the ambitions of the Kremlin better than for our military forces to be committed to a full-scale war with Red China?

It may well be that, in spite of our best efforts, the Communists may spread the war. But it would be wrong—tragically wrong—for us to take the initiative in extending the war.

The dangers are great. Make no mistake about it. Behind the North Koreans and Chinese Communists in the front lines stand additional millions of Chinese soldiers. And behind the Chinese stand the tanks, the planes, the submarines, the soldiers and the scheming rulers of the Soviet Union.

Our aim is to avoid the spread of the conflict.

The course we have been following is the one best calculated to avoid an all-out war. It is the course consistent with our obligation to do all we can to maintain international peace and security. Our experience in Greece and Berlin shows that it is the most effective course of action we can follow.

First of all, it is clear that our efforts in Korea can blunt the will of the Chinese Communists to continue the struggle. The United Nations forces have put up a tremendous fight in Korea and have inflicted very heavy casualties on the enemy. Our forces are stronger now than they have been before. These are plain facts which may discourage the Chinese Communists from continuing their attack.

Second, the free world as a whole is growing in military strength every day. In the United States, in Western Europe and throughout the world, free men are alert to the Soviet threat and are building their defenses. This may discourage the Communist rulers from continuing the war in Korea—and from undertaking new acts of aggression elsewhere.

If the Communist authorities realize that they cannot defeat us in Korea, if they realize it would be foolhardy to widen the hostilities beyond Korea, then they may recognize the folly of continuing their aggression. A peaceful settlement may then be possible. The door is always open....

I believe that we must try to limit the war to Korea for these vital reasons: To make sure that the precious lives of our fighting men are not wasted; to see that the security of our country and the free world is not needlessly jeopardized; and to prevent a third world war.

A number of events have made it evident that General MacArthur did not agree with that policy. I have therefore considered it essential to relieve General MacArthur so that there would be no doubt or confusion as to the real purpose and aim of our policy.

It was with the deepest personal regret that I found myself compelled to take this action. General MacArthur is one of our greatest military commanders. But the cause of world peace is more important than any individual. *"*

United Nations troops eventually held under the biggest Communist offensive of the war and armistice negotiations commenced in July 1951. The terms: A full ceasefire, the retention of the 38th Parallel as a permanent border and the repatriation of prisoners—dragged the war on for another 15 months.

Harry Truman was defeated by Dwight D. Eisenhower in the 1952 Presidential election and Russian leader, Josef Stalin, died the following year. An armistice was signed in 1953 but no formal peace treaty has ever been signed to end the Korean War.

One hundred and eighty thousand United Nations troops were lost; the majority of them American (three million Korean military and civilian lost their lives).

In the years that have passed, Harry Truman's direct, plain-speaking rhetoric has made him something of a folk hero with the American public—but not until long after he left office in 1952 with one of the lowest approval ratings of any American president this century.

Douglas MacArthur

'Old Soldiers Never Die'

Address to US Congress, Washington DC, 20 April 1951.

D ouglas MacArthur (1880-1964), the hero of the Pacific during World War II, fell spectacularly from grace during the Korean War. Despite being relieved of his command, he was given a hero's homecoming, and is today remembered as a modern military icon.

After serving in the Philippines and France in World War I, he became Commander in Chief of US army forces in the Pacific theater of World War II. Forced to retreat from the Philippines in March 1942, he conducted the liberation of the southwest Pacific from his Australian base during the next three years. In September 1945, MacArthur formally accepted the Japanese surrender aboard the *USS Missouri* and as the head of occupied forces in Japan earned the unflattering empirical mantle of 'Viceroy of Japan' for his superior single-mindedness in doing things his own way. MacArthur was even considered as a Republican presidential candidate but his defeat in the Wisconsin primary in 1948 eroded his support base.

During World War II, Korea had been divided into two states along the invisible 38th Parallel, with Russia protecting the northern section and America the southern. Both sections held 'elections' in the late 1940s but North Korea had become dominated by communists and unification with the (southern-based) 'Republic of Korea' seemed as far as away as ever. In June 1950, 80 000 North Korean troops backed by Russian tanks launched a surprise invasion of South Korea. US President Harry S Truman immediately dispatched American troops based in Japan and was able to garner support from the United Nations to undertake a 'police action' under the control of General Douglas MacArthur to recapture Seoul.

After early success pushing North Korean troops back past the 38th Parallel, MacArthur rashly pressed on towards the northern capital Pyongyang. Sure that Russian and Chinese troops would not support the North Koreans, MacArthur bombed bridges on the Yula which prompted China's Chairman Mao to send 300 000 troops to support the North Koreans. United Nations forces were then forced to retreat.

The hero of World War II was determined to this conflict and openly criticised President Truman, his own military superiors and America's allies for their lack of support in the face of Chinese aggression. He made his intentions clear in the press—blockade the Chinese mainland, use atomic weapons to suppress the enemy and invade both China and Korea with the help of Chiang Kai-shek's Nationalist forces. When he independently invited the Chinese leadership to meet with him in April 1951, Truman removed MacArthur from his command.

On his return to the United States, General Douglas MacArthur was invited to address a joint session of Congress. He condemned America's 'blackmail of appeasement' and ended with one of the most-quoted epitaphs of the twentieth century—old soldiers never die; they just fade away.

❛I stand on this rostrum with a sense of deep humility and great pride—humility in the wake of those great architects of our history who have stood here before me, pride in the reflection that this home of legislative debate represents human liberty in the purest form yet devised.

Here are centered the hopes and aspirations and faith of the entire human race.

I do not stand here as advocate for any partisan cause, for the issues are fundamental and reach quite beyond the realm of partisan considerations. They must be resolved on the highest plane of national interest, if our course is to prove sound and our future protected.

I trust, therefore, that you will do me the justice of receiving that which I have to say as solely expressing the considered viewpoint of a fellow American.

I address you with neither rancor nor bitterness in the fading twilight of life, with but one purpose in mind: To serve my country.

The issues are global, and so interlocked that to consider the problems of one sector oblivious to those of another is to court disaster for the whole. While Asia is commonly referred to as the gateway to Europe, it is no less true that Europe is the gateway to Asia, and the broad influence of the one cannot fail to have its impact upon the other.

There are those who claim our strength is inadequate to protect on both fronts, that we cannot divide our effort. I can think of no greater expression of defeatism.

If a potential enemy can divide his strength on two fronts, it is for us to counter his efforts. The Communist threat is a global one. Its successful advance in one sector threatens the destruction of every other sector. You cannot appease or otherwise surrender to Communism in Asia without simultaneously undermining our efforts to halt its advance in Europe.

Beyond pointing out these general truisms, I shall confine my discussion to the general areas of Asia.

While I was not consulted prior to the President's decision to intervene in support of the Republic of Korea, that decision, from a military standpoint, proved a sound one. As I say, it proved a sound one, as we hurled back the invader and decimated his forces. Our victory was complete, and our objectives within reach, when Red China intervened with numerically superior ground forces.

This created a new war and an entirely new situation, a situation not contemplated when our forces were committed against the North Korean invaders; a situation which called for new decisions in the diplomatic sphere to permit the realistic adjustment of military strategy. Such decisions have not been forthcoming. While no man in his right mind would advocate sending our ground forces into continental China, and such was never given a thought, the new situation did urgently demand a drastic revision of strategic planning, if our political aim was to defeat this new enemy as we had defeated the old.

Apart from the military need, as I saw it, to neutralize the sanctuary protection given the enemy north of the Yalu, I felt that military necessity in the conduct of the war made necessary:

1. The intensification of our economic blockade against China.

2. The imposition of a naval blockade against the China coast.
3. Removal of restrictions on air reconnaissance of China's coastal area and of Manchuria.
4. Removal of restrictions on the forces of the Republic of China on Formosa, with logistical support to contribute to their effective operations against the Chinese mainland.

For entertaining these views, all professionally designed to support our forces committed to Korea and to bring hostilities to an end with the least possible delay and at a saving of countless American and Allied lives, I have been severely criticized in lay circles, principally abroad, despite my understanding that, from a military standpoint, the above views have been fully shared in the past by practically every military leader concerned with the Korean campaign, including our own Joint Chiefs of Staff.

I called for reinforcements, but was informed that reinforcements were not available. I made clear that if not permitted to destroy the enemy built-up bases north of the Yalu, if not permitted to utilize the friendly Chinese force of some 600 000 men on Formosa, if not permitted to blockade the China coast to prevent the Chinese Reds from getting succor from without, and if there were to be no hope of major reinforcements, the position of the command from the military standpoint forbade victory.

We could hold in Korea by constant manoeuvre and at an approximate area where our supply-line advantages were in balance with the supply-line disadvantages of the enemy, but we could hope at best for only an indecisive campaign with its terrible and constant attrition upon our forces if the enemy utilized his full military potential.

I have constantly called for the new political decisions essential to a solution. Efforts have been made to distort my position. It has been said, in effect, that I was a warmonger. Nothing could be further from the truth.

I know war as few other men now living know it, and nothing to me is more revolting! I have long advocated its complete abolition, as its very destructiveness on both friend and foe has rendered it useless as a means of settling international disputes.

Indeed, on the second day of September, 1945, just following the surrender of the Japanese nation on the battleship Missouri, I formally cautioned as follows:

'Men since the beginning of time have sought peace. Various methods through the ages have been attempted to devise an international process to prevent or settle disputes between nations. From the very start, workable methods were found in so far as individual citizens were concerned, but the mechanics of an instrumentality of larger international scope have never been successful.

Military alliances, balances of power, leagues of nations, all in turn failed, leaving the only path to be by way of the crucible of war. The utter destructiveness of war now blocks out this alternative. We have had our last chance. If we will not devise some greater and more equitable system, our Armageddon will be at our door. The problem basically is theological and involves a spiritual recrudescence, an improvement of human character that will synchronize with our almost matchless advances in science, art, literature, and all material and cultural developments of the past two thousand years. It must be of the spirit if we are to save the flesh.

But once war is forced upon us, there is no other alternative than to apply every available means to bring it to a swift end. War's very object is victory, not prolonged indecision. In war, there is no substitute for victory.

There are some who, for varying reasons, would appease Red China. They are blind to history's clear lesson, for history teaches with unmistakable emphasis that appeasement but begets new and bloodier war. It points to no single instance where this end has justified that means, where appeasement has led to more than a sham peace. Like blackmail, it lays the basis for new and successively greater demands until, as in blackmail, violence becomes the only other alternative.

Why, my soldiers asked of me, surrender military advantages to an enemy in the field? I could not answer.

Some may say to avoid spread of the conflict into an all-out war with China. Others, to avoid Soviet intervention. Neither explanation seems valid, for China is already engaging with the maximum power it can commit, and the Soviet [Union] will not necessarily mesh its actions with our moves. Like a cobra, any new enemy will more likely strike whenever it feels that the relativity in military or other potential is in its favor on a world-wide basis.

The tragedy of Korea is further heightened by the fact that its military action is confined to its territorial limits. It condemns that nation, which it is our purpose to save, to suffer the devastating impact of full naval and air bombardment, while the enemy's sanctuaries are fully protected from such attack and devastation.

Of the nations of the world Korea alone, up to now, is the sole one which has risked its all against communism. The magnificence of the courage and fortitude of the Korean people defies description. They have chosen to risk death rather than slavery. Their last words to me were: "Don't scuttle the Pacific."

I have just left your fighting sons in Korea. They have met all tests there, and I can report to you without reservation that they are splendid in every way. It was my constant effort to preserve them and end this savage conflict honorably and with the least loss of time and a minimum sacrifice of life. Its growing bloodshed has caused me the deepest anguish and anxiety. Those gallant men will remain often in my thoughts and in my prayers always.

I am closing my 52 years of military service. When I joined the army, even before the turn of the century, it was the fulfillment of all of my boyish hopes and dreams.

The world has turned over many times since I took the oath on the plain at West Point, and the hopes and dreams have long since vanished, but I still remember the refrain of one of the most popular barracks ballads of that day which proclaimed most proudly that 'old soldiers never die; they just fade away.' And like the old soldier of that ballad, I now close my military career and just fade away, an old soldier who tried to do his duty as God gave him the light to see that duty. Good-bye. **'**

General MacArthur retired to private life when he was defeated by another war hero—Dwight D. Eisenhower—for the Republican nomination for the 1952 presidential race. MacArthur later worked on the boards of several companies before passing away in Washington DC on 5 April, 1964, aged 84.

Dwight D Eisenhower

'Cross of Iron'

Speech to the American Society of Newspaper Editors, 16 April 1953.

Dwight D 'Ike' Eisenhower (1890-1969) was the Supreme Commander of Allied forces during World War II and was perceived by the American public as a living hero. After first declining to run as a Democratic presidential nominee, 'Ike' accepted the Republican Party's nomination as presidential candidate in 1952. After winning the New Hampshire Republican primary without even campaigning, his presidential victory became a formality when he used a new communication medium—television—to sell his candidacy to the American public. Eisenhower's magnetism as a leader, running a campaign that addressed the issues of 'Communism, Corruption and Korea', overcame the potential scandal concerning his running mate, Richard M Nixon.

Eisenhower's presidency received an immediate boost when relations with Russia mellowed following the death of Soviet dictator Josef Stalin in March 1953. However Eisenhower's greatest fear remained that America would 'spend itself broke' in an arms race before a threat from Russia ever eventuated. In this speech of 1953, Eisenhower demonstrated the futility of a 'cold war' arms race. He compared William Jennings Bryan's phrase, a 'cross of gold'—first used in 1896 at the Democratic National Convention to criticise public monetary policy—to a 'cross of iron' to describe the expenditures of both the United States and the Soviet Union on armaments.

The following speech was broadcast over television and radio from the Statler Hotel in Washington.

❦ In this spring of 1953 the free world weighs one question above all others: the chance for a just peace for all peoples.

To weigh this chance is to summon instantly to mind another recent moment of great decision. It came with that yet more hopeful spring of 1945, bright with the promise of victory and of freedom. The hope of all just men in that moment too was a just and lasting peace.

The eight years that have passed have seen that hope waver, grow dim, and almost die. And the shadow of fear again has darkly lengthened across the world.

Today the hope of free men remains stubborn and brave, but it is sternly disciplined by experience. It shuns not only all crude counsel of despair but also the self-deceit of easy illusion. It weighs the chance for peace with sure, clear knowledge of what happened to the vain hope of 1945.

In that spring of victory the soldiers of the Western Allies met the soldiers of Russia in the center of Europe. They were triumphant comrades in arms. Their peoples shared the joyous prospect of building, in honor of their dead, the only fitting monument—an age of just peace. All these war-weary peoples shared too this concrete, decent purpose: to guard vigilantly against the domination ever again of any part of the world by a single, unbridled aggressive power.

This common purpose lasted an instant and perished. The nations of the world divided to follow two distinct roads.

The United States and our valued friends, the other free nations, chose one road.

The leaders of the Soviet Union chose another.

The way chosen by the United States was plainly marked by a few clear precepts, which govern its conduct in world affairs.

First: No people on earth can be held, as a people, to be enemy, for all humanity shares the common hunger for peace and fellowship and justice.

Second: No nation's security and well-being can be lastingly achieved in isolation but only in effective cooperation with fellow-nations.

Third: Any nation's right to a form of government and an economic system of its own choosing is inalienable.

Fourth: Any nation's attempt to dictate to other nations their form of government is indefensible.

And fifth: A nation's hope of lasting peace cannot be firmly based upon any race in armaments but rather upon just relations and honest understanding with all other nations.

In the light of these principles the citizens of the United States defined the way they proposed to follow, through the aftermath of war, toward true peace.

This way was faithful to the spirit that inspired the United Nations: to prohibit strife, to relieve tensions, to banish fears. This way was to control and to reduce armaments. This way was to allow all nations to devote their energies and resources to the great and good tasks of healing the war's wounds, of clothing and feeding and housing the needy, of perfecting a just political life, of enjoying the fruits of their own free toil.

The Soviet government held a vastly different vision of the future.

In the world of its design, security was to be found, not in mutual trust and mutual aid but in force: huge armies, subversion, rule of neighbor nations. The goal was power superiority at all costs. Security was to be sought by denying it to all others.

The result has been tragic for the world and, for the Soviet Union, it has also been ironic.

The amassing of the Soviet power alerted free nations to a new danger of aggression. It compelled them in self-defence to spend unprecedented money and energy for armaments. It forced them to develop weapons of war now capable of inflicting instant and terrible punishment upon any aggressor.

It instilled in the free nations—and let none doubt this—the unshakable conviction that, as long as there persists a threat to freedom, they must, at any cost, remain armed, strong, and ready for the risk of war. It inspired them—and let none doubt this—to attain a unity of purpose and will beyond the power of propaganda or pressure to break, now or ever.

There remained, however, one thing essentially unchanged and unaffected by Soviet conduct: the readiness of the free nations to welcome sincerely any genuine evidence of peaceful purpose enabling all peoples again to resume their common quest of just peace.

The free nations, most solemnly and repeatedly, have assured the Soviet Union that their firm association has never had any aggressive purpose whatsoever. Soviet leaders, however, have seemed to persuade themselves, or tried to persuade their people, otherwise.

And so it has come to pass that the Soviet Union itself has shared and suffered the very fears it has fostered in the rest of the world.

This has been the way of life forged by eight years of fear and force.

What can the world, or any nation in it, hope for if no turning is found on this dread road?

The worst to be feared and the best to be expected can be simply stated.

The worst is atomic war.

The best would be this: a life of perpetual fear and tension; a burden of arms draining the wealth and the labor of all peoples; a wasting of strength that defies the American system or the Soviet system or any system to achieve true abundance and happiness for the peoples of this earth.

Every gun that is made, every warship launched, every rocket fired signifies, in the final sense, a theft from those who hunger and are not fed, those who are cold and are not clothed.

This world in arms is not spending money alone.

It is spending the sweat of its laborers, the genius of its scientists, the hopes of its children.

The cost of one modern heavy bomber is this: a modern brick school in more than 30 cities.

It is two electric power plants, each serving a town of 60 000 population.

It is two fine, fully equipped hospitals.

It is some 50 miles of concrete highway.

We pay for a single fighter with a half million bushels of wheat.

We pay for a single destroyer with new homes that could have housed more than 8000 people.

This, I repeat, is the best way of life to be found on the road the world has been taking.

This is not a way of life at all, in any true sense. Under the cloud of threatening war, it is humanity hanging from a cross of iron.

These plain and cruel truths define the peril and point the hope that comes with this spring of 1953.

This is one of those times in the affairs of nations when the gravest choices must be made, if there is to be a turning toward a just and lasting peace.

It is a moment that calls upon the governments of the world to speak their intentions with simplicity and with honesty.

It calls upon them to answer the questions that stirs the hearts of all sane men: is there no other way the world may live? The world knows that an era ended with the death of Joseph Stalin. The extraordinary 30-year span of his rule saw the Soviet Empire expand to reach from the Baltic Sea to the Sea of Japan, finally to dominate 800 million souls.

The Soviet system shaped by Stalin and his predecessors was born of one World War. It survived the stubborn and often amazing courage of a second World War. It has lived to threaten a third.

Now, a new leadership has assumed power in the Soviet Union. It links to the past, however strong, cannot bind it completely. Its future is, in great part, its own to make.

This new leadership confronts a free world aroused, as rarely in its history, by the will to stay free.

This free world knows, out of bitter wisdom of experience, that vigilance and sacrifice are the price of liberty.

It knows that the defence of Western Europe imperatively demands the unity of purpose and action made possible by the North Atlantic Treaty Organization, embracing a European Defense Community.

It knows that Western Germany deserves to be a free and equal partner in this community and that this, for Germany, is the only safe way to full, final unity.

It knows that aggression in Korea and in Southeast Asia are threats to the whole free community to be met by united action.

This is the kind of free world which the new Soviet leadership confront. It is a world that demands and expects the fullest respect of its rights and interests. It is a world that will always accord the same respect to all others.

So the new Soviet leadership now has a precious opportunity to awaken, with the rest of the world, to the point of peril reached and to help turn the tide of history.

Will it do this?

We do not yet know. Recent statements and gestures of Soviet leaders give some evidence that they may recognize this critical moment.

This we do know: a world that begins to witness the rebirth of trust among nations can find its way to a peace that is neither partial nor punitive.

The first great step along this way must be the conclusion of an honorable armistice in Korea. This means the immediate cessation of hostilities and the prompt initiation of political discussions leading to the holding of free elections in a united Korea.

It should mean, no less importantly, an end to the direct and indirect attacks upon the security of Indochina and Malaya. For any armistice in Korea that merely released aggressive armies to attack elsewhere would be fraud. We seek, throughout Asia as throughout the world, a peace that is true and total.

Out of this can grow a still wider task—the achieving of just political settlements for the other serious and specific issues between the free world and the Soviet Union.

None of these issues, great or small, is insoluble-given only the will to respect the rights of all nations.

Again we say: the United States is ready to assume its just part.

We are ready not only to press forward with the present plans for closer unity of the nations of Western Europe by also, upon that foundation, to strive to foster a broader European community, conducive to the free movement of persons, of trade, and of ideas.

As progress in all these areas strengthens world trust, we could proceed concurrently with the next great work—the reduction of the burden of armaments now weighing upon the world. To this end we would welcome and enter into the most solemn agreements. These could properly include:

1. The limitation, by absolute numbers or by an agreed international ratio, of the sizes of the military and security forces of all nations.

2. A commitment by all nations to set an agreed limit upon that proportion of total production of certain strategic materials to be devoted to military purposes.

3. International control of atomic energy to promote its use for peaceful purposes only and to insure the prohibition of atomic weapons.

4. A limitation or prohibition of other categories of weapons of great destructiveness.

5. The enforcement of all these agreed limitations and prohibitions by adequate safeguards, including a practical system of inspection under the United Nations.

The peace we seek, founded upon decent trust and cooperative effort among nations, can be fortified, not by weapons of war but by wheat and by cotton, by milk and by wool, by meat and by timber and by rice. These are words that translate into every language on earth. These are needs that challenge this world in arms.

We are prepared to reaffirm, with the most concrete evidence, our readiness to help build a world in which all peoples can be productive and prosperous.

The monuments to this new kind of war would be these: roads and schools, hospitals and homes, food and health.

We are ready, in short, to dedicate our strength to serving the needs, rather than the fears, of the world.

We are ready, by these and all such actions, to make of the United Nations an institution that can effectively guard the peace and security of all peoples.

The test of truth is simple. There can be no persuasion but by deeds.

Is the new leadership of Soviet Union prepared to use its decisive influence in the Communist world, including control of the flow of arms, to bring not merely an expedient truce in Korea but genuine peace in Asia?

Is it prepared to allow other nations, including those of Eastern Europe, the free choice of their own forms of government?

Is it prepared to act in concert with others upon serious disarmament proposals to be made firmly effective by stringent U.N. control and inspection?

If not, where then is the concrete evidence of the Soviet Union's concern for peace?

The test is clear. There is, before all peoples, a precious chance to turn the black tide of events. If we failed to strive to seize this chance, the judgment of future ages would be harsh and just.

If we strive but fail and the world remains armed against itself, it at least need be divided no longer in its clear knowledge of who has condemned humankind to this fate.

The purpose of the United States, in stating these proposals, is simple and clear. These proposals spring, without ulterior purpose or political passion, from our calm conviction that the hunger for peace is in the hearts of all peoples—those of Russia and of China no less than of our own country.

They conform to our firm faith that God created men to enjoy, not destroy, the fruits of the earth and of their own toil.

They aspire to this: the lifting, from the backs and from the hearts of men, of their burden of arms and of fears, so that they may find before them a golden age of freedom and of peace. **'**

Despite an end to fighting in Korea in 1953, the Cold War atmosphere of the mid-1950s did little to slow the arms race. In December 1953 Eisenhower proposed the ideal of 'Atoms for Peace' to the United Nations—even going so far as suggesting that atomic materials be managed by a single international agency—but the brutal repression of rebellious eastern bloc countries Poland and Hungary (both in 1958) meant that the US felt that it had to be 'ready' for any conflict. Although he avoided a Third World War, Eisenhower warned America in his final address as president that 'security and liberty' must learn to prosper together. The arms race would continue for another three decades.

After eight years in the White House, Dwight D Eisenhower left Washington DC in 1961 and retired with his wife Mamie to their farm in Gettysburg, Pennsylvania, overlooking the famous Civil War battlefield. The former two-term US President died there on 28 March, 1969, aged 78.

Fidel Castro

'United Nations Address'

United Nations General Assembly, New York, 26 September 1960.

In 1959 Cuban exile Fidel Castro Ruz invaded his homeland with a band of 80 men trained in guerrilla warfare and overturned the rule of General Fulgencio Batista backed by popular support of his countrymen.

Born in 1926, near Birán, Cuba, Castro graduated from the University of Havana with a law degree in 1950. He intended to stand for parliament but the Cuban government was overthrown in a coup led by General Batista. In 1953 Castro was jailed for 15 years after launching a July 26 attack on Batista's army. 'History will absolve me,' he famously declared at his trial. Castro was released after only two years in a general amnesty. He immediately went into exile and started training a small group of guerrillas near Mexico City.

After invading Cuba in 1956, Castro waged a guerrilla war in the Cuban hills alongside protégé Che Guevara, gathering support from the people as they defeated Batista's army, before capturing Havana in January 1959.

Originally, the United States recognised the new Cuban Government in which Castro had assumed the role of Prime Minister by popular mandate on July 26, 1959. Here was a shining example of true democracy, he said, and quoted Abraham Lincoln: 'a government of the people, by the people, and for the people'. He gestured dramatically toward his audience. 'This,' he said, 'is real democracy'. The Cuban dictator quickly became a vocal critic of US foreign policy. As a committed Marxist, Castro sought to expropriate foreign-owned companies and the United States instigated economic sanctions (especially against the lucrative sugar market) and banned all travel to Cuba. Castro responded by nationalising some $850 million worth of

American-owned properties and companies.

In the longest speech in the history of the United Nations, Castro addressed the General Assembly in September 1960 and argued that 'the case of Cuba is the case of all underdeveloped countries'. The Cuban revolutionary leader also used this platform to attack American colonial aggression internationally. In conclusion, Castro publicly stated the revolutionary aims of the Republic of Cuba before the world leadership and made clear his opposition to American colonial interests.

'In conclusion, we are going to place our trust in reason and in the decency of all. We wish to sum up our ideas regarding some aspects of these world problems about which there should be no doubt. The problem of Cuba, which we have set forth here, is a part of the problems of the world. Those who attack us today are those who are helping to attack others in other parts of the world.

The United States Government cannot be on the side of the Algerian people, it cannot be on the side of the Algerian people because it is allied to metropolitan France. It cannot be on the side of the Congolese people, because it is allied to Belgium. It cannot be on the side of the Spanish people, because it is allied to Franco. It cannot be on the side of the Puerto Rican people, whose nationhood it has been destroying for fifty years. It cannot be on the side of the Panamanians, who claim the Canal. It cannot support the ascendancy of civil power in Latin America, Germany or Japan. It cannot be on the side of the peasants who want land, because it is allied to the big landowners. It cannot be on the side of the workers who are demanding better living conditions in all parts of the world, because it is allied to the monopolies. It cannot be on the side of the colonies which want their freedom, because it is allied to the colonizers.

That is to say, it is for France, for the colonization of Algeria for the colonization of the Congo; it is for the maintenance of its privileges and interests in the Panama Canal, for colonialism through the world. It is for the German militarism and for the resurgence of German militarism. It is for Japanese militarism and for the resurgence of Japanese militarism.

The Government of the United States forgets the millions of Jews murdered in European concentration camps by the Nazis, who are today regaining their influence in the German army. It forgets the Frenchmen who were killed in their heroic struggle against the occupation; it forgets the American soldiers who died on the Siegfried Line, in the Ruhr, on the Rhine, and on the Asian fronts. The United States Government cannot be for the integrity and sovereignty of nations. Why? Because it must curtail the sovereignty of nations in order to keep its military bases, and each base is a dagger thrust into sovereignty; each base is a limitation on sovereignty.

That is why it has to be against the sovereignty of nations, because it must constantly limit sovereignty in order to maintain its policy of encircling the Soviet Union with bases. We believe that these problems are not properly explained to the American people. But the American people need only imagine how uneasy they would feel if the Soviet Union began to establish a ring of atomic bases in Cuba, Mexico, or Canada. The population would not feel secure or calm. World opinion, including American opinion, must be taught to see the other person's point of view.

The underdeveloped peoples should not always be represented as aggressors; revolutionaries should not be presented as aggressors, as enemies of the American people, because we have seen American like Carleton Beals, Waldo Frank, and others, famous and distinguished intellectuals, shed tears at the thought of the mistakes that are being made, at the breach of hospitality towards us; there are many Americans, the most humane, the most progressive, and the most esteemed writers, in whom I see the nobility of this country's early leaders, the Washingtons, the Jeffersons, and the Lincolns. I say this in no spirit of demagogy, but with the sincere admiration that we feel for those who once succeeded in freeing their people from colonial status and who did not fight in order that their country might today be the ally of all the reactionaries, the gangsters, the big landowners, the monopolists, the exploiters, the militarists, the fascists in the world, that is to say, the ally of the most reactionary forces, but rather in order that their country might always be the champion of noble and just ideals.

We know well what will be said about us, today, tomorrow, every day, to deceive the American people. But it does not matter. We are doing our duty by stating our views in this historic Assembly. We proclaim the right of people to freedom, the right of people to nationhood; those who know that nationalism means the desire of the people to regain what is rightly theirs, their wealth, their natural resources, conspire against nationalism.

We are, in short, for all the noble aspirations of all the peoples. That is our position. We are, and always shall be for everything that is just: against colonialism, exploitation, monopolies, militarism, the armaments race, and warmongering. We shall always be against such things. That will be our position.

And to conclude, fulfilling what we regard as our duty, I am going to quote to this Assembly the key part of the Declaration of Havana. As you all know, the Declaration of Havana was the Cuban people's answer to the Declaration of San Jose, Costa Rica. Nor 10, nor 100, nor 100 000, but more than one million Cubans gathered together.

At that Assembly, which was convened as an answer to the Declaration of San Jose, the following principles were proclaimed, in consultation with the people and by acclamation of the people, as the principles of the Cuban Revolution:

"The National General Assembly of the Cuban people condemns large-scale landowning as a source of poverty for the peasant and a backward and inhuman system of agricultural production; it condemns starvation wages and the iniquitous exploitation of human work by illegitimate and privileged interests; it condemns illiteracy, the lack of teachers, of schools, doctor and hospitals; the lack of old-age security in the countries of America; it condemns discrimination against the Negro and the Indian'; it condemns the inequality and the exploitation of women; it condemns political and military oligarchies, which keep our peoples in poverty, prevent their democratic development and the full exercise of their sovereignty; it condemns concessions of the natural resources of our countries as a policy of surrender which betrays the interests of the peoples; it condemns the governments which ignore the demands of their people in order to obey orders from abroad; it condemns the systematic deception of the people by mass communications media which serve the interests of the oligarchies and the policy of imperialist oppression; it condemns the monopoly held by news agencies, which are instruments of monopolist trusts and agents of such interests; it condemns the repressive laws which prevent the workers, the peasants, the students and the intellectuals, the great majorities in each country, from organizing themselves to fight for their social and national rights; it condemns the imperialist monopolies and enterprises which continually plunder our wealth, exploit our workers and peasants, bleed our economies to keep them in a backward state, and subordinate Latin American politics to their designs and interests.

"In short, The National General Assembly of the Cuban People condemns the exploitation of man by man, and the exploitations of underdeveloped countries by imperialists capital.

"Therefore, the National General Assembly of the Cuban People proclaims before America, and proclaims here before the world, the right of the peasants to the land; the right of the workers to the fruits of their labor; the right of the children to education: the right of the sick to medical care and hospitalization; the right of young people to work; the right of students to free vocational training and scientific education; the right of Negroes, and Indians to full human dignity; the right of women to civil, social and political equality; the right of the elderly to security in their old age; the right of intellectuals, artists and scientists to fight through their works for a better world; the right of States to nationalize imperialist monopolies, thus rescuing their national wealth and resources; the right of nations to their full sovereignty; the right of peoples to convert their military fortresses into schools, and to arm their workers—because in this we too have to be arms-conscious, to arm our people in defense against imperialist attacks—their peasants, their students, their intellectuals, Negroes, Indians, women, young people, old people, all the oppressed and exploited, so that they themselves can defend their rights and their destinies."

Some people wanted to know what the policy of the Revolutionary Government of Cuba was. Very well, then, this is our policy. '

Fidel Castro survived an aborted American-backed invasion in the Bay of Pigs in 1961, the Cuban Missile Crisis the following year and even the collapse of the Soviet Union in 1991. The revolutionary leader maintained his dictatorship of Cuba—and an awkward neighbour for the capitalist USA—until his retirement due to ill-health in 2011, age 85, fifty years after coming to power.

After handing over the presidency to his brother Raul (b.1931), Fidel Castro slipped into retirement as his country reopened diplomatic ties with the US after diplomatic overtures from the Obama administration.

Harold MacMillan

'The Wind of Change'

Address to the South African Parliament in Cape Town, 3 February 1960.

Harold MacMillan (1894-1986) was British Prime Minister from 1957 to 1963 at a time when the black independence movement was sweeping the African continent. In 1960 MacMillan visited the African Commonwealth states of Ghana and Nigeria and addressed the South African Parliament. Acknowledging the rights of African nations to rule their own affairs, he stated that it was his government's responsibility to promote the creation of societies that upheld the rights of individuals. This was the first public statement by a British government in this vein and signalled a major shift in attitude not only towards the Commonwealth's colonial past, but towards the apartheid regime in South Africa.

❛As I've travelled around the Union I have found everywhere, as I expected, a deep preoccupation with what is happening in the rest of the African continent. I understand and sympathise with your interests in these events and your anxiety about them.

Ever since the break-up of the Roman Empire one of the constant facts of political life in Europe has been the emergence of independent nations. They have come into existence over the centuries in different forms, with different kinds of Government, but all have been inspired by a deep, keen feeling of nationalism, which has grown as the nations have grown.

In the twentieth century, and especially since the end of the war, the processes which gave birth to the nation states of Europe have been repeated all over the world. We have seen the awakening of national consciousness in peoples who have for centuries lived in dependence upon some other power. Fifteen years ago this movement spread through Asia. Many countries there of different races and civilizations pressed their claim to an independent national life. Today the same thing is happening in Africa, and the most striking of all the impressions I have formed is of the strength of this African national consciousness. In different places it takes different forms, but it is happening everywhere. The wind of change is blowing through this continent, and, whether we like it or not, this growth of national consciousness is a political fact. We must all accept it as a fact, and our national policies must take account of it.

Of course, you understand this better than anyone. You are sprung from Europe, the home of nationalism, and here in Africa you have yourselves created a new nation. Indeed, in the history of our times yours will be recorded as the first of the African nationalisms, and this tide of national consciousness which is now rising in Africa is a fact for which you and we and the other nations of the Western World are ultimately responsible. For its causes are to be found in the achievements of Western civilization, in the pushing forward of the frontiers of knowledge, in the applying of science in the service of human needs, in the expanding of food production, in the speeding and multiplying of the means of communication, and perhaps, above all, the spread of education ...

As I see it the great issue in this second half of the twentieth century is whether the uncommitted peoples of Asia and Africa will swing to the East or to the West. Will they be drawn into the Communist camp? Or will the great experiments in self-government that are now being made in Asia and Africa, especially within the Commonwealth, prove so successful, and by their example so compelling, that the balance will come down in favour of freedom and order and justice?

The struggle is joined, and it is a struggle for the minds of men. What is now on trial is much more than our military strength or our diplomatic and administrative skill. It is our way of life. The uncommitted nations want to see before they choose.

What can we show them to help them choose right? Each of the independent members of the Commonwealth must answer that question for itself. It is a basic principle of our modern Commonwealth that we respect each other's sovereignty in matters of internal policy. At the same time we must recognize that in this shrinking world in which we live today the internal policies of one nation may have effects outside it. We may sometimes be tempted to say to each other, 'Mind your own business,' but in these days I would myself expand the old saying so that it runs: 'Mind your own business, but mind how it affects my business, too.'

Let me be very, frank with you, my friends. What governments and Parliaments in the United Kingdom have done since the war in according independence to India, Pakistan, Ceylon, Malaya and Ghana, and what they will do for Nigeria and other countries now nearing independence, all this, though we take full and sole responsibility for it, we do in the belief that it is the only way to establish the future of the Commonwealth and of the Free World on sound foundations. All this of course is also of deep and close concern to you for nothing we do in this small world can be done in a corner or remain hidden. What we do today in West, Central and East Africa becomes known tomorrow to everyone in the Union, whatever his language, colour or traditions. Let me assure you, in all friendliness, that we are well aware of this and that we have acted and will act with full knowledge of the responsibility we have to all our friends.

Nevertheless I am sure you will agree that in our own areas of responsibility we must each do what we think right. What we think right derives from a long experience both of failure and success in the management of our own affairs. We have tried to learn and apply the lessons of our judgement of right and wrong. Our justice is rooted in the same soil as yours—in Christianity and in the rule of law as the basis of a free society. This experience of our own explains why it has been our aim in the countries for which we have borne responsibility, not only to raise the material standards of living, but also to create a society which respects the rights of individuals, a society in which men are given the opportunity to grow to their full stature—and that must in our view include the opportunity to have an increasing share in political power and responsibility, a society in which individual merit and individual merit alone is the criterion for a man's advancement, whether political or economic ...

The attitude of the United Kingdom towards this problem was clearly expressed by the Foreign Secretary, Mr Selwyn Lloyd, speaking at the United Nations General Assembly on 17 September 1959. These were his words:

"In those territories where different races or tribes live side by side the task is to ensure that all the people may enjoy security and freedom and the chance to contribute as individuals to the progress and well being of these countries. We reject the idea of any inherent superiority of one race over another. Our policy therefore is non-racial. It offers a future in which Africans, Europeans, Asians, the peoples of the Pacific and others with whom we are concerned, will all play their full part as citizens in the countries where they live, and in which feelings of race will be submerged in loyalty to new nations.

I have thought you would wish me to state plainly and with full candour the policy for which we in Britain stand. It may well be that in trying to do our duty as we see it we shall sometimes make difficulties for you. If this proves to be so we shall regret it. But I know that even so you would not ask us to flinch from doing our duty.

As a fellow member of the Commonwealth it is our earnest desire to give South Africa our support and encouragement, but I hope you won't mind my saying frankly that there are some aspects of your policies which make it impossible for us to do this without being false to our own deep convictions about the political destinies of free men to which in our own territories we are trying to give effect. I think we ought, as friends, to face together, without seeking to apportion credit or blame, the fact that in the world of today this difference of outlook lies between us ..."

The fact is that in this modern world no country, not even the greatest, can live for itself alone. Nearly two thousand years ago, when the whole of the civilized world was comprised within the confines of the Roman Empire, St Paul proclaimed one of the great truths of history—we are all members one of another. During this twentieth century that eternal truth has taken on a new and exciting significance. It has always been impossible for the individual man to live in isolation from his fellows, in the home, the tribe, the village, or the city. Today it is impossible for nations to live in isolation from one another. What Dr John Donne said of individual men three hundred years ago is true today of my country, your country, and all the countries of the world:

"Any man's death diminishes me, because I am involved in Mankind. And therefore never send to know for whom the bell tolls; it tolls for thee."

All nations now are interdependent one upon another, and this is generally realized throughout the Western World ... Those of us who by grace of the electorate are temporarily in charge of affairs in your country and in mine, we fleeting transient phantoms on the great stage of history, we have no right to sweep aside on this account the friendship that exists between our countries, for that is the legacy of history. It is not ours alone to deal with as we wish. To adapt a famous phrase, it belongs to those who are living, but it also belongs to those who are dead and to those who are yet unborn. We must face the differences, but let us try to see beyond them down the long vista of the future.

I hope—indeed, I am confident—that in another 50 years we shall look back on the differences that exist between us now as matters of historical interest, for as time passes and one generation yields to another, human problems change and fade. Let us remember these truths. Let us resolve to build, not to destroy, and let us remember always that weakness comes from division, strength from unity. '

The great fear of the British and other Western governments was that newly-independent African nations would align themselves with the Communist East and upset the balance of power during the Cold War. A fortnight after this historic speech, Britain announced a power-sharing agreement with Kenyan nationalists before that country's independence in 1963. By 1961 Nigeria, Somalia, Sierra Leone and Tanzania would also gain their independence.

However, South African Prime Minister Hendrik Verwoerd responded to McMillan's speech by stating that 'justice to all, does not only mean being just to the black man of Africa, but also to the white man of Africa' because it was the white man who 'historically brought civilisation to a bare continent'. On 31 May, 1961—largely in response to domestic civil unrest and the fear of political interference from Britain—the white South African regime pushed through its declaration of independence and created a republic founded on systemic apartheid.

In 1964 several high-profile black nationalists (including Nelson Mandela) were jailed for treason, Prime Minister Verwoerd was assassinated by a mentally disturbed white parliamentary clerk in 1966, and South Africa gradually became the pariah of western democracies during the next three decades.

After the finest moment of his political career, Harold MacMillan resigned his position as Prime Minister because of ill health in 1963 and left parliament the following year. He was made an Earl on his 90th birthday in 1984, two years before his death.

John F Kennedy

'The Cuban Missile Crisis'

National television broadcast, 22 October 1962.

John F. Kennedy (1917-63) was regarded as the 'new generation' of US leader—young, charismatic and a powerful communicator. The second son of a former US Ambassador to England, JFK was a Harvard graduate, a war hero, a Democratic Representative (1947) and Senator (1952), whose book, *Profiles in Courage*, won the 1956 Pulitzer Prize for Literature.

It is hard to believe that Kennedy was the underdog to Republican Party candidate, Vice-President Richard Nixon, in the 1960 presidential race. But Kennedy's charisma translated well on television and the medium became an important factor in his election victory when he outpointed the more-experienced Richard Nixon in the first televised series of debates.

Nixon looked decidedly nervous—and untrustworthy—next to the debonair Senator from Massachusetts (interestingly, television viewers thought Kennedy had easily won the debates while radio listeners put Nixon ahead).

On a cold January morning in 1961, John F. Kennedy took the oath of office and became the 35th President of the United States of America. His inauguration speech—with a bold challenge for all Americans and the 'citizens of the world'—signalled the birth of one of the most historic, controversial and mythical periods in American politics. Kennedy's time as president, barely 1000 days, was known as 'Camelot'.

On 16 October 1962, President Kennedy was shown aerial photos taken by an American U-2 spy plane over Cuba—just ninety miles off the coast of Florida—of the Soviet installation of offensive nuclear missiles.

Four days later he summoned the Soviet Minister of Foreign Affairs, Andrei Gromyko, who informed him that the weapons were for defensive purposes only.

The President then met with top military aides—and his brother, Attorney General Robert Kennedy—to discuss America's response. On Sunday October 21, Kennedy and his advisors spent the entire day considering two main military options—an air strike against the bases or a naval blockade of Cuba. The President chose the latter option, which would be referred to by the less provocative term 'quarantine', and forced a stand-off with the Russians.

At 7 pm (EST) on 22 October 1962, President Kennedy informed the American people on national television of the recently discovered Soviet military build-up in Cuba.

'This Government, as promised, has maintained the closest surveillance of the Soviet Military build-up on the island of Cuba. Within the past week, unmistakable evidence has established the fact that a series of offensive missile sites is now in preparation on that imprisoned island. The purpose of these bases can be none other than to provide a nuclear strike capability against the Western Hemisphere.

Upon receiving the first preliminary hard information of this nature last Tuesday morning at 9 am, I directed that our surveillance be stepped up. And having now confirmed and completed our evaluation of the evidence and our decision on a course of action, this Government feels obliged to report this new crisis to you in fullest detail.

The characteristics of these new missile sites indicate two distinct types of installations. Several of them include medium range ballistic missiles capable of carrying a nuclear warhead for a distance of more than 1 000 nautical miles. Each of these missiles, in short, is capable of striking Washington, DC, the Panama Canal, Cape Canaveral, Mexico City, or any other city in the south-eastern part of the United States, in Central America, or in the Caribbean area.

Additional sites not yet completed appear to be designed for intermediate range ballistic missiles—capable of traveling more than twice as far—and thus capable of striking most of the major cities in the Western Hemisphere, ranging as far north as Hudson Bay, Canada, and as far south as Lima, Peru. In addition, jet bombers, capable of carrying nuclear weapons, are now being uncrated and assembled in Cuba, while the necessary air bases are being prepared.

This urgent transformation of Cuba into an important strategic base—by the presence of these large, long range, and clearly offensive weapons of sudden mass destruction—constitutes an explicit threat to the peace and security of all the Americas, in flagrant and deliberate defiance of the Rio Pact of 1947, the traditions of this Nation and hemisphere, the joint resolution of the 87th Congress, the Charter of the United Nations, and my own public warnings to the Soviets on September 4 and 13. This action also contradicts the repeated assurances of Soviet spokesmen, both publicly and privately delivered, that the arms build-up in Cuba would retain its original defensive character, and that the Soviet Union had no need or desire to station strategic missiles on the territory of any other nation.

The size of this undertaking makes clear that it has been planned for some months. Yet only last month, after I had made clear the distinction between any introduction of ground-to-ground missiles and the existence of defensive antiaircraft missiles, the Soviet Government publicly stated on September 11, and I quote, "the armaments and military equipment sent to Cuba are designed exclusively for defensive purposes," that, and I quote the Soviet Government, "there is no need for the Soviet Government to shift its weapons . . . for a retaliatory blow to any other country, for instance Cuba," and that, and I quote their government, "the Soviet Union has no powerful rockets to carry these nuclear warheads that there is no need to search for sites for them beyond the boundaries of the Soviet Union." That statement was false.

Only last Thursday, as evidence of this rapid offensive build-up was already in my hand, Soviet Foreign Minister Gromyko told me in my office that he was instructed to make it clear once again, as he said his government had already done, that Soviet assistance to Cuba, and I quote, "pursued solely the purpose of contributing to the defense capabilities of Cuba," that, and I quote him, "training by Soviet specialists of Cuban nationals in handling defensive armaments was by no means offensive, and if it were otherwise," Mr. Gromyko went on, "the Soviet Government would never become involved in rendering such assistance." That statement also was false.

Neither the United States of America nor the world community of nations can tolerate deliberate deception and offensive threats on the part of any nation, large or small. We no longer live in a world where only the actual firing of weapons represents a sufficient challenge to a nation's security to constitute maximum peril. Nuclear weapons are so destructive and ballistic missiles are so swift, that any substantially increased possibility of their use or any sudden change in their deployment may well be regarded as a definite threat to peace.

For many years both the Soviet Union and the United States, recognizing this fact, have deployed strategic nuclear weapons with great care, never upsetting the precarious status quo which insured that these weapons would not be used in the absence of some vital challenge. Our own strategic missiles have never been transferred to the territory of any other nation under a cloak of secrecy and deception; and our history—unlike that of the Soviets since the end of World War II—demonstrates that we have no desire to dominate or conquer any other nation or impose our system upon its people. Nevertheless, American citizens have become adjusted to living daily on the bull's-eye of Soviet missiles located inside the USSR or in submarines.

In that sense, missiles in Cuba add to an already clear and present danger—although it should be noted the nations of Latin America have never previously been subjected to a potential nuclear threat.

But this secret, swift, and extraordinary build-up of Communist missiles—in an area well known to have a special and historical relationship to the United States and the nations of the Western Hemisphere, in violation of Soviet assurances, and in defiance of American and hemispheric policy—this sudden, clandestine decision to station strategic weapons for the first time outside of Soviet soil—is a deliberately provocative and unjustified change in the status quo which cannot be accepted by this country, if our courage and our commitments are ever to be trusted again by either friend or foe.

The 1930's taught us a clear lesson: aggressive conduct, if allowed to go unchecked and unchallenged ultimately leads to war. This nation is opposed to war. We are also true to our word. Our unswerving objective, therefore, must be to prevent the use of these missiles against this or any other country, and to secure their withdrawal or elimination from the Western Hemisphere.

Our policy has been one of patience and restraint, as befits a peaceful and powerful nation, which leads a worldwide alliance. We have been determined not to be diverted from our central concerns by mere irritants and fanatics. But now further action is required—and it is under way; and these actions may only be the beginning. We will not prematurely or unnecessarily risk the costs of worldwide nuclear war in which even the fruits of victory would be ashes in our mouth—but neither will we shrink from that risk at any time it must be faced.

Acting, therefore, in the defense of our own security and of the entire Western Hemisphere, and under the authority entrusted to me by the Constitution as endorsed by the resolution of the Congress, I have directed that the following initial steps be taken immediately:

First: To halt this offensive build-up, a strict quarantine on all offensive military equipment under shipment to Cuba is being initiated. All ships of any kind bound for Cuba from whatever nation or port will, if found to contain cargoes of offensive weapons, be turned back. This quarantine will be extended, if needed, to other types of cargo and carriers. We are not at this time, however, denying the necessities of life as the Soviets attempted to do in their Berlin blockade of 1948.

Second: I have directed the continued and increased close surveillance of Cuba and its military build-up. The foreign ministers of the OAS, in their communique of October 6, rejected secrecy in such matters in this hemisphere. Should these offensive military preparations continue, thus increasing the threat to the hemisphere, further action will be justified. I have directed the Armed Forces to prepare for any eventualities; and I trust that in the interest of both the Cuban people and the Soviet technicians at the sites, the hazards to all concerned in continuing this threat will be recognized.

Third: It shall be the policy of this Nation to regard any nuclear missile launched from Cuba against any nation in the Western Hemisphere as an attack by the Soviet Union on the United States, requiring a full retaliatory response upon the Soviet Union.

Fourth: As a necessary military precaution, I have reinforced our base at Guantanamo, evacuated today the dependents of our personnel there, and ordered additional military units to be on a standby alert basis.

Fifth: We are calling tonight for an immediate meeting of the Organ of Consultation under the Organization of American States, to consider this threat to hemispheric security and to invoke articles 6 and 8 of the Rio Treaty in support of all necessary action. The United Nations Charter allows for regional security arrangements—and the nations of this hemisphere decided long ago against the military presence of outside powers. Our other allies around the world have also been alerted.

Sixth: Under the Charter of the United Nations, we are asking tonight that an emergency meeting of the Security Council be convoked without delay to take action against this latest Soviet threat to world peace. Our resolution will call for the prompt dismantling and withdrawal of all offensive weapons in Cuba, under the supervision of U.N. observers, before the quarantine can be lifted.

Seventh and finally: I call upon Chairman Khrushchev to halt and eliminate this clandestine, reckless and provocative threat to world peace and to stable relations between our two nations. I call upon him further to abandon this course of world domination, and to join in an historic effort to end the perilous arms race and to transform the history of man. He has an opportunity now to move the world back from the abyss of destruction— by returning to his government's own words that it had no need to station missiles outside its own territory, and withdrawing these weapons from Cuba—by refraining from any action which will widen or deepen the present crisis—and then by participating in a search for peaceful and permanent solutions.

This Nation is prepared to present its case against the Soviet threat to peace, and our own proposals for a peaceful world, at any time and in any forum—in the OAS, in the United Nations, or in any other meeting that could be useful—without limiting our freedom of action. We have in the past made strenuous efforts to limit the spread of nuclear weapons. We have proposed the elimination of all arms and military bases in a fair and effective disarmament treaty. We are prepared to discuss new proposals for the removal of tensions on both sides—including the possibility of a genuinely independent Cuba, free to determine its own destiny. We have no wish to war with the Soviet Union— for we are a peaceful people who desire to live in peace with all other peoples.

But it is difficult to settle or even discuss these problems in an atmosphere of intimidation. That is why this latest Soviet threat—or any other threat which is made independently or in response to our actions this week—must and will be met with determination. Any hostile move anywhere in the world against the safety and freedom of peoples to whom we are committed—including in particular the brave people of West

Berlin—will be met by whatever action is needed.

Finally, I want to say a few words to the captive people of Cuba, to whom this speech is being directly carried by special radio facilities. I speak to you as a friend, as one who knows of your deep attachment to your fatherland, as one who shares your aspirations for liberty and justice for all. And I have watched and the American people have watched with deep sorrow how your nationalist revolution was betrayed—and how your fatherland fell under foreign domination. Now your leaders are no longer Cuban leaders inspired by Cuban ideals. They are puppets and agents of an international conspiracy which has turned Cuba against your friends and neighbors in the Americas—and turned it into the first Latin American country to become a target for nuclear war—the first Latin American country to have these weapons on its soil.

These new weapons are not in your interest. They contribute nothing to your peace and well-being. They can only undermine it. But this country has no wish to cause you to suffer or to impose any system upon you. We know that your lives and land are being used as pawns by those who deny your freedom.

Many times in the past, the Cuban people have risen to throw out tyrants who destroyed their liberty. And I have no doubt that most Cubans today look forward to the time when they will be truly free—free from foreign domination, free to choose their own leaders, free to select their own system, free to own their own land, free to speak and write and worship without fear or degradation. And then shall Cuba be welcomed back to the society of free nations and to the associations of this hemisphere.

My fellow citizens: let no one doubt that this is a difficult and dangerous effort on which we have set out. No one can see precisely what course it will take or what costs or casualties will be incurred. Many months of sacrifice and self-discipline lie ahead -months in which our patience and our will be tested—months in which many threats and denunciations will keep us aware of our dangers. But the greatest danger of all would be to do nothing.

The path we have chosen for the present is full of hazards, as all paths are—but it is the one most consistent with our character and courage as a nation and our commitments around the world. The cost of freedom is always high—and Americans have always paid it. And one path we shall never choose, and that is the path of surrender or submission.

Our goal is not the victory of might, but the vindication of right—not peace at the expense of freedom, but both peace and freedom, here in this hemisphere, and, we hope, around the world. God willing, that goal will be achieved.

Thank you and good night.'

The 'Missiles of October' brought the world to the brink of nuclear war, but Kennedy's steel will and unequivocal diplomacy forced the USSR's mighty hand. The Soviets backed down and removed the missiles.

Although his legislative career during his time as President was not extensive, John Kennedy can be seen as a leader for his time—a man who was able to divine the mood of the people, synthesise the major issues of the day and move government policy towards an ideal—especially regarding civil rights.

On Friday, 22 November 1963 JFK was killed by an assassin's bullet as he rode in a motorcade through Dallas, Texas. Later that afternoon, Lee Harvey Oswald was implicated in the President's death when he was arrested in a theater and charged with the murder of a Dallas policeman (see Lyndon Johnson, 'Let Us Continue', p 215).

Martin Luther King

'I Have a Dream'
Lincoln Memorial, Washington DC, 28 August 1963.

Atlanta-born Martin Luther King Jnr (1929-68) is rightly regarded by historians as one of the most significant civil rights leaders of the 20th Century—arguably the most significant in the modern history of the United States—and one whose lifetime achievements and lasting impact ranks him alongside that of Mohandas Gandhi.

King graduated from Crozer Theological Seminary in Chester, Pennsylvania in 1953 and was granted his doctorate two years later after completing his dissertation. That same year, he became pastor of the Dexter Avenue Baptist Church in Montgomery, Alabama, at a time when the local black community had a formed a boycott of local bus companies because of the South's strict code of racial segregation. The boycott lasted 382 days, King was arrested and his home was bombed but ultimately, the Supreme Court declared bus segregation unconstitutional and outlawed racial segregation on public transportation.

In August 1963, the Reverend Martin Luther King Jnr led a march to Washington DC to demonstrate the commitment of the American people— of all creeds and religions—to seek equal rights in every facet of American society. King's speech, delivered before hundreds of thousands of followers assembled on the steps of the Lincoln Memorial, is one of the greatest speeches of the twentieth century.

‘I am happy to join with you today in what will go down in history as the greatest demonstration for freedom in the history of our nation.

Five score years ago, a great American, in whose symbolic shadow we stand today, signed the Emancipation Proclamation. This momentous decree came as a great beacon light of hope to millions of Negro slaves, who had been seared in the flames of withering injustice. It came as a joyous daybreak to end the long night of their captivity.

But one hundred years later, the Negro still is not free. One hundred years later, the life of the Negro is still sadly crippled by the manacles of segregation and the chains of discrimination. One hundred years later, the Negro lives on a lonely island of poverty in the midst of a vast ocean of material prosperity. One hundred years later, the Negro still languishes in the corners of American society and finds himself an exile in his own land.

So we've come here today to dramatize a shameful condition. In a sense, we've come to our nation's capital to cash a check. When the architects of our Republic wrote the magnificent words of the Constitution and the Declaration of Independence, they were signing a promissory note to which every American was to fall heir. This note was a promise that all men—yes, black men as well as white men—would be guaranteed the unalienable rights of life, liberty, and the pursuit of happiness.

It is obvious today that America has defaulted on this promissory note insofar as her citizens of color are concerned. Instead of honoring this sacred obligation, America has given the Negro people a bad check, a check which has come back marked "insufficient funds." But we refuse to believe that the bank of justice is bankrupt. We refuse to believe that there are insufficient funds in the great vaults of opportunity of this nation. So we've come to cash this check—a check that will give us upon demand the riches of freedom and the security of justice.

We have also come to this hallowed spot to remind America of the fierce urgency of "now." This is no time to engage in the luxury of cooling off or to take the tranquilizing drug of gradualism. Now is the time to make real the promises of democracy. Now is the time to rise from the dark and desolate valley of segregation to the sunlit path of racial justice. Now is the time to lift our nation from the quicksand of racial injustice to the solid rock of brotherhood. Now is the time to make justice a reality for all of God's children.

It would be fatal for the nation to overlook the urgency of the moment. This sweltering summer of the Negro's legitimate discontent will not pass until there is an invigorating autumn of freedom and equality. Nineteen sixty-three is not an end, but a beginning. Those who hope that the Negro needed to blow off steam and will now be content will have a rude awakening if the nation returns to business as usual. There will be neither rest nor tranquillity in America until the Negro is granted his citizenship rights. The whirlwinds of revolt will continue to shake the foundations of our nation until the bright day of justice emerges.

But that is something that I must say to my people who stand on the warm threshold which leads into the palace of justice. In the process of gaining our rightful place we must not be guilty of wrongful deeds. Let us not seek to satisfy our thirst for freedom by drinking from the cup of bitterness and hatred.

We must forever conduct our struggle on the high plane of dignity and discipline. We must not allow our creative protest to degenerate into physical violence. Again and again we must rise to the majestic heights of meeting physical force with soul force. The marvelous new militancy which has engulfed the Negro community must not lead us to a distrust of all white people, for many of our white brothers, as evidenced by their presence here today, have come to realize that their destiny is tied up with our destiny. And they have come to realize that their freedom is inextricably bound to our freedom. We cannot walk alone.

As we walk, we must make the pledge that we shall always march ahead. We cannot turn back.

There are those who are asking the devotees of civil rights, "When will you be satisfied?" We can never be satisfied as long as the Negro is the victim of the unspeakable horrors of police brutality. We can never be satisfied as long as our bodies, heavy with the fatigue of travel, cannot gain lodging in the motels of the highways and the hotels of the cities. We cannot be satisfied as long as the Negro's basic mobility is from a smaller ghetto to a larger one. We can never be satisfied as long as our children are stripped of their selfhood and robbed of their dignity by signs stating "For Whites Only." We cannot be satisfied as long as a Negro in Mississippi cannot vote and a Negro in New York believes he has nothing for which to vote. No, no, we are not satisfied, and we will not be satisfied until justice rolls down like waters and righteousness like a mighty stream!

I am not unmindful that some of you have come here out of great trials and tribulations. Some of you have come fresh from narrow jail cells. Some of you have come from areas where your quest for freedom left you battered by the storms of persecution and staggered by the winds of police brutality. You have been the veterans of creative suffering. Continue to work with the faith that unearned suffering is redemptive.

Go back to Mississippi, go back to Alabama, go back to South Carolina, go back to Georgia, go back to Louisiana, go back to the slums and ghettos of our Northern cities, knowing that somehow this situation can and will be changed. Let us not wallow in the valley of despair.

I say to you today, my friends, so even though we face the difficulties of today and tomorrow, I still have a dream. It is a dream deeply rooted in the American dream.

I have a dream that one day this nation will rise up and live out the true meaning of its creed: "We hold these truths to be self-evident; that all men are created equal."

I have a dream that one day on the red hills of Georgia the sons of former slaves and the sons of former slave owners will be able to sit down together at the table of brotherhood.

I have a dream that one day even the state of Mississippi, a state sweltering with the heat of injustice, sweltering with the heat of oppression, will be transformed into an oasis of freedom and justice.

I have a dream that my four little children will one day live in a nation where they will not be judged by the color of their skin but by the content of their character.

I have a dream today!

I have a dream that one day, down in Alabama, with its vicious racists, with its governor having his lips dripping with the words of interposition and nullification, one day right there in Alabama little black boys and black girls will be able to join hands with little white boys and white girls as sisters and brothers ... I have a dream today!

I have a dream that one day every valley shall be exalted, every hill and mountain shall be made low, the rough places will be made plain and the crooked places will be made straight, and the glory of the Lord shall be revealed, and all flesh shall see it together!

This is our hope. This is the faith that I go back to the South with. With this faith, we will be able to hew out of the mountain of despair a stone of hope. With this faith we will be able to transform the jangling discords of our nation into a beautiful symphony of brotherhood. With this faith we will be able to work together, to pray together, to struggle together, to go to jail together, to stand up for freedom together, knowing that we will be free one day!

This will be the day ... this will be the day when all of God's children will be able to sing with new meaning. "My country 'tis of thee, sweet land of liberty, of thee I sing. Land where my fathers died, land of the Pilgrims' pride, from every mountainside, let freedom ring," and if America is to be a great nation, this must become true.

So let freedom ring! From the prodigious hilltops of New Hampshire, let freedom ring. From the mighty mountains of New York, let freedom ring, from the heightening Alleghenies of Pennsylvania!

Let freedom ring from the snow-capped Rockies of Colorado!

Let freedom ring from the curvaceous slopes of California! But not only that.

Let freedom ring from Stone Mountain of Georgia!

Let freedom ring from Lookout Mountain in Tennessee!

Let freedom ring from every hill and mole hill of Mississippi. From every mountainside, let freedom ring, and when this happens ... when we allow freedom to ring, when we let it ring from every village and every hamlet, from every state and every city, we will be able to speed up that day when all of God's children, black men and white men, Jews and Gentiles, Protestants and Catholics, will be able to join hands and sing in the words of the old Negro spiritual, "Free at last! Free at last! Thank God Almighty, we are free at last!" **)**

Dr Martin Luther King Jnr was named *Time Magazine*'s 'Person of the Year' in 1963 and, a few months later, received the 1964 Nobel Peace Prize—at the time the youngest man to be so honoured. On his return from Norway, King threw himself into a new cause—voter registration in Selma Alabama.

In 1965, President Johnson asked Congress to ratify a tough voting rights bill in his State of the Union speech. When Congress stalled, King and over 500 supporters marched from Selma to Montgomery to register African-Americans to vote. Alabama police attacked the marchers and the violence shown on national television shocked the country. It took government intervention—the 'federalising' of the Alabama National Guard and the addition of another 2000 guards—to allow a second, 3000 strong, march to Montgomery to begin on March 21, 1965. Congress finally passed the bill (known as the Civil Rights Act of 1965 or the Voting Rights Act of 1965) on 5 August 1965.

Dr King went on to battle other issues—domestic poverty, Chicago slums and the war in Vietnam—as well as factions within the equal rights movement in the remaining years of his short life.

In 1968 King was planning another massive march on Washington—'a demonstration of such intensity and size' that Congress would have to finally take notice of the nation's poor—when he was invited to Memphis, Tennessee to support striking sanitation workers. He gave his famous 'I have seen the Promised Land' speech at the Mason Temple in Memphis on the evening of 3 April, 1968.

The following day Martin Luther King Jnr was shot and killed as he stood on the balcony of the black-owned Lorraine Hotel, just off Beale Street. He was talking to Ralph Abernathy and Jesse Jackson when he was struck in the neck and died at the scene soon after.

For a man of peace, Reverend Martin Luther King Jnr died a violent death and his passing caused a wave of destruction in major cities across the United States.

Lyndon B Johnson

'Let Us Continue'

US Congress, Washington DC, 27 November 1963.

On Friday, 22 November 1963 Vice President Lyndon Johnson took the oath of office aboard Air Force One at 2:38pm with the body of the slain president John F Kennedy on board, and in front of JFK's widow Jackie and his own wife, Bird.

Before his unexpected ascension to the presidency, Lyndon Baines Johnson (1908-1973) was a Democratic Representative for ten years before being elected to the US Senate in 1948.

The world stood still on Monday, 25 November 1963 as John F Kennedy was laid to rest. The previous day his alleged assassin Lee Harvey Oswald was himself gunned down by Dallas night-club owner Jack Ruby. The motivations and circumstances surrounding this 'second assassination' raised just as many questions as Kennedy's death. Three days later Lyndon Johnson, the 36th President of the United States, addressed the US Congress. Johnson's words would have to heal a nation ... and the entire world.

❝Mr. Speaker, Mr. President, Members of the House, Members of the Senate, my fellow Americans:

All I have I would have given gladly not to be standing here today.

The greatest leader of our time has been struck down by the foulest deed of our time. Today, John Fitzgerald Kennedy lives on in the immortal words and works that he left behind. He lives on in the mind and memories of mankind. He lives on in the hearts of his countrymen. No words are sad enough to express our sense of loss. No words are strong enough to express our determination to continue the forward thrust of America that he began.

The dream of conquering the vastness of space, the dream of partnership across the Atlantic—and across the Pacific as well—the dream of a Peace Corps in less developed nations, the dream of education for all of our children, the dream of jobs for all who seek them and need them, the dream of care for our elderly, the dream of an all-out attack on mental illness, and above all, the dream of equal rights for all Americans, whatever their race or color. These and other American dreams have been vitalized by his drive and by his dedication. And now the ideas and the ideals which he so nobly represented must and will be translated into effective action.

Under John Kennedy's leadership, this nation has demonstrated that it has the courage to seek peace, and it has the fortitude to risk war. We have proved that we are a good and reliable friend to those who seek peace and freedom. We have shown that we can also be a formidable foe to those who reject the path of peace and those who seek to impose upon us or our allies the yoke of tyranny. This nation will keep its commitments from South Vietnam to West Berlin. We will be unceasing in the search for peace, resourceful in our pursuit of areas of agreement —even with those with whom we differ—and generous and loyal to those who join with us in common cause.

In this age when there can be no losers in peace and no victors in war, we must recognize the obligation to match national strength with national restraint. We must be prepared at one and the same time for both the confrontation of power and the limitation of power. We must be ready to defend the national interest and to negotiate the common interest. This is the path that we shall continue to pursue. Those who test our courage will find it strong, and those who seek our friendship will find it honorable. We will demonstrate anew that the strong can be just in the use of strength, and the just can be strong in the defense of justice.

And let all know we will extend no special privilege and impose no persecution. We will carry on the fight against poverty, and misery, and disease, and ignorance, in other lands and in our own. We will serve all the nation, not one section or one sector, or one group, but all Americans.

These are the United States: A united people with a united purpose.

Our American unity does not depend upon unanimity. We have differences; but now, as in the past, we can derive from those differences strength, not weakness, wisdom, not despair. Both as a people and a government, we can unite upon a program, a program which is wise and just, enlightened and constructive.

For 32 years Capitol Hill has been my home. I have shared many moments of pride with you, pride in the ability of the Congress of the United States to act, to meet any crisis, to distill from our differences strong programs of national action. An assassin's bullet has thrust upon me the awesome burden of the Presidency. I am here today to say I need your help. I cannot bear this burden alone. I need the help of all Americans, and all America.

This nation has experienced a profound shock, and in this critical moment, it is our duty, yours and mine, as the Government of the United States, to do away with uncertainty and doubt and delay, and to show that we are capable of decisive action; that from the brutal loss of our leader we will derive not weakness, but strength; that we can and will act and act now.

From this chamber of representative government, let all the world know and none misunderstand that I rededicate this Government to the unswerving support of the United Nations, to the honorable and determined execution of our commitments to our allies, to the maintenance of military strength second to none, to the defense of the strength and the stability of the dollar, to the expansion of our foreign trade, to the reinforcement of our programs of mutual assistance and cooperation in Asia and Africa, and to our Alliance for Progress in this hemisphere.

On the 20th day of January, in 1961, John F. Kennedy told his countrymen that our national work would not be finished "in the first thousand days, nor in the life of this administration, nor even perhaps in our lifetime on this planet." "But," he said, "let us begin."

Today in this moment of new resolve, I would say to all my fellow Americans, let us continue.

This is our challenge—not to hesitate, not to pause, not to turn about and linger over this evil moment, but to continue on our course so that we may fulfill the destiny that history has set for us.

Our most immediate tasks are here on this Hill. First, no memorial oration or eulogy could more eloquently honor President Kennedy's memory than the earliest possible passage of the Civil Rights Bill for which he fought so long. We have talked long enough in this country about equal rights. We have talked for a hundred years or more. It is time now to write the next chapter, and to write it in the books of law. I urge you again, as I did in 1957 and again in 1960, to enact a civil rights law so that we can move forward to eliminate from this nation every trace of discrimination and oppression that is based upon race or color. There could be no greater source of strength to this nation both at home and abroad.

And second, no act of ours could more fittingly continue the work of President Kennedy than the early passage of the tax bill for which he fought all this long year. This is a bill designed to increase our national income and Federal revenues, and to provide insurance against recession. That bill, if passed without delay, means more security for those now working, more jobs for those now without them, and more incentive for our economy.

In short, this is no time for delay. It is a time for action—strong, forward-looking action on the pending education bills to help bring the light of learning to every home and hamlet in America; strong, forward-looking action on youth employment opportunities; strong, forward-looking action on the pending foreign aid bill, making clear that we are not forfeiting our responsibilities to this hemisphere or to the world, nor erasing Executive flexibility in the conduct of our foreign affairs; and strong, prompt, and forward-looking action on the remaining appropriation bills.

In this new spirit of action, the Congress can expect the full cooperation and support of the executive branch. And, in particular, I pledge that the expenditures of your Government will be administered with the utmost thrift and frugality. I will insist that the Government get a dollar's value for a dollar spent. The Government will set an example of prudence and economy.

This does not mean that we will not meet our unfilled needs or that we will not honor our commitments. We will do both.

As one who has long served in both Houses of the Congress, I firmly believe in the independence and the integrity of the legislative branch. And I promise you that I shall always respect this. It is deep in the marrow of my bones. With equal firmness, I believe in the capacity and I believe in the ability of the Congress, despite the divisions of opinions which characterize our nation, to act—to act wisely, to act vigorously, to act speedily when the need arises.

The need is here. The need is now. I ask your help.

We meet in grief, but let us also meet in renewed dedication and renewed vigor. Let us meet in action, in tolerance, and in mutual understanding.

John Kennedy's death commands what his life conveyed—that America must move forward.

The time has come for Americans of all races and creeds and political beliefs to understand and to respect one another. So let us put an end to the teaching and the preaching of hate and evil and violence. Let us turn away from the fanatics of the far left and the far right, from the apostles of bitterness and bigotry, from those defiant of law, and those who pour venom into our nation's bloodstream.

I profoundly hope that the tragedy and the torment of these terrible days will bind us together in new fellowship, making us one people in our hour of sorrow. So let us here highly resolve that John Fitzgerald Kennedy did not live or die in vain. And on this Thanksgiving eve, as we gather together to ask the Lord's blessing, and give Him our thanks, let us unite in those familiar and cherished words:

America, America, God shed His grace on thee,

And crown thy good, With brotherhood

From sea to shining sea. '

Johnson proved to be both an enigmatic and contradictory President. He was a great domestic reformer who was returned to power with an increased majority in 1964 but a flawed commander-in-chief who escalated the conflict in Vietnam.

The President of the United States pushed Congress to ratify the tough voting rights bill in his State of the Union speech, and the Civil Rights Act of 1965 was finally passed on 5 August that year.

However, any gains Johnson had made on civil issues were brought undone by the escalation of America's commitment to the Vietnam War. In January 1968 the 'Tet' Offensive (launched on the Vietnamese New Year holiday) reiterated North Vietnamese determination to win its civil war at all costs. Just as importantly, uncensored news coverage shown on nightly news programs and in American newspapers reinforced the growing perception that this was not a winnable war. Congressional opposition, media scrutiny and domestic unrest—especially among students—brought President Lyndon Johnson to make the gravest of decisions. In March 1968 Johnson stunned the world with the surprise announcement that he would not seek re-election as president. The Vietnam War had claimed its highest ranking victim.

Malcolm X

'The Bullet or the Ballot'

Cleveland, Ohio, 3 April 1964

Malcolm X was born Malcolm Little on 19 May 1925, in Omaha Nebraska. One of eight children of outspoken Baptist Minister Earl Little, the family home in Lansing Michigan was burnt to the ground in 1929 because of Little Senior's support of black nationalist leader, Marcus Garvey.

Two years later, Earl Little's body was found lying on a trolley track—the victim of white supremacist group, the Black Legion—but at the time his death was ruled an accident.

Malcolm's mother suffered the first of several nervous breakdowns and he and his siblings were placed in foster homes and orphanages.

Although he was a bright student, Malcolm drifted into petty crime and, after moving to Boston in 1946, was sentenced to ten years jail on burglary charges. Malcolm used his time in jail to rekindle his interest in education and converted to Islam. By the time he was paroled in 1952, Malcolm was a firm follower of 'Nation of Islam' leader, Elijah Muhammad, and forsook his slave name 'Little' for the letter 'X' to symbolise the loss of his African identity.

His ability to articulate Elijah Muhammad's sternest teachings—to despise the white society that had enslaved African-Americans and was actively working against them in achieving equality and a separate NOI State within America—portrayed Malcolm X as a stark alternative for African Americans to the non-violent leadership of Martin Luther King.

Malcolm X emerged as the Nation of Islam's most important leader in the late 1950s and early 1960s—eventually eclipsing his mentor, Elijah

Muhammad, whom Malcolm considered a living prophet. When he discovered that Elijah Muhammad was conducting affairs with as many as six women (and had fathered several children) in his organisation, he broke away from NOI in March 1964 and founded his own religious organisation, the Muslim Mosque, Inc.

In this famous speech in Cleveland, Ohio, the following month, Malcolm X gave a scathing account of democratic politics in the United States as that year's presidential race began. At the end of the speech he reiterated his position—if politicians did not grant equality through the ballot then African Americans should fight for their civil rights with bullets if need be.

'...Our gospel is black nationalism. We're not trying to threaten the existence of any organization, but we're spreading the gospel of black nationalism. Anywhere there's a church that is also preaching and practicing the gospel of black nationalism, join that church. If the NAACP is preaching and practicing the gospel of black nationalism, join the NAACP. If CORE is spreading and practicing the gospel of black nationalism, join CORE. Join any organization that has a gospel that's for the uplift of the black man. And when you get into it and see them pussyfooting or compromising, pull out of it because that's not black nationalism. We'll find another one.

And in this manner, the organizations will increase in number and in quantity and in quality and by August, it is then our intention to have a black nationalist convention which will consist of delegates from all over the country who are interested in the political, economic and social philosophy of black nationalism. After these delegates convene, we will hold a seminar; we will hold discussions; we will listen to everyone. We want to hear new ideas and new solutions and new answers. And at that time, if we see fit then to form a black nationalist party, we'll form a black nationalist party. If it's necessary to form a black nationalist army, we'll form a black nationalist army. It'll be the ballot or the bullet. It'll be liberty or it'll be death.

It's time for you and me to stop sitting in this country, letting some cracker senators, Northern crackers and Southern crackers, sit there in Washington, DC and come to a conclusion in their mind that you and I are supposed to have civil rights. There's no white man going to tell me anything about my rights. Brothers and sisters, always remember, if it doesn't take senators and congressmen and presidential proclamations to give freedom to the white man, it is not necessary for legislation or proclamation or Supreme Court decisions to give freedom to the black man. You let that white man know, if this is a country of freedom, let it be a country of freedom; and if it's not a country of freedom, change it.

We will work with anybody, anywhere, at any time, who is genuinely interested in tackling the problem head-on, non-violently as long as the enemy is non-violent, but violent when the enemy gets violent. We'll work with you on the voter-registration drive, we'll work with you on rent strikes, we'll work with you on school boycotts.

I don't believe in any kind of integration. I'm not even worried about it, because I know you're not going to get it anyway. You're not going to get it because you're afraid to die. You've got to be ready to die if you try and force yourself on the white man, because he'll get just as violent as those crackers in Mississippi, right here in Cleveland.

But we will still work with you on the school boycotts because we're against a segregated school system. A segregated school system produces children who, when they graduate, graduate with crippled minds. But this does not mean that a school is segregated because it's all black. A segregated school means a school that is controlled by people who have no real interest in it whatsoever.

Let me explain what I mean. A segregated district or community is a community in which people live, but outsiders control the politics and the economy of that community. They never refer to the white section as a segregated community. It's the all-Negro section that's a segregated community. Why? The white man controls his own school, his own bank, his own economy, his own politics, his own everything, his own community; but he also controls yours.

When you're under someone else's control, you're segregated. They'll always give you the lowest or the worst that there is to offer, but it doesn't mean you're segregated just because you have your own. You've got to control your own. Just like the white man has control of his, you need to control yours.

You know the best way to get rid of segregation? The white man is more afraid of separation than he is of integration. Segregation means that he puts you away from him, but not far enough for you to be out of his jurisdiction; separation means you're gone. And the white man will integrate faster than he'll let you separate. So we will work with you against the segregated school system because it's criminal, because it is absolutely destructive, in every way imaginable, to the minds of the children who have to be exposed to that type of crippling education.

Last but not least, I must say this concerning the great controversy over rifles and shotguns. The only thing that I've ever said is that in areas where the government has proven itself either unwilling or unable to defend the lives and the property of Negroes, it's time for Negroes to defend themselves. Article number two of the constitutional amendments provides you and me the right to own a rifle or a shotgun. It is constitutionally legal to own a shotgun or a rifle. This doesn't mean you're going to get a rifle and form battalions and go out looking for white folks, although you'd be within your rights—I mean, you'd be justified—but that would be illegal and we don't do anything illegal. If the white man doesn't want the black man buying rifles and shotguns, then let the government do its job.

That's all. And don't let the white man come to you and ask you what you think about what Malcolm says—why, you old Uncle Tom. He would never ask you if he thought you were going to say: "Amen!" No, he is making a Tom out of you.

So, this doesn't mean forming rifle clubs and going out looking for people, but it is time, in 1964, if you are a man, to let that man know, if he's not going to do his job in running the government and providing you and me with the protection that our taxes are supposed to be for, since he spends all those billions for his defense budget, he certainly can't begrudge you and me spending $12 or $15 for a single-shot, or double-action.

I hope you understand. Don't go out shooting people, but any time—brothers and sisters and especially the men in this audience—some of you wearing Congressional Medals of Honor, with shoulders this wide, chests this big, muscles that big—any time you and I sit around and read where they bomb a church and murder in cold blood, not some grown-ups, but four little girls while they were praying to the same God the white man taught them to pray to, and you and I see the government go down and can't find who did it.

Why, this man—he can find Eichmann hiding down in Argentina somewhere. Let two or three American soldiers, who are minding somebody else's business way over in South

Vietnam, get killed, and he'll send battleships, sticking his nose in their business. He wanted to send troops down to Cuba and make them have what he calls free elections—this old cracker who doesn't have free elections in his own country.

No, if you never see me another time in your life, if I die in the morning, I'll die saying one thing: The ballot or the bullet, the ballot or the bullet.

If a Negro in 1964 has to sit around and wait for some cracker senator to filibuster when it comes to the rights of black people, why, you and I should hang our heads in shame. You talk about a march on Washington in 1963, you haven't seen anything. There's some more going down in 64.

And this time they're not going like they went last year. They're not going singing "We Shall Overcome." They're not going with white friends. They're not going with placards already painted for them. They're not going with round-trip tickets. They're going with one-way tickets. And if they don't want that non-non-violent army going down there, tell them to bring the filibuster to a halt.

The black nationalists aren't going to wait. Lyndon B. Johnson is the head of the Democratic Party. If he's for civil rights, let him go into the Senate next week and declare himself. Let him go in there right now and declare himself. Let him go in there and denounce the Southern branch of his party. Let him go in there right now and take a moral stand—right now, not later. Tell him, don't wait until election time. If he waits too long, brothers and sisters, he will be responsible for letting a condition develop in this country which will create a climate that will bring seeds up out of the ground with vegetation on the end of them looking like something these people never dreamed of. In 1964, it's the ballot or the bullet.

Thank you. ❜

In May 1964 Malcolm X established the Organisation of Afro-American Unity (OAAU), a secular political group.

A pilgrimage to Mecca that year softened his political approach and upon his return to the United States, he saw integration as the real hope for the future.

Slowly, his message started to reach all races and creeds.

But Malcolm X's denouncement of Elijah Muhammad created powerful enemies with the Nation of Islam and his family home in East Elmhurst, New York, was firebombed in February 1964.

One week later, on 21 February, Malcolm X was shot by three members of NOI as he began an address at the Audubon Ballroom, New York. He was just 39 years old when he died.

Robert F Kennedy

'Announcement of Martin Luther King's Death'

Rally for presidential votes, Indianapolis, Indiana, 4 April 1968.

Robert Francis Kennedy (1925-68) served on the Select Committee for Improper Activities in the late 1950s—taking on Teamster Union boss Jimmy Hoffa—before being appointed Attorney General during the presidency of his older brother, John. After John Kennedy's death in 1963, Bobby Kennedy left the White House in 1964 and became the Democratic Senator for New York the following year. When President Johnson announced that he would not seek re-election in March 1968, the younger Kennedy stepped up his bid for the Democratic Party nomination and began a hectic schedule of campaigning—largely on an anti-Vietnam war platform.

On 4 April, 1968 Bobby Kennedy arrived by plane into Indianapolis, Indiana, to address a largely black rally to promote 'RFK for President'. On that same day Dr Martin Luther King Jnr had been murdered in Memphis. On his arrival Kennedy asked the rally organiser, 'Do they know about Martin Luther King?' The man responded by saying, 'No. We've left that up to you.' Kennedy asked the crowd to lower their pro-Kennedy placards and then addressed them in this heartfelt, spontaneous speech that evoked the memory of his own slain brother.

'I have bad news for you, for all of our fellow citizens, and people who love peace all over the world, and that is that Martin Luther King was shot and killed tonight.

Martin Luther King dedicated his life to love and to justice for his fellow human beings, and he died because of that effort.

In this difficult day, in this difficult time for the United States, it is perhaps well to ask what kind of a nation we are and what direction we want to move in. For those of you who are black—considering the evidence there evidently is, that there were white people who were responsible—you can be filled with bitterness, with hatred, and a desire for revenge. We can move in that direction as a country, in great polarization—black people amongst black, white people amongst white, filled with hatred toward one another.

Or we can make an effort, as Martin Luther King did, to understand and to comprehend, and to replace that violence, that stain of blood shed that has spread across our land, with an effort to understand with compassion and love.

For those of you who are black and are tempted to be filled with hatred and distrust at the injustice of such an act, against all white people, I can only say that I feel in my own heart that same kind of feeling. I had a member of my family killed, but he was killed by a white man. But we have to make an effort in the United States, we have to make an effort to understand, to go beyond these rather difficult times.

My favorite poet was Aeschylus. He wrote: "In our sleep, pain which cannot forget falls drop by drop upon the heart until, in our own despair, against our will, comes wisdom through the awful grace of God."

What we need in the United States is not division; what we need in the United States is not hatred; what we need in the United States is not violence or lawlessness; but love and wisdom, and compassion toward one another, and a feeling of justice toward those who still suffer within our country, whether they be white or they be black.

So I shall ask you tonight to return home, to say a prayer for the family of Martin Luther King, that's true, but more importantly, to say a prayer for our own country, which all of us love—a prayer for understanding and that compassion of which I spoke.

We can do well in this country. We will have difficult times; we've had difficult times in the past; we will have difficult times in the future. It is not the end of violence; it is not the end of lawlessness; it is not the end of disorder.

But the vast majority of white people and the vast majority of black people in this country want to live together, want to improve the quality of our life, and want justice for all human beings who abide in our land.

Let us dedicate ourselves to what the Greeks wrote so many years ago: to tame the savageness of man and make gentle the life of this world.

Let us dedicate ourselves to that, and say a prayer for our country and for our people. *

Ten weeks later, on 4 June 1968, Robert F.Kennedy won the California Primary for the Democratic nomination and pulled away from his closest rivals, Eugene McCarthy and Hubert Humphrey. His short victory speech, delivered at the Ambassador Hotel's Embassy Ballroom just before midnight, constituted his final public appearance:

*I think we can end the divisions within the United States. What I think is quite clear is that we can work together in the last analysis. And that what has been going on with the United States over the period of that last three years, the divisions, the violence, the disenchantment with our society, the divisions—whether it's between blacks and whites, between the poor and the more affluent, or between age groups, or in the war in Vietnam—that we can work together. We are a great country, an unselfish country and a compassionate country. And I intend to make that my basis for running. *

Kennedy then left the rostrum, behind a curtain, taking a back route to the press room via the hotel kitchen. There, at 12:23 am on the morning of 5 June, Kennedy was shot in the head by Jordanian immigrant Sirhan Sirhan. The 24-year-old assassin was allegedly upset by Kennedy's support of Israel during the Six-Day War the previous year, but as was the case with the death of John Kennedy and Martin Luther King, Sirhan's crime started a conspiracy industry (Sirhan was sentenced to death but this was commuted to life imprisonment). Robert Kennedy was taken to the nearby Good Samaritan Hospital where on the fifth floor, surrounded by family and friends, Kennedy, and his unfulfilled potential, died the following day.

Edward 'Teddy' Kennedy

'Eulogy for Robert F Kennedy'

St. Patrick's Cathedral, New York, 8 June 1968.

Edward Moore 'Teddy' Kennedy was born in 1932, the youngest of four sons and five daughters born to Joseph and Rose Kennedy. After studying at Harvard and the Virginia University Law School, he was admitted to the bar in 1959. Teddy Kennedy was elected Democratic Senator for Massachusetts in 1962—the position vacated by his brother John F. Kennedy when he became President in 1961—at the young age of 30. The youngest Kennedy was an important part of the mythical Kennedy political 'dynasty' but even more pressure was placed on the last of the family line following the assassinations of his brothers in 1963 and 1968. (The Kennedy's oldest brother, Joe Jnr, was killed in World War II while another sister, Kathleen, died in a plane accident).

Senator Teddy Kennedy delivered the eulogy for his brother Bobby at St Patrick's Cathedral, New York, on 8 June 1968. Towards the end of this speech Kennedy's voice strained under the emotion—highlighting the poignancy of the occasion.

❝On behalf of Mrs Robert Kennedy, her children and the parents and sisters of Robert Kennedy, I want to express what we feel to those who mourn with us today in this cathedral and around the world. We loved him as a brother and father and son. From his parents, and from his older brothers and sisters—Joe, Kathleen and Jack—he received inspiration which he passed on to all of us. He gave us strength in time of trouble, wisdom in time of uncertainty, and sharing in time of happiness. He was always by our side.

Love is not an easy feeling to put into words. Nor is loyalty, or trust or joy. But he was all of these. He loved life completely and lived it intensely.

A few years back, Robert Kennedy wrote some words about his own father and they expressed the way we in his family feel about him. He said of what his father meant to him:

"What it really all adds up to is love—not love as it is described with such facility in popular magazines, but the kind of love that is affection and respect, order, encouragement, and support. Our awareness of this was an incalculable source of strength, and because real love is something unselfish and involves sacrifice and giving, we could not help but profit from it.

"Beneath it all, he has tried to engender a social conscience. There were wrongs which needed attention. There were people who were poor and who needed help. And we have a responsibility to them and to this country. Through no virtues and accomplishments of our own, we have been fortunate enough to be born in the United States under the most comfortable conditions. We, therefore, have a responsibility to others who are less well off."

This is what Robert Kennedy was given. What he leaves us is what he said, what he did and what he stood for. A speech he made to the young people of South Africa on their Day of Affirmation in 1966 sums it up best, and I would read it now:

"There is discrimination in this world, and slavery and slaughter and starvation. Governments repress their people; and millions are trapped in poverty while the nation grows rich; and wealth is lavished on armaments everywhere.

"These are differing evils, but they are common works of man. They reflect the imperfection of human justice, the inadequacy of human compassion, our lack of sensibility toward the sufferings of our fellows.

"But we can perhaps remember—even if only for a time—that those who live with us are our brothers; that they share with us the same short moment of life; that they seek—as we do—nothing but the chance to live out their lives in purpose and happiness, winning what satisfaction and fulfillment they can.

"Surely this bond of common faith, this bond of common goal, can begin to teach us something. Surely, we can learn, at least, to look at those around us as fellow men. And surely we can begin to work a little harder to bind up the wounds among us and to become in our own hearts brothers and countrymen once again.

"Our answer is to rely on youth—not a time of life but a state of mind, a temper of the will, a quality of imagination, a predominance of courage over timidity, of the appetite for adventure over the love of ease. The cruelties and obstacles of this swiftly changing planet will not yield to obsolete dogmas and outworn slogans. They cannot be moved by those who cling to a present that is already dying, who prefer the illusion of security to the excitement and danger that come with even the most peaceful progress. It is a revolutionary world we live in; and this generation, at home and around the world, has had thrust upon it a greater burden of responsibility than any generation that has ever lived.

"Some believe there is nothing one man or one woman can do against the enormous array of the world's ills. Yet many of the world's great movements, of thought and action, have flowed from the work of a single man. A young monk began the Protestant reformation, a young general extended an empire from Macedonia to the borders of the earth, and a young woman reclaimed the territory of France. It was a young Italian explorer who discovered the New World, and the thirty-two-year-old Thomas Jefferson who proclaimed that all men are created equal.

"These men moved the world, and so can we all. Few will have the greatness to bend history itself, but each of us can work to change a small portion of events, and in the total of all those acts will be written the history of this generation. It is from numberless diverse acts of courage and belief that human history is shaped. Each time a man stands up for an ideal, or acts to improve the lot of others, or strikes out against injustice, he sends forth a tiny ripple of hope, and crossing each other from a million different centers of energy and daring, those ripples build a current that can sweep down the mightiest walls of oppression and resistance.

"Few are willing to brave the disapproval of their fellows, the censure of their colleagues, the wrath of their society. Moral courage is a rarer commodity than bravery in battle or great intelligence. Yet it is the one essential, vital quality for those who seek to change a world that yields most painfully to change. And I believe that in this generation those with the courage to enter the moral conflict will find themselves with companions in every corner of the globe.

"For the fortunate among us, there is the temptation to follow the easy and familiar paths of personal ambition and financial success so grandly spread before those who enjoy the privilege of education. But that is not the road history has marked out for us. Like it or not, we live in times of danger and uncertainty. But they are also more open to the creative energy of men than any other time in history. All of us will ultimately be judged, and as the years pass, we will surely judge ourselves on the effort we have contributed to building a new world society and the extent to which our ideals and goals have shaped that effort.

"The future does not belong to those who are content with today, apathetic toward common problems and their fellow man alike, timid and fearful in the face of new ideas and bold projects. Rather it will belong to those who can blend vision, reason and courage in a personal commitment to the ideals and great enterprises of American society.

"Our future may lie beyond our vision, but it is not completely beyond our control. It is the shaping impulse of America that neither fate nor nature nor the irresistible tides of history, but the work of our own hands, matched to reason and principle, that will determine our destiny. There is pride in that, even arrogance, but there is also experience and truth. In any event, it is the only way we can live."

This is the way he lived. My brother need not be idealized, or enlarged in death beyond what he was in life, to be remembered simply as a good and decent man, who saw wrong and tried to right it, saw suffering and tried to heal it, saw war and tried to stop it.

Those of us who loved him and who take him to his rest today, pray that what he was to us and what he wished for others will some day come to pass for all the world. As he said many times, in many parts of this nation, to those he touched and who sought to touch him:

"Some men see things as they are and say why.

I dream things that never were and say why not." **)**

Within a year, Teddy Kennedy's dream of following his slain brothers into the White House disappeared in the murky waters off Chappaquiddick Island. Kennedy's conduct regarding the death of party secretary Mary Jo Kopechne in a submerged car after a night of partying at Martha's Vineyard did not endear him to the American public. He ultimately ran for President in 1980 but his loss to Jimmy Carter at the Democratic National Convention in New York in August 1980 confirmed what the American public already knew— Teddy Kennedy would never become President. It was the end of the dream of a 'Kennedy dynasty'.

In 1999 Teddy Kennedy—still the Democratic Senator for Massachusetts but promoted by fate from kid brother to family patriarch and eulogiser—was again called upon after his nephew, 38 year-old John Kennedy Jnr, his wife Carolyn and sister-in-law Lauren Bessette, were killed in a light plane crash off the coast of Massachusetts.

Teddy Kennedy died in 2009, aged 77.

John Kerry

'Against the War in Vietnam'

House Foreign Relations Committee, Washington DC, 22 April 1971.

John F Kerry was the Democratic presidential candidate against George W Bush in 2004. During that campaign, at a time when America was fighting an unpopular war in Iraq, Kerry's Vietnam War experiences became a major issue in his bid to become president. Kerry was both lauded by ex-comrades and publicly vilified by his Republican opponents about his war record. (He accepted the Democratic nomination in July 2004 by stating 'I'm John Kerry … reporting for duty' as he saluted the party faithful.) President George Bush ultimately won the November elections, but the Vietnam veteran pushed Bush to the narrowest margin of primary votes by any sitting president in American history.

Kerry was born on 11 December, 1943 in Colorado, the son of an Army Air Corps test pilot who flew DC-3s and B-29s during World War II. Kerry's father, Richard, was a Foreign Service Officer in the Eisenhower administration. After graduating from Yale University, Kerry—a liberal, well-to-do Catholic with a military heritage—volunteered to serve in Vietnam because he felt it was 'the right thing to do'. Kerry completed two tours of duty and on the latter, volunteered to serve on a patrol boat scouring the Vietnamese river deltas. His leadership and courage under fire earned him a Silver Star, a Bronze Star with Combat V, and three Purple Hearts.

Along with many Vietnam veterans, Kerry's wartime experience led him to speak out against the war. He joined Vietnam Veterans Against the War (VVAW) and was later co-founded Vietnam Veterans of America. In April 1971, the then 27 year-old testified before the House Foreign Relations Committee and openly questioned America's involvement in the civil war in Vietnam.

❝I would like to say for the record, and also for the men sitting behind me who are also wearing the uniforms and their medals, that my sitting here is really symbolic. I am not here as John Kerry. I am here as one member of a group of 1,000, which is a small representation of a very much larger group of veterans in this country, and were it possible for all of them to sit at this table, they would be here and have the same kind of testimony. I would simply like to speak in general terms. I apologize if my statement is general because I received notification [only] yesterday that you would hear me, and, I am afraid, because of the injunction I was up most of the night and haven't had a great deal of chance to prepare.

I would like to talk, representing all those veterans, and say that several months ago, in Detroit, we had an investigation at which over 150 honorably discharged, and many very highly decorated, veterans testified to war crimes committed in Southeast Asia. These were not isolated incidents, but crimes committed on a day-to-day basis, with the full awareness of officers at all levels of command. It is impossible to describe to you exactly what did happen in Detroit—the emotions in the room, and the feelings of the men who were reliving their experiences in Vietnam. They relived the absolute horror of what this country, in a sense, made them do.

They told stories that, at times, they had personally raped, cut off ears, cut off heads, taped wires from portable telephones to human genitals and turned up the power, cut off limbs, blown up bodies, randomly shot at civilians, razed villages in fashion reminiscent of Ghengis Khan, shot cattle and dogs for fun, poisoned food stocks, and generally ravaged the countryside of South Vietnam, in addition to the normal ravage of war and the normal and very particular ravaging which is done by the applied bombing power of this country.

We call this investigation the Winter Soldier Investigation. The term "winter soldier" is a play on words of Thomas Paine's in 1776, when he spoke of the "sunshine patriots," and "summertime soldiers" who deserted at Valley Forge because the going was rough.

We who have come here to Washington have come here because we feel we have to be winter soldiers now. We could come back to this country, we could be quiet, we could hold our silence, we could not tell what went on in Vietnam, but we feel, because of what threatens this country, not the reds, but the crimes which we are committing that threaten it, that we have to speak out.

I would like to talk to you a little bit about what the result is of the feelings these men carry with them after coming back from Vietnam. The country doesn't know it yet, but it has created a monster, a monster in the form of millions of men who have been taught to deal and to trade in violence, and who are given the chance to die for the biggest nothing in history; men who have returned with a sense of anger and a sense of betrayal which no one has yet grasped.

As a veteran and one who felt this anger, I would like to talk about it. We are angry because we feel we have been used in the worst fashion by the administration of this country.

In 1970, at West Point, Vice President Agnew said, "some glamorize the criminal misfits of society while our best men die in Asian rice paddies to preserve the freedom which most of those misfits abuse," and this was used as a rallying point for our effort in Vietnam.

But for us, as boys in Asia whom the country was supposed to support, his statement is a terrible distortion from which we can only draw a very deep sense of revulsion. Hence the anger of some of the men who are here in Washington today. It is a distortion because we in no way consider ourselves the best men of this country, because those he calls misfits were standing up for us in a way that nobody else in this country dared to, because so many who have died would have returned to this country to join the misfits in their efforts to ask for an immediate withdrawal from South Vietnam, because so many of those best men have returned as quadriplegics and amputees, and they lie forgotten in Veterans' Administration hospitals in this country which fly the flag which so many have chosen as their own personal symbol. And we cannot consider ourselves America's best men when we are ashamed of and hated what we were called on to do in Southeast Asia.

In our opinion, and from our experience, there is nothing in South Vietnam which could happen that realistically threatens the United States of America. And to attempt to justify the loss of one American life in Vietnam, Cambodia, or Laos by linking such loss to the preservation of freedom, which those misfits supposedly abuse, is to us the height of criminal hypocrisy, and it is that kind of hypocrisy which we feel has torn this country apart.

We found that not only was it a civil war, an effort by a people who had for years been seeking their liberation from any colonial influence whatsoever, but, also, we found that the Vietnamese, whom we had enthusiastically molded after our own image, were hard-put to take up the fight against the threat we were supposedly saving them from.

We found most people didn't even know the difference between communism and democracy. They only wanted to work in rice paddies without helicopters strafing them and bombs with napalm burning their villages and tearing their country apart. They wanted everything to do with the war, particularly with this foreign presence of the United States of America, to leave them alone in peace, and they practiced the art of survival by siding with whichever military force was present at a particular time, be it Viet Cong, North Vietnamese or American.

We found also that, all too often, American men were dying in those rice paddies for want of support from their allies. We saw first hand how monies from American taxes were used for a corrupt dictatorial regime. We saw that many people in this country had a one-sided idea of who was kept free by the flag, and blacks provided the highest percentage of casualties. We saw Vietnam ravaged equally by American bombs and search-and-destroy missions as well as by Viet Cong terrorism—and yet we listened while this country tried to blame all of the havoc on the Viet Cong.

We rationalized destroying villages in order to save them. We saw America lose her sense of morality as she accepted very coolly a My Lai, and refused to give up the image of American soldiers who hand out chocolate bars and chewing gum.

We learned the meaning of free-fire zones—shooting anything that moves—and we watched while America placed a cheapness on the lives of Orientals.

We watched the United States falsification of body counts, in fact the glorification of body counts. We listened while, month after month, we were told the back of the enemy was about to break. We fought using weapons against "Oriental human beings" with quotation marks around that. We fought using weapons against those people which I do not believe this country would dream of using, were we fighting in the European theater. We watched while men charged up hills because a general said that hill has to be taken, and, after losing one platoon, or two platoons, they marched away to leave the hill for reoccupation by the North Vietnamese. We watched pride allow the most unimportant battles to be blown into extravaganzas, because we couldn't lose, and we couldn't retreat, and because it didn't matter how many American bodies were lost to prove that point, and so there were Hamburger Hills and Khe Sanhs and Hill 81s and Fire Base 6s, and so many others.

Now we are told that the men who fought there must watch quietly while American lives are lost so that we can exercise the incredible arrogance of "Vietnamizing" the Vietnamese.

146

Each day, to facilitate the process by which the United States washes her hands of Vietnam, someone has to give up his life so that the United States doesn't have to admit something that the entire world already knows, so that we can't say that we have made a mistake. Someone has to die so that President Nixon won't be, and these are his words, "the first President to lose a war."

We are asking Americans to think about that, because how do you ask a man to be the last man to die in Vietnam? How do you ask a man to be the last man to die for a mistake? We are here in Washington to say that the problem of this war is not just a question of war and diplomacy. It is part and parcel of everything that we are trying, as human beings, to communicate to people in this country—the question of racism, which is rampant in the military, and so many other questions, such as the use of weapons: the hypocrisy in our taking umbrage at the Geneva Conventions and using that as justification for a continuation of this war, when we are more guilty than any other body of violations of those Geneva Conventions; in the use of free-fire zones; harassment-interdiction fire, search-and-destroy missions; the bombings; the torture of prisoners; all accepted policy by many units in South Vietnam. That is what we are trying to say. It is part and parcel of everything.

An American Indian friend of mine who lives in the Indian Nation of Alcatraz put it to me very succinctly. He told me how, as a boy on an Indian reservation, he had watched television, and he used to cheer the cowboys when they came in and shot the Indians, and then suddenly one day he stopped in Vietnam and he said, "my God, I am doing to these people the very same thing that was done to my people," and he stopped. And that is what we are trying to say, that we think this thing has to end.

We are here to ask, and we are here to ask vehemently, where are the leaders of our country? Where is the leadership? We're here to ask where are McNamara, Rostow, Bundy, Gilpatrick, and so many others? Where are they now that we, the men they sent off to war, have returned? These are the commanders who have deserted their troops. And there is no more serious crime in the laws of war. The Army says they never leave their wounded. The Marines say they never even leave their dead. These men have left all the casualties and retreated behind a pious shield of public rectitude. They've left the real stuff of their reputations bleaching behind them in the sun in this country....

We wish that a merciful God could wipe away our own memories of that service as easily as this administration has wiped away their memories of us. But all that they have done, and all that they can do by this denial, is to make more clear than ever our own determination to undertake one last mission: to search out and destroy the last vestige of this barbaric war; to pacify our own hearts; to conquer the hate and fear that have driven this country these last ten years and more. And more. And so, when, thirty years from now, our brothers go down the street without a leg, without an arm, or a face, and small boys ask why, we will be able to say "Vietnam" and not mean a desert, not a filthy obscene memory, but mean instead where America finally turned, and where soldiers like us helped it in the turning. **'**

After delivering this speech, Kerry went to work as a high-profile prosecutor in Middlesex County, Massachusetts. He was elected Lieutenant Governor in 1982 and became a US Senator two years later. In 1988 Senator Kerry chaired the Senate Foreign Relations Subcommittee's investigation into the 'Iran/Contra Affair'. He was serving his fourth term when he announced his candidacy for the Democratic presidential nomination in 2003.

What happened to the earnest young man with the mop of black hair who dared to confront the US military leadership three decades before? Time knocked the edges off the young Vietnam Veteran and the American public ultimately rejected the smoothed-over politician that stood before them in 2004 in favour of four more years of George W Bush.

John Kerry later served President Obama as US Secretary of State at the conclusion of Hillary Clinton's term in February 2013.

Richard M Nixon

'Farewell to the Whitehouse'
Washington DC, 9 August 1974.

Richard Milhous Nixon (1913-94) enjoyed a spectacular rise to prominence in US politics in the late 1940s and early 1950s. After his return from the political graveyard in 1968, six years later he became the first president in the history of the United States to resign from office.

Elected to the US Congress in 1946 after serving in the Navy during World War II, he had made a name for himself as a fervent 'anti-Communist' on the House Committee on Un-American Activities. In 1950 he was elected to the US Senate and as a high-profile opponent of President Truman's handling of the Korean War, he had enough clout to persuade the Californian delegation to throw their support behind Republican candidate Dwight D. Eisenhower in the 1952 presidential race. Eisenhower rewarded Nixon by choosing him as his running mate.

While the Republicans were holding their National Convention in September 1952 a sensational story appeared in the *New York Post* alleging that a 'secret rich men's trust fund' had kept Nixon in financial style far beyond his congressional salary. There was immediate pressure to remove Nixon from the Republican ticket but in a brilliant tactical move, Nixon appeared on national television in California to 'explain' to the American people his financial situation. Now known as the 'Checkers Speech' because of the reference to a pet dog given to his daughters by a Republican supporter, Richard Nixon turned the performance—part drama, part pathos—into a political triumph.

The Republican Party went on to win the election by a landslide but

Nixon could not capitalise on his eight years as vice president and lost the 1960 presidential race to Senator John F. Kennedy. After a failed bid for the governorship of California in 1962 a bitter Nixon told the press, 'You won't have Nixon to kick around any more, gentlemen. This is my last Press Conference.' Almost seven years later to the day, Nixon was elected the 37th President of the United States.

In 1968 Richard Nixon returned from the political scrapheap and the anonymity of corporate life to win the Republican nomination and defeat a decimated Democratic Party to win the presidency. In January 1969 Nixon halted the bombing of North Vietnam but a year later only a token withdrawal of troops had taken place. Under Nixon the Vietnam War entered a new phase when he ordered troops into neighbouring Cambodia to clear out Vietcong training grounds, invaded Laos then resumed the bombing of North Vietnam. By 1972, Dr Henry Kissinger, Nixon's special representative at the Paris Peace talks, declared that peace was 'at hand'. This premature announcement, timed to make maximum impact on that year's presidential race, saw Nixon re-elected in a land-slide victory.

Nixon's second term as president was engulfed by 'Watergate'. The scandal grew from a bungled break-in by five burglars who entered the Democratic National Committee offices at the Watergate complex in Washington on the night of 17 June, 1972. Subsequent investigations, most famously by *Washington Post* reporters Carl Bernstein and Bob Woodward, linked the break-in to President Nixon's top aides, who were involved in an extensive cover-up of politically-sanctioned illegal activities. After a two year investigation by the news media, government agencies, the US Senate, the House of Representatives and the US Supreme Court, the extent of the White House cover-up consumed Nixon's Presidency. It gradually became apparent that Nixon would not survive a full impeachment vote in the Congress despite using the prestige and power of the presidency to stonewall the judicial process.

On August 8, 1974, President Richard M. Nixon appeared on television and became the first President in the history of the United States to resign from office. At 11:35 am the following day Nixon's assistant, Alexander Haig Jnr, tended the President's letter of resignation to Secretary of State Henry A. Kissinger in his White House office. Members of Nixon's staff then assembled to farewell the man they had served—in some cases stretching back to Nixon's time as Vice-President in the early 1950s. Nixon then delivered this revealing speech.

❦I think the record should show that this is one of those spontaneous things that we always arrange whenever the President comes in to speak, and it will be so reported in the press, and we don't mind, because they have to call it as they see it.

But on our part, believe me, it is spontaneous.

You are here to say goodbye to us, and we don't have a good word for it in English—the best is au revoir. We'll see you again.

I just met with the members of the White House staff, you know, those who serve here in the White House day in and day out, and I asked them to do what I ask all of you to do to the extent that you can and, of course, are requested to do so: to serve our next President as you have served me and previous Presidents—because many of you have been here for many years—with devotion and dedication, because this office, great as it is, can only be as great as the men and women who work for and with the President.

This house, for example—I was thinking of it as we walked down this hall, and I was comparing it to some of the great houses of the world that I have been in. This isn't the biggest house. Many, and most, in even smaller countries, are much bigger. This isn't the finest house. Many in Europe, particularly, and in China, Asia, have paintings of great, great value, things that we just don't have here and, probably, will never have until we are 1,000 years old or older.

But this is the best house. It is the best house, because it has something far more important than numbers of people who serve, far more important than numbers of rooms or how big it is, far more important than numbers of magnificent pieces of art.

This house has a great heart, and that heart comes from those who serve. I was rather sorry they didn't come down. We said goodbye to them upstairs. But they are really great.

And I recall after so many times I have made speeches, and some of them pretty tough, yet, I always come back, or after a hard day—and my days usually have run rather long—I would always get a lift from them, because I might be a little down but they always smiled.

And so it is with you. I look around here, and I see so many on this staff that, you know, I should have been by your offices and shaken hands, and I would love to have talked to you and found out how to run the world—everybody wants to tell the President what to do, and boy, he needs to be told many times—but I just haven't had the time. But I want you to know that each and every one of you, I know, is indispensable to this Government.

I am proud of this Cabinet. I am proud of all the members who have served in our Cabinet. I am proud of our sub-Cabinet. I am proud of our White House Staff. As I pointed out last night, sure, we have done some things wrong in this Administration, and the top man always takes the responsibility, and I have never ducked it. But I want to say one thing: We can be proud of it—five and a half years. No man or no woman came into this Administration and left it with more of this world's goods than when he came in. No man or no woman ever profited at the public expense or the public till. That tells something about you.

Mistakes, yes. But for personal gain, never. You did what you believed in. Sometimes right, sometimes wrong. And I only wish that I were a wealthy man—at the present time, I have got to find a way to pay my taxes—and if I were, I would like to recompense you for the sacrifices that all of you have made to serve in government.

But you are getting something in government—and I want you to tell this to your children, and I hope the Nation's children will hear it, too—something in government service that is far more important than money. It is a cause bigger than yourself. It is the cause of making this the greatest nation in the world, the leader of the world, because without our leadership, the world will know nothing but war, possibly starvation or worse, in the years ahead. With our leadership it will know peace, it will know plenty.

We have been generous, and we will be more generous in the future as we are able to. But most important, we must be strong here, strong in our hearts, strong in our souls, strong in our belief, and strong in our willingness to sacrifice, as you have been willing to sacrifice, in a pecuniary way, to serve in government.

There is something else I would like for you to tell your young people. You know, people often come in and say, "What will I tell my kids?" They look at government and say, sort of a rugged life, and they see the mistakes that are made. They get the impression that everybody is here for the purpose of feathering his nest. That is why I made this earlier point—not in this Administration, not one single man or woman.

And I say to them, there are many fine careers. This country needs good farmers, good businessmen, good plumbers, good carpenters.

I remember my old man. I think that they would have called him sort of a little man, common man. He didn't consider himself that way. You know what he was? He was a streetcar motorman first, and then he was a farmer, and then he had a lemon ranch. It was the poorest lemon ranch in California, I can assure you. He sold it before they found oil on it. [Laughter] And then he was a grocer. But he was a great man, because he did his job, and every job counts up to the hilt, regardless of what happens.

Nobody will ever write a book, probably, about my mother. Well, I guess all of you would say this about your mother—my mother was a saint. And I think of her, two boys dying of tuberculosis, nursing four others in order that she could take care of my older brother for three years in Arizona, and seeing each of them die, and when they died, it was like one of her own.

Yes, she will have no books written about her. But she was a saint.

Now, however, we look to the future. I had a little quote in the speech last night from T.R. [Theodore Roosevelt]. As you know, I kind of like to read books. I am not educated, but I do read books—and the T.R. quote was a pretty good one. Here is another one I found as I was reading, my last night in the White House, and this quote is about a young man. He was a young lawyer in New York. He had married a beautiful girl, and they had a lovely daughter, and then suddenly she died, and this is what he wrote. This was in his diary.

He said, "She was beautiful in face and form and lovelier still in spirit. As a flower she grew and as a fair young flower she died. Her life had been always in the sunshine. There had never come to her a single great sorrow. None ever knew her who did not love and revere her for her bright and sunny temper and her saintly unselfishness. Fair, pure and joyous as a maiden, loving, tender and happy as a young wife. When she had just become a mother, when her life seemed to be just begun and when the years seemed so bright before her, then by a strange and terrible fate death came to her. And when my heart's dearest died, the light went from my life forever."

That was T.R. in his twenties. He thought the light had gone from his life forever—but he went on. And he not only became President but, as an ex-President, he served his country, always in the arena, tempestuous, strong, sometimes wrong, sometimes right, but he was a man.

And as I leave, let me say, that is an example I think all of us should remember. We think sometimes when things happen that don't go the right way; we think that when you don't pass the bar exam the first time—I happened to, but I was just lucky; I mean, my writing was so poor the bar examiner said, "We have just got to let the guy through." We think that when someone dear to us dies, we think that when we lose an election, we think that when we suffer a defeat that all is ended. We think, as T.R. said, that the light had left his life forever. Not true.

It is only a beginning, always. The young must know it; the old must know it. It must always sustain us, because the greatness comes not when things go always good for you, but the greatness comes and you are really tested, when you take some knocks, some disappointments, when sadness comes, because only if you have been in the deepest valley can you ever know how magnificent it is to be on the highest mountain.

And so I say to you on this occasion, as we leave, we leave proud of the people who have stood by us and worked for us and served this country. We want you to be proud of what you have done. We want you to continue to serve in government, if that is your wish.

Always give your best, never get discouraged, never be petty; always remember, others may hate you, but those who hate you don't win unless you hate them, and then you destroy yourself.

And so, we leave with high hopes, in good spirit, and with deep humility, and with very much gratefulness in our hearts. I can only say to each and every one of you, we come from many faiths, we pray perhaps to different gods—but really the same God in a sense—but I want to say for each and every one of you, not only will we always remember you, not only will we always be grateful to you but always you will be in our hearts and you will be in our prayers.

Thank you very much. **)**

Richard Nixon's spontaneous speech exposed a flawed contradiction. Much was made of Nixon's references to his mother and his self-demeaning attitude towards his academic ability but his attempt to explain his behaviour as being 'not for personal gain' did not sit well with those who still remembered the 'Checkers' speech. (By choosing resignation over impeachment, Nixon also kept his presidential pension for the rest of his life.) Unlike Teddy Roosevelt, to whom he alluded in his speech, Nixon did not enjoy a vigorous public life in retirement. Although he re-entered the spotlight under the sponsorship of the Clinton administration—writing books, commenting on political issues and even attending official functions—he remained a national ghost, haunting the public from a time long gone.

Richard M. Nixon died in 1994, aged 81. Someone once wrote that the only thing history owes us is the truth. History will judge Nixon harshly.

Gough Whitlam

'Well May We Say, God Save the Queen'

Parliament House Steps, Canberra, Australia, 11 November 1975.

E dward Gough Whitlam, born in Melbourne on 11 July, 1916, is the only Australian Prime Minister to be dismissed from office. Moving to Sydney at the age of two, Whitlam studied law at Sydney University before joining the Royal Australian Air Force in World War II. In 1945, just before leaving the RAAF, he joined the Labor Party in Sydney. After unsuccessful forays into local and state politics, Whitlam won a seat in federal politics in 1952. He was Deputy Opposition leader to Arthur Calwell from 1960-66 but once he took control of the party, Whitlam swept through the old guard of 'laborites' and established a more democratic style of socialist leadership that appealed to Labor's left-wing and centre-right factions.

In December 1972—on the back of a memorable slogan 'It's Time'— the Labor Party was returned to government after 23 years in opposition. Whitlam's sharp wit and charismatic presence provided many Australians with the hope that the 1970s would be a progressive era after decades of conservative government.

Once in government, Whitlam's initial reforms took Australia by storm— removing race as a criterion for immigration (the 'White Australia' policy was still in unofficial operation), ending conscription, abolishing the British honours system, increasing government support for the arts (and reinvigorating the Australian film industry), reforming health services (and putting contraceptives on the medical benefits list), increasing social and educational opportunities for Aborigines and instituting equal pay for women. He was the first Prime Minister in 24 years to visit China, and he re-opened the

Australian Embassey in Peking. Perhaps he moved too quickly.

Despite a booming economy and low inflation when he came to office Australia, like the rest of the world in the mid-1970s, was beset by international economic constraints—especially fuel prices and overseas loans. Whitlam's biggest failing as Prime Minister was that he did not control his ministers, and with a mandate to conduct 'open' government, their economic mismanagement severely embarrassed him and eroded public confidence in his leadership.

Despite this perception, Whitlam was re-elected to a second three-year term in 1974 but with a greatly reduced majority.

The events leading up Whitlam's dismissal have become part of Australian political history. In 1974 Whitlam's Minister for Minerals and Energy, Rex Connor, negotiated a $4 billion loan (incredibly, to be repaid over 20 years) to finance the government's ambitious development projects. Although Whitlam knew of the negotiations, his cabinet did not. When the press reported the story the Federal Opposition, under Liberal leader Malcolm Fraser, went on the attack. Whitlam was then forced to sack his treasurer, Deputy Prime Minister Jim Cairns, who was involved in a messy affair with his Secretary (Juni Morosi) and Rex Connor resigned in October 1975 for misleading the parliament over his negotiations with Pakistani financier Tirath Khemlani.

When Malcolm Fraser used the Liberals' majority in the Senate to block the government's money bills—threatening to bring the country to halt in a bid to force an election in both houses of government—Whitlam had a constitutional crisis on his hands.

One of the quirks of Australia's parliamentary system, which is modelled on Britain's Westminster system, is that the head of state is actually the representative of the ruling monarch of England ... the Governor-General. In 1975, Queen Elizabeth II's representative was Sir John Kerr, the jurist and barrister who had been appointed to the post by his former law colleague, Gough Whitlam.

The Governor-General, in consultation with the Queen, asserted the power to dissolve both houses of parliament—effectively dismissing the elected government of the land—and appoint an interim government of his choosing. This Kerr did on 11 November 1975—a date that had long resonated with the Australian public. It was the date, in 1880, that bushranger Ned Kelly was hanged. It was the date, in 1918, that World War I ended. Now the country had another reason to remember it.

On advice of the Chief Justice of the High Court, Sir John Kerr called Gough Whitlam to Government House at 1:00 pm that afternoon. What Whitlam didn't know was that Liberal leader Malcolm Fraser was waiting in another room, although allegations of collusion between the Governor-General and the Opposition Leader proved unfounded.

Whitlam was dismissed at 1:15 pm, Fraser was commissioned as Prime Minister at 1:30 pm and barely half an hour later the Senate passed the Supply Bill that it had been blocking since October 16. Almost comically, when Fraser announced to the House of Representatives that he was the new Prime Minister and put forward the motion to adjourn the session, the move was defeated by the dismissed former government which still maintained a slender majority in the lower house.

Then, at 3:16 pm, Gough Whitlam sponsored a motion of no-confidence in the new Prime Minister which was passed. Parliament was patently unworkable and the Speaker of the House sought an urgent meeting with the Governor-General but was told that Kerr was not available until 4:45 pm. For the next hour, Australia effectively had no federal government.

At 4:50 pm that afternoon, the Governor-General's secretary, David Smith, went to the steps of Parliament House and read the proclamation dissolving Parliament.

A large, angry crowd mostly made up of Labor supporters had gathered at the base of the original Parliament House steps, with Gough Whitlam standing silently at Smith's shoulder. The proclamation concluded:

'Now therefore, I Sir John Robert Kerr, the Governor General of Australia, do by this my

Proclamation dissolve the Senate and the House of Representatives.
Given under my Hand and the Great Seal of Australia on 11 November 1975.
By His Excellency's Command,
Malcolm Fraser
Prime Minister.
God Save the Queen!'

Gough Whitlam immediately addressed the crowd when David Smith finished. His spontaneous speech—a mixture of sarcastic word-play and controlled venom—has since passed into Australian folklore.

❛Well may we say "God Save the Queen" because nothing will save the Governor-General. The proclamation which you have just heard read by the Governor-General's official secretary was countersigned "Malcolm Fraser" who will undoubtedly go down in Australian history from Remembrance Day, 1975 as "Kerr's cur". They won't silence the outskirts of Parliament House, even if the inside has been silenced for the next few weeks. The Governor-General's proclamation was signed after he already made an appointment to meet the Speaker at a quarter to five. The House of Representatives had requested the Speaker to give the Governor-General its decision that Mr Fraser did not have the confidence of the House and that the Governor-General should call me to form the Government … Maintain your rage and enthusiasm through the campaign for the election now to be held and until polling day.❜

But Whitlam misjudged the mood of the Australian people and the Labor Party lost the 13 December elections by the biggest majority in electoral history. Malcolm Fraser remained Prime Minister until defeated by Bob Hawke in 1983. Although Whitlam and many of Labor's hardcore supporters 'maintained the rage' in the three decades since, Whitlam's relationship towards Malcolm Fraser softened after he left politics in 1977. (Needless to say, Whitlam never again spoke to his former friend, Sir John Kerr, who died in London in 1993.)

The two former Prime Ministers formed something of an 'odd couple' during Australia's Republican debate in the late 1990s, but interestingly, given the opportunity to change the Head of State to an elected or nominated Australian representative, the nation opted to stay part of the British Commonwealth.

Gough Whitlam died on October 21, 2016, aged 98 … political foe Malcolm Fraser followed him suddenly in March 2015, aged 84.

Anwar el-Sadat

'Peace With Justice'

Address to the Israeli Knesset, Tel Aviv, 20 November 1977.

Mohammed Anwar el-Sadat (1918-81) was born in the Tala District of Egypt. After the coup that ousted King Farouk in 1952, he succeeded Gamal Abdel Nasser as Egyptian president in 1970. As early as 1971 Sadat had raised the issue of signing a peace agreement with Israel providing that all occupied territories captured during the Six-Day War in 1967 were returned to neighbouring Arab states. During 1972-73 Sadat stated that war was inevitable unless the US forced Israel to accept the United Nations resolution to withdraw from occupied territories.

In 1973-74 Sadat also assumed the role of prime minister—a period in which he presided over Egyptian involvement in the 'Yom Kippur War' against Israel. On the feast of Yom Kippur, 6 October, 1973, the holiest day of the Jewish calendar, Egypt and Syria (backed by nine other Arab states) launched a surprise attack on Israel. The Israeli army recovered brilliantly and Egypt was on the brink of a disastrous defeat when, on 22 October, the United Nations directed all parties to immediately 'terminate all military activity'. With war a diplomatic and military failure, Sadat sought a peaceful end to the conflict by continuing to negotiate with the Israeli government and announced he would be willing to enter into a peace agreement with his country's former enemy.

In an historic move for both Egypt and Israel, Sadat was invited to address the Israeli parliament on 20 November 1977.

❪ In the name of God, Mr. Speaker of the Knesset, ladies and gentlemen, allow me first to thank deeply the Speaker of the Knesset for affording me this opportunity to address you.

As I begin my address I wish to say, peace and the mercy of God Almighty be upon you and may peace be with us all, God willing. Peace for us all, of the Arab lands and in Israel, as well as in every part of this big world, which is so beset by conflicts, perturbed by its deep contradictions, menaced now and then by destructive wars launched by man to annihilate his fellow men.

Finally, amidst the ruins of what man has built among the remains of the victims of mankind there emerges neither victor nor vanquished. The only vanquished remains always a man, God's most sublime creation. Man, whom God has created, as Gandhi, the apostle of peace puts it, to forge ahead, to mold the way of life and to worship God Almighty.

I come to you today on solid ground to shape a new life and to establish peace. We all love this land, the land of God, we all, Moslems, Christians and Jews, all worship God.

Under God, God's teachings and commandments are: love, sincerity, security and peace.

I do not blame all those who received my decision when I announced it to the entire world before the Egyptian People's Assembly. I do not blame all those who received my decision with surprise and even with amazement—some gripped even by violent surprise. Still others interpreted it as political, to camouflage my intentions of launching a new war.

I would go so far as to tell you that one of my aides at the presidential office contacted me at a late hour following my return home from the People's Assembly and sounded worried as he asked me: "Mr. President, what would be our reaction if Israel actually extended an invitation to you?"

I replied calmly: 'I would accept it immediately. I have declared that I would go to the ends of the earth. I would go to Israel, for I want to put before the people of Israel all the facts."

I can see the faces of all those who were astounded by my decision and had doubts as to the sincerity of the intentions behind the declaration of my decision. No one could have ever conceived that the President of the biggest Arab state, which bears the heaviest burden and the main responsibility pertaining to the cause of war and peace in the Middle East, should declare his readiness to go to the land of the adversary while we were still in a state of war.

We all still bear the consequences of four fierce wars waged within 30 years. All this at the time when the families of the 1973 October war are still mourning under the cruel pain of bereavement of father, son, husband and brother.

As I have already declared, I have not consulted as far as this decision is concerned with any of my colleagues or brothers, the Arab heads of state or the confrontation states.

Most of those who contacted me following the declaration of this decision expressed their objection because of the feeling of utter suspicion and absolute lack of confidence between the Arab states and the Palestine people on the one hand and Israel on the other that still surges in us all.

Many months in which peace could have been brought about have been wasted over differences and fruitless discussions on the procedure of convening the Geneva conference. All have shared suspicion and absolute lack of confidence.

But to be absolutely frank with you, I took this decision after long thought, knowing that it constitutes a great risk, for God Almighty has made it my fate to assume responsibility on behalf of the Egyptian people, to share in the responsibility of the Arab nation, the main duty of which, dictated by responsibility, is to exploit all and every means in a bid to save my Egyptian Arab people and the pan-Arab nation from the horrors of new suffering and destructive wars, the dimensions of which are foreseen only by God Himself.

After long thinking, I was convinced that the obligation of responsibility before God and before the people make it incumbent upon me that I should go to the far corners of the world—even to Jerusalem to address members of the Knesset and acquaint them with all the facts surging in me, then I would let you decide for yourselves.

Following this, may God Almighty determine our fate.

Ladies and gentlemen, there are moments in the lives of nations and peoples when it is incumbent upon those known for their wisdom and clarity of vision to survey the problem, with all its complexities and vain memories, in a bold drive toward new horizons.

Those who like us are shouldering the same responsibilities entrusted to us are the first who should have the courage to make determining decisions that are consonant with the magnitude of the circumstances. We must all rise above all forms of obsolete theories of superiority, and the most important thing is never to forget that infallibility is the prerogative of God alone.

If I said that I wanted to avert from all the Arab people the horrors of shocking and destructive wars I must sincerely declare before you that I have the same feelings and bear the same responsibility toward all and every man on earth, and certainly toward the Israeli people.

Any life that is lost in war is a human life, be it that of an Arab or an Israeli. A wife who becomes a widow is a human being entitled to a happy family life, whether she be an Arab or an Israeli.

Innocent children who are deprived of the care and compassion of their parents are ours. They are ours, be they living on Arab or Israeli land.

They command our full responsibility to afford them a comfortable life today and tomorrow.

For the sake of them all, for the sake of the lives of all our sons and brothers, for the sake of affording our communities the opportunity to work for the progress and happiness of man, feeling secure and with the right to a dignified life, for the generations to come, for a smile on the face of every child born in our land—for all that I have taken my decision to come to you, despite all the hazards, to deliver my address.

I have shouldered the prerequisites of the historic responsibility and therefore I declared on February 4, 1971, that I was willing to sign a peace agreement with Israel. This was the first declaration made by a responsible Arab official since the outbreak of the Arab-Israeli conflict. Motivated by all these factors dictated by the responsibilities of leadership on October 16, 1973, before the Egyptian People's Assembly, I called for an international conference to establish permanent peace based on justice. I was not heard.

I was in the position of man pleading for peace or asking for a cease-fire, motivated by the duties of history and leadership, I signed the first disengagement agreement, followed by the second disengagement agreement in Sinai.

Then we proceeded, trying both open and closed doors in a bid to find a certain road leading to a durable and just peace.

We opened our heart to the peoples of the entire world to make them understand our motivations and objectives and actually to convince them of the fact that we are advocates of justice and peacemakers. Motivated by all these factors, I also decided to come to you with an open mind and an open heart and with a conscious determination so that we might establish permanent peace based on justice.

It is so fated that my trip to you, which is a journey of peace, coincided with the Islamic feast the holy Feast of the Sacrifice when Abraham—peace be upon him—forefather of the Arabs and Jews, submitted to God, I say, when God Almighty ordered him not out of weakness, but through a giant spiritual force and by free will to sacrifice his very own son, personified a firm and unshakeable belief in ideals that had for mankind a profound significance.

Ladies and gentlemen, let us be frank with each other. Using straightforward words and a clear conception with no ambiguity, let us be frank with each other today while the entire world, both East and West, follows these unparalleled moments which could prove to be a radical turning point in the history of this part of the world if not in the history of the world as a whole.

Let us be frank with each other, let us be frank with each other as we answer this important question:

How can we achieve permanent peace based on justice? Well, I have come to you carrying my clear and frank answer to this big question, so that the people in Israel as well as the entire world may hear it. All those devoted prayers ring in my ears, pleading to God Almighty that this historic meeting may eventually lead to the result aspired to by millions.

Before I proclaim my answer, I wish to assure you that in my clear and frank answer I am availing myself of a number of facts which no one can deny.

The first fact is that no one can build his happiness at the expense of the misery of others.

The second fact: never have I spoken, nor will I ever speak, with two tongues; never have I adopted, nor will I ever adopt, two policies. I never deal with anyone except in one tongue, one policy and with one face.

The third fact: direct confrontation is the nearest and most successful method to reach a clear objective.

The fourth fact: the call for permanent and just peace based on respect for United Nations resolutions has now become the call of the entire world. It has become the expression of the will of the international community, whether in official capitals where policies are made and decisions taken, or at the level of world public opinion, which influences policymaking and decision-taking.

The fifth fact, and this is probably the clearest and most prominent, is that the Arab nation, in its drive for permanent peace based on justice, does not proceed from a position of weakness. On the contrary, it has the power and stability for a sincere will for peace.

The Arab declared intention stems from an awareness prompted by a heritage of civilization, that to avoid an inevitable disaster that will befall us, you and the whole world, there is no alternative to the establishment of permanent peace based on justice, peace that is not swayed by suspicion or jeopardized by ill intentions.

In the light of these facts which I meant to place before you the way I see them, I would also wish to warn you, in all sincerity I warn you, against some thoughts that could cross your minds.

Frankness makes it incumbent upon me to tell you the following:

First, I have not come here for a separate agreement between Egypt and Israel. This is not part of the policy of Egypt. The problem is not that of Egypt and Israel.

An interim peace between Egypt and Israel, or between any Arab confrontation state and Israel, will not bring permanent peace based on justice in the entire region.

Rather, even if peace between all the confrontation states and Israel were achieved in the absence of a just solution of the Palestinian problem, never will there be that durable and just peace upon which the entire world insists.

Second, I have not come to you to seek a partial peace, namely to terminate the state of belligerency at this stage and put off the entire problem to a subsequent stage. This is not the radical solution that would steer us to permanent peace.

Equally, I have not come to you for a third disengagement agreement in Sinai or in Golan or the West Bank. For this would mean that we are merely delaying the ignition of the fuse. It would also mean that we are lacking the courage to face peace, that we are too weak to shoulder the burdens and responsibilities of a durable peace based upon justice.

I have come to you so that together we should build a durable peace based on justice to avoid the shedding of one single drop of blood by both sides. It is for this reason that I have proclaimed my readiness to go to the farthest corner of the earth...

....I repeat with Zachariah: "Love, right and justice." From the holy Koran I quote the following verses: "We believe in God and in what has been revealed to us and what was revealed to Abraham, Ishmael, Isaac, Jacob and the 13 Jewish tribes. And in the books given to Moses and Jesus and the Prophets from their Lord, who made no distinction between them." So we agree, Salam Aleikum—peace be upon you. '

The peace agreement between Egypt and Israel was sponsored by newly-elected US President Jimmy Carter in 1978. Carter invited the Egyptian President and Israeli Prime Minister Menachem Begin to his presidential retreat at Camp David, resulting in the 1978 Camp David Accord. Sadat and Begin were jointly awarded the Nobel Peace Prize for their efforts, but Sadat was severely criticised for his initiative by other Arab leaders and hard-line Muslims from within his own country. On 6 October, 1981 Sadat was attending a military parade when he was fired upon by five gunmen dressed in black ceremonial uniforms who were part of the official parade. The Egyptian president and five other people were killed in the attack. Sadat's successor, former vice-president Hosni Mubarak, pledged to honour all treaties with the Israelis.

Indira Gandhi

'True Liberation of Women'
New Delhi, India, 26 March 1980.

The Nehru-Gandhi 'dynasty' in modern Indian politics is as important—and equally tragic—as the Kennedy family in the United States of America. Indira Gandhi (1917-84) was the daughter of Jawaharla Nehru, the first Prime Minister of India. After studying at Oxford she married Feroze Jehangir Gandhi (a member of a well-known Parsi family originally named Ghandy, and no relation to Mahatma Gandhi) in 1942, against the wishes of her parents. In order to facilitate the inter-caste marriage, Mahatma Gandhi 'adopted' Khan (whose mother's maiden name was the Persian derivative 'Ghandy') but although the marriage produced two sons (Rajiv and Sanjay) it was not a success. Indira Gandhi later became president of the Indian Congress Party (1959-60) and following the death of Lal Shastri, Prime Minister of India in 1966. During the 1970s she struggled to contain national sectarian violence. After her conviction for electoral malpractice in 1975, she declared a state of emergency that was kept in place for two years. Defeated in 1977 she returned for a second term as Prime Minister in 1980.

In March 1980 she outlined the true liberation of women at the inauguration of the All-India Women's Conference Building Complex in New Delhi.

‘ For several decades the All-India Women's Conference has been the organized voice of the women of India. I have never been a member of any women's organization but have been interested enough to keep track of their activities and to lend the helping hand whenever I could.

I am glad that at long last the All-India Women's Conference has a home of its own and it is named after one of the best known and most remarkable women of our times, Sarojini Naidu, feminine to the core but well able to hold her own in the world of men, whether in letters or in politics.

To add to the importance of the occasion and to give it a touch of elegance, we have in our midst His Highness the Aga Khan and Her Highness the Begum Aga Khan. They are friends of India and have founded or encouraged many projects for education, health and other aspects of welfare. But for their timely and generous help, this complex would not have been ready today. Nor would we have before us the attractive Aga Khan Hall. We welcome them and wish them well in their work.

I see before me a number of eminent women who have distinguished themselves in various professions—in social work, in education, in science, in administration, in law and, of course, in politics. They must all feel gratified to see the completion of this building. I have often said that I am not a feminist. Yet, in my concern for the underprivileged, how can I ignore women who, since the beginning of history, have been dominated over and discriminated against in social customs and in laws. How insidious and all-pervasive is this attitude of male' superiority is revealed in the vocabulary of the languages the world over. And this is unquestioningly accepted and acquiesced in by all but a minuscule minority of men and also women. Currently I am reading a book titled World and Women. I learned from it what Mr. Ling White, the President of Mills College in the USA, wrote of the use of masculine generic pronouns. I quote: "The penetration of the habit of language into the minds of little girls as they grow up to be women is more profound than most people, including most women, have realized. For, it implies that personality is really a male attribute and that women are a sub or a human sub-species." The author goes on to say that it is time we looked more carefully where the thoughtless use of stereotypes is taking us. "Man as leader, woman as follower; man as producer, woman as consumer; man as strength, woman as weakness; this is the cosmography that has brought us to man as aggressor and humanity the victim."

Hence, by excluding women, men are depriving themselves of a fuller emancipation or growth for themselves.

In the West, women's so-called freedom is often equated with imitation of man. Frankly, I feel that is merely an exchange of one kind of bondage for another. To be liberated, woman must feel free to be herself, not in rivalry to man but in the context of her own capacity and her personality. We need women to be more interested, more alive and more active not because they are women but because they do comprise half the human race. Whether they like it or not, they cannot escape their responsibility nor should they be denied its benefits. Indian women are traditionally conservative but they also have the genius of synthesis, to adapt and to absorb. That is what gives them resilience to face suffering and to meet upheavals with a degree of calm, to change constantly and yet remain changeless, which is the quality of India herself.

Today's major concerns are: first, economic and social inequality and injustice between the affluent and developing countries and within countries. Secondly, the anxiety whether human wisdom will prevail over what can only be called a death wish in which the desire to dominate expresses itself in countless ways, the most dangerous being the armament race. And, thirdly, the need to protect this, our only Earth, from human rapacity and exploitation. Only recently have we awakened to the awareness of ancient truths regarding our own utter dependence on the balance of Nature and its resources.

These enormous challenges cannot be met only by some sections, however advanced they may be, while others pull in different directions or watch apathetically. The effort has to be a universal one, conscious and concerted, considering no one too small to contribute. The effort must embrace all nationalities and all classes regardless of religion, caste or sex.

There is no time to lose and it involves a tremendous task of educating. We want to walk together and in step with all others, but if men hesitate, should not women show the way? So, while complimenting the All-India Women's Conference, especially its President, Smt. Lakshmi Raghuramaiah, on their achievements, I dedicate to the nation this building complex of the All-India Women's Conference. '

One of the great ironies of Indira Gandhi's political career was that a predominantly non-Christian country (Hindu/Muslim) would democratically elect a woman as its leader (twice) when some western governments (USA and Australia) have yet to cross that gender barrier. On 31 October 1984

Indira Gandhi was gunned down by her Sikh body guards as she walked through the garden of her New Delhi home to meet with actor Peter Ustinov who was making a documentary about her.

In June that year, Indian troops had stormed the Golden Temple in Amristar in order to end a four-day siege by Sikh militants. (Most commentators saw this as the reason for her murder.) She was succeeded as Prime Minister by her eldest son, Rajiv Gandhi. The elder Gandhi heir was a pilot of India Airlines but his mother sponsored his political career following the death of his younger brother Sanjiv, in 1980.

When general elections were held later that year, Gandhi's Congress Party won with a record majority. In November 1989, Rajiv Gandhi resigned as Premier but suffered a similar fate to his mother when he was assassinated by Tamil separatists in May 1991 while campaigning in Madras.

Archbishop Óscar Romero

'Stop the Repression!'
San Salvador, El Salvador, 23 March 1980

Óscar Romero y Galdámez (1917–80) became the Roman Catholic Archbishop of San Salvador, the capital of war-torn Latin American country, El Salvador, in 1977.

Following the overthrow of the Carlos Romero (no relation) military dictatorship in 1979, the US-backed Revolutionary Government Junta targeted members of the Catholic Church, trade unionists and the peasant population whom they felt were sympathetic to their left-wing military and political opponents.

In the previous three years, six Catholic priests had been assassinated—others had been jailed, tortured and expelled from the country—and death squads attached to the military dictatorship were responsible for the murder and abduction of thousands of Salvadorean citizens.

Óscar Romero was viewed as a conservative compromise candidate as Archbishop of San Salvador, but once in office he became the voice of the voiceless.

Despite Pope John Paul II's warning to the Latin American Catholic Church not to become involved in social activism in their homelands, Archbishop Romero felt that not to speak out against violence and injustice would be a legitimisation of the military persecution of the innocent.

In his sermon at the Metropolitan Cathedral of the Holy Saviour in San Salvador on Sunday, 23 March 1980, Archbishop Romero reviewed the tragic events of the week and finished with a heartfelt, impassioned appeal to the men of the armed forces on both sides.

❛Every country lives its own "exodus". Today El Salvador is living its own exodus. Today we are passing to our liberation through a desert strewn with bodies and where anguish and pain are devastating us. Many suffer the temptation of those who walked with Moses and wanted to turn back and did not work together. It is the same old story. God, however, wants to save the people by making a new history...

History will not fail. God sustains it. That is why I say that insofar as historical projects attempt to reflect the eternal plan of God, to that extent they reflect the kingdom of God. This attempt is the work of the church. Because of this, the church, the people of God in history, is not attached to any one social system, to any political organization, to any party. The church does not identify herself with any of those forces because she is the eternal pilgrim of history and is indicating at every historical moment what reflects the kingdom of God and what does not reflect the kingdom of God. She is the servant of the kingdom of God.

The great task of Christians must be to absorb the spirit of God's kingdom and, with souls filled with the kingdom of God, to work on the projects of history. It's fine to be organized in popular groups; it's all right to form political parties; it's all right to take part in the government. It's fine as long as you are a Christian who carries the reflection of the kingdom of God and tries to establish it where you are working and as long as you are not being used to further worldly ambitions.

This is the great duty of the people of today. My dear Christians, I have always told you, and I will repeat, that the true liberators of our people must come from us Christians, from the people of God. Any historical plan that's not based on what we spoke of in the first point—the dignity of the human being, the love of God, the kingdom of Christ among people—will be a fleeting project. Your project, however, will grow in stability the more it reflects the eternal design of God. It will be a solution of the common good of the people every time, if it meets the needs of the people...

Now I invite you to look at things through the eyes of the church, which is trying to be the kingdom of God on earth and so often must illuminate the realities of our national situation.

We have lived through a tremendously tragic week. I could not give you the facts before, but a week ago last Saturday, on 15 March, one of the largest and most distressing military operations was carried out in the countryside. The villages affected were La Laguna, Plan de Ocotes and El Rosario. The operation brought tragedy. A lot of ranches were burned. There was looting and inevitably people were killed.

In La Laguna, the attackers killed a married couple, Ernesto Navas and Audelia Mejia de Navas, their little children, Martin and Hilda, thirteen and seven years old, and eleven more peasants.

Other deaths have been reported, but we do not know the names of the dead. In Plan de Ocotes, two children and four peasants were killed, including two women. In El Rosario, three more peasants were killed. That was last Saturday.

Last Sunday, the following were assassinated in Arcatao by four members of ORDEN: Peasants Marcelino Serrano, Vincente Ayala, 24 years old, and his son, Freddy. That same day, Fernando Hernandez Navarro, a peasant, was assassinated in Galera de Jutiapa, when he fled from the military.

Last Monday, 17 March, was a tremendously violent day. Bombs exploded in the capital as well as in the interior of the country. The damage was very substantial at the headquarters of the Ministry of Agriculture. The campus of the national university was under armed siege from dawn until 7.00 pm. Throughout the day, constant bursts of machine-gun fire were heard in the university area. The Archbishop's office intervened to protect people who found themselves caught inside.

On the Hacienda Colima, eighteen persons died, at least fifteen of whom were peasants. The administrator and the grocer of the ranch also died. The armed forces confirmed that there was a confrontation. A film of the events appeared on TV and many analyzed interesting aspects of the situation.

At least 50 people died in serious incidents that day. In the capital, seven persons died in events at the Colonia Santa Lucia; on the outskirts of Tecnillantas, five people died; and in the area of the rubbish dump, after the evacuation of the site by the military, were found the bodies of four workers who had been captured in that action.

Sixteen peasants died in the village of Montepeque, 38 kilometers along the road to Suchitoto. That same day, two students at the University of Central America were captured in Tecnillantas: Mario Nelson and Miguel Alberto Rodriguez Velado, who were brothers. The first one, after four days of illegal detention, was handed over to the courts. Not so his brother, who was wounded and is still held in illegal detention. Legal Aid is intervening on his behalf.

Amnesty International issued a press release in which it described the repression of the peasants, especially in the area of Chalatenango. The week's events confirm this report in spite of the fact the government denies it. As I entered the church, I was given a cable that says: "Amnesty International confirmed today [that was yesterday] that in El Salvador human rights are violated to extremes that have not been seen in other countries."

That is what Patricio Fuentes (spokesman for the urgent action section for Central America in Swedish Amnesty International) said at a press conference in Managua, Nicaragua.

Fuentes confirmed that, during two weeks of investigations he carried out in El Salvador, he was able to establish that there had been 83 political assassinations between 10 and 14 March. He pointed out that Amnesty International recently condemned the government of El Salvador, alleging that it was responsible for 600 political assassinations. The Salvadorean government defended itself against the charges, arguing that Amnesty International based its condemnation on unproved assumptions.

Fuentes said that Amnesty had established that in El Salvador human rights are violated to a worse degree than the repression in Chile after the coup d'etat. The Salvadorean government also said that the 600 dead were the result of armed confrontations between army troops and guerrillas. Fuentes said that during his stay El Salvador, he could see that the victims had been tortured before their deaths and mutilated afterward.

The spokesman of Amnesty International said that the victims' bodies characteristically appeared with the thumbs tied behind their backs. Corrosive liquids had been applied to the corpses to prevent identification of the victims by their relatives and to prevent international condemnation, the spokesman added. Nevertheless, the bodies were exhumed and the dead have been identified. Fuentes said that the repression carried out by the Salvadorean army was aimed at breaking the popular organizations through the assassination of their leaders in both town and country.

According to the spokesman of Amnesty International, at least 3500 peasants have fled from their homes to the capital to escape persecution. "We have complete lists in London and Sweden of young children and women who have been assassinated for being organized," Fuentes stated...

I would like to make a special appeal to the men of the army, and specifically to the ranks of the National Guard, the police and the military.

Brothers, you come from our own people. You are killing your own brother peasants when any human order to kill must be subordinate to the law of God which says; "Thou shalt not kill."

No soldier is obliged to obey an order contrary to the law of God. No one has to obey an immoral law. It is high time you recovered your consciences and obeyed your consciences rather than a sinful order. The church, the defender of the rights of God, of the law of God, of human dignity, of the person, cannot remain silent before such an abomination. We want the government to face the fact that reforms are valueless if they are to be carried out at the cost of so much blood. In the name of God, in the name of this suffering people whose cries rise to heaven more loudly each day, I implore you, I beg you, I order you in the name of God: Stop the repression.

The church preaches your liberation just as we have studied it in the holy Bible today. It is a liberation that has, above all else, respect for the dignity of the person, hope for humanity's common good, and the transcendence that looks before all to God and only from God derives its hope and its strength. '

The following day, Archbishop Romero was assassinated while he celebrated mass in the small chapel attached to the Divina Providencia Cancer Hospital which he had called home for several years.

In the sermon just minutes before his death, he spoke of the parable of the wheat. 'Those who surrender to the service of the poor through love of Christ, will live like the grains of wheat that die. It only apparently dies. If it were not to die, it would remain a solitary grain. The harvest comes because of the grain that dies'.

At 6.25 pm, as he prayed over the gifts of bread and wine for Communion, he was shot through the heart by unknown members of a Salvadorean military death squad.

Archbishop Romero's funeral the following week attracted more than 250,000 mourners from all over the world and resulted in more bloodshed when a bomb exploded on the steps of the Cathedral and 44 mourners were shot or trampled to death in the ensuing panic.

The civil war in El Salvador lasted for another twelve years (1980-92) but for Óscar Romero, life, not death, would be the final word.

'I do not believe in death without resurrection,' he once said. 'If they kill me, I will be resurrected in the Salvadorean people.'

Margaret Thatcher

'The Falklands War'
Cheltenham, England, 3 July 1982.

The 'Iron Lady' of world politics during the 1980s and Britain's first female Prime Minister was born Margaret Hilda Roberts above a shop in Grantham, Lincolnshire in 1925. An Oxford graduate and research chemist, she married Dennis Thatcher in 1951 before becoming a lawyer. The Conservative Party member for Finchley in 1959, she replaced Edward Heath as Opposition Leader in 1975. In 1979, the Conservative Party was swept to power and Margaret Thatcher duly became Britain's first female Prime Minister.

Under Thatcher's leadership, the Conservative Party privatised national industries and institutions such as education, health care and local government services. Despite presiding over the worst unemployment figures since the Depression, Thatcher's government was re-elected with an increased majority in 1983. The reasons for this were two-fold: the lack of an organised Opposition Party and public support for her after the Falklands War in 1982.

On 2 April, 1982 Argentinean troops invaded the Falkland Islands in the southern Atlantic Ocean. The Falklands, 770 kilometres north-east of Cape Horn, had been a British Crown Colony since 1833 but for many years Argentina had laid claim to the islands (which they called Islas Malvines). As Prime Minister, Margaret Thatcher immediately sent a task force of 30 warships, and some 10 000 troops, to liberate the two larger islands, East and West Falkland.

By 12 April Britain had established a 200-mile exclusion zone around the islands and had recaptured South Georgia, a Falklands dependency to the south-west, by the end of the month. On 1 May the RAF conducted a Vulcan bomber raid on Stanley, the islands' capital, on East Falkland. Many lives were lost on both sides; most notably for Britain on the *HMS Antelope* and *HMS Coventry*, while the *HMS Sheffield* was hit by Exocet missile and the *Atlantic Conveyor* was also sunk. Then, on 28 May, the second battalion of the Parachute Regiment recaptured Goose Green, on the south-west part of East Falkland, and infantry brigades landed at San Carlos, in the north-west corner, three days later.

Although the war had turned in Britain's favour it suffered massive losses on 8 June when the RFA Sir Galahad and RFA Sir Tristram were attacked during the transfer of troops to Fitzroy, south-west of Stanley, and the HMS Fearless was sunk in Choiseul Sound. Within a week, General Mario Menendez, the leader of the Argentinean troops in the Falklands surrendered. The Falklands were recaptured, at a price—255 Britains killed and 777 wounded, 635 Argentineans killed and 1068 wounded.

This speech exemplifies the way Margaret Thatcher used Britain's military success to reverse her polls rating as the 'least popular' Prime Minister of modern times to win the 1983 general election. Thatcher remarked at the time: 'It's exciting to have a real crisis on your hands, when you have spent half your political life dealing with humdrum issues like the environment.'

❛Today we meet in the aftermath of the Falklands Battle. Our country has won a great victory and we are entitled to be proud. This nation had the resolution to do what it knew had to be done—to do what it knew was right.

We fought to show that aggression does not pay, and that the robber cannot be allowed to get away with his swag. We fought with the support of so many throughout the world: the Security Council, the Commonwealth, the European Community, and the United States. Yet we also fought alone—for we fought for our own people and for our own sovereign territory.

Now that it is all over, things cannot be the same again, for we have learnt something about ourselves -a lesson which we desperately needed to learn. When we started out, there were the waverers and the faint-hearts: the people who thought that Britain could no longer seize the initiative for herself; the people who thought we could no longer do the great things which we once did; and those who believed that our decline was irreversible—that we could never again be what we were. There were those who would not admit it—even perhaps some here today—people who would have strenuously denied the suggestion but—in their heart of hearts—they too had their secret fears that it was true: that Britain was no longer the nation that had built an Empire and ruled a quarter of the world.

Well, they were wrong. The lesson of the Falklands is that Britain has not changed and that this nation still has those sterling qualities which shine through our history. This generation can match their fathers and grandfathers in ability, in courage, and in resolution. We have not changed. When the demands of war and the dangers to our own people call us to arms—then we British are as we have always been—competent, courageous and resolute.

When called to arms—ah, that's the problem. It took the battle in the South Atlantic for the shipyards to adapt ships way ahead of time; for dockyards to refit merchantmen and cruise liners, to fix helicopter platforms, to convert hospital ships—all faster than was thought possible; it took the demands of war for every stop to be pulled out and every man and woman to do their best.

British people had to be threatened by foreign soldiers and British territory invaded and then—why then—the response was incomparable. Yet why does it need a war to bring out our qualities and reassert our pride? Why do we have to be invaded before we throw aside our selfish aims and begin to work together as only we can work, and achieve as only we can achieve?

That really is the challenge we as a nation face today. We have to see that the spirit of the South Atlantic—the real spirit of Britain—is kindled not only by war but can now be fired by peace.

We have the first prerequisite. We know we can do it-we haven't lost the ability. That is the Falklands Factor. We have proved ourselves to ourselves. It is a lesson we must not now forget. Indeed, it is a lesson which we must apply to peace just as we have learnt it in war. The faltering and the self-doubt has given way to achievement and pride. We have the confidence and we must use it.

Just look at the Task Force as an object lesson. Every man had his own task to do and did it superbly. Officers and men, senior NCO and newest recruit—every one realized that his contribution was essential for the success of the whole. All were equally valu¬able—each was differently qualified. By working together, each was able to do more than his best. As a team they raised the average to the level of the best and by each doing his utmost together they achieved the impossible. That's an accurate picture of Britain at war—not yet of Britain at peace. But the spirit has stirred and the nation has begun to assert itself. Things are not going to be the same again. **'**

In 1987 Margaret Thatcher became the first Prime Minister since the nineteenth century to win three consecutive elections. But Thatcher's autocratic prime ministerial style and her attitude towards the European Community ultimately split her own cabinet and led to her downfall. When Sir Geoffrey Howe, the Leader of the Commons and the last remaining member of her original cabinet in 1979, was publicly critical of her when announcing his resignation in November 1990, Thatcher's days as Prime Minister were numbered. Michael Heseltine was the first to challenge for the leadership of the Conservative Party and when Thatcher could not gather the necessary support to survive the first round of voting, she withdrew from the leadership race. John Major was elected her eventual successor.

Margaret Thatcher was made a life peer of the realm, becoming Lady Thatcher, in 1992. After a series of strokes in 2002, she withdrew from public life. Her death in 2011, aged 87, divided both historians and the public regarding her true legacy, much as she had done in her political life.

David Lange

'Nuclear Weapons are Morally Indefensible'
Oxford Union, Oxford UK, 1 March 1985

D avid Lange (1942–2005) served as New Zealand Prime Minister from 1984 to 1989. Lange's Labour Party was elected with an anti nuclear mandate when long-serving conservative Prime Minister, Sir Robert Muldoon, misjudged the mood of the people on the issue and called a snap election.

Former lawyer David Lange, a large man with an even larger intellect, was swept into government and led only the fourth Labour government in New Zealand's 130-year parliamentary history.

Although New Zealand's nuclear-free stance did not become law until 1987, US-New Zealand relationships deteriorated rapidly and by the time Prime Minister David Lange ventured to England in February 1985, the postwar ANZUS alliance was effectively over.

A guest at the famous Oxford Union debating society in Great Britain, Lange spoke for the affirmative team in favour of the topic, 'Nuclear Weapons Are Morally Indefensible'. The world was listening.

❢ Mr President, honourable members of the union, ladies and gentlemen… in fact if I could greet straight away—because I understand there is a direct feed to the White House tonight—if I could greet the President of the United States, who is of course of the very genesis of the proposition we are debating tonight.

A quote in *Time* magazine last year, an assertion by the President of the United States that nuclear weapons were immoral; his avowal reiterated in January this year in a statement over the space initiative known as SDI. And there again, he asserted that this system of the nuclear stare-out cannot be sustained morally.

May I say to the honourable gentleman who preceded me, there is nothing of what I am about to say which has been conditioned in any way by my meeting with the Prime Minister of the United Kingdom yesterday… I did not meet her yesterday… I am meeting her on Monday. But I know the apprehension that he feels at his constant fear of being summoned to that carpet.

I also feel a considerable sympathy for the members of the opposite side, who have this extraordinary sense of destabilisation at the imminent prospect of peace breaking out.

The character of the argument, sir, is something which I find regrettable. So I can say very simply that it is my conviction that there is no moral case for nuclear weapons. That the best defence which can be made of their existence and the threat of their use is, as we have heard tonight, that they are a necessary evil; an abhorrent means to a desirable end.

I hold that the character of nuclear weapons is such that their very existence corrupts the best of intentions; that the means in fact perverts the end. And I hold that their character is such that they have brought us to the greatest of all perversions: The belief that this evil is necessary—as it has been stated tonight—when in fact it is not.

And I make my case against nuclear weapons the more vigorously because I distinguish between them and all other forms of coercive or deterrent power. I've got no case to make against the policeman's truncheon. And the people tonight who have argued that you must go to the ultimate in force every time you seek to embark upon it, is of course a surrender to the worst of morality.

I accept, and do not wish to be heard arguing here against any proposition that the state must arm itself with military force to protect its citizens against aggression or to defend the weak and the helpless against aggression.

But I do not accept that the state must for those reasons arm itself with nuclear weapons. That is a case I do not easily or lightly make in Europe where governments have held it their duty to arm themselves with nuclear weapons. I do not doubt for one moment the quality of the intention which led to that decision or that series of decisions.

And I freely acknowledge that that decision is pursued in good conscience with the honourable intention of preserving the life and freedom of the people of Western Europe. Because those governments are faced with the close presence of an alien and relentlessly oppressive regime and obviously feel it their duty to prepare for their own defence by membership in what for most governments' policy now is straightforwardly a nuclear alliance. That is an assessment I understand and I do not come here to argue for any proposition in favour of unilateral disarmament.

And if I make that acknowledgement, I must then deal with the argument that it is the intention which determines the moral character of the action. My contention is very simply that the character of nuclear weapons is such that it is demonstrably the case that they subvert the best of intentions. And the snuggling up to the nuclear arsenal which has gone on with my friends on the opposite side tonight shows at what level of sophistication and refinement that subversion takes place.

There is, Mr President, a quality of irrationality about nuclear weapons which does not sit well with good intentions. A system of defence serves its purpose if it guarantees the security of those it protects. A system of nuclear defence guarantees only insecurity. The means of defence terrorise as much as the threat of attack. In Europe, it is impossible to be unaware of the intensity of military preparedness. In New Zealand, the visitor must make an effort to find a military installation or indeed any sign of military activity, although it does exist. There is no imperative in New Zealand to prepare for war. The result is that I feel safer in Wellington than I ever could in London or New York or Oxford.

The fact is that Europe and the United States are ringed about with nuclear weapons and your people have never been more at risk. There is simply only one thing more terrifying than nuclear weapons pointed in your direction and that is nuclear weapons pointed in your enemy's direction. The outcome of their use would be the same in either case, and that is the annihilation of you and all of us. That is a defence which is no defence; it is a defence which disturbs far more than it reassures. The intention of those who for honourable motives use nuclear weapons to deter is to enhance security. Notwithstanding that intention, they succeed only in enhancing insecurity. Because the machine has perverted the motive.

The President of the United States has acknowledged that, notwithstanding that my honourable friend opposite does not, and the weapon has installed mass destruction as the objective of the best-intentioned.

The weapon simply has its own relentless logic and it is inhuman. It is the logic of escalation, the logic of the arms race. Nuclear weapons make us insecure and to compensate for our insecurity we build and deploy more nuclear weapons. We know that we are seized by irrationality—and every now and then some new generation technology comes in, the argument for which is that it will cause us to draw back from the nuclear precipice. And we are seeing right now another initiative, under a new title. The title of course in dispute as much as its efficiency will be. And that, Mr President, is the story of the whole saga of the nuclear escalation.

We know, all of us, that it is wholly without logic or reason, any sense at all, to have the means at the disposal of two particular sets of powers to turn this world into rubble time and time again. And yet in spite of that awareness, the world watches as two enormous machines enhance, refine their capacity to inflict destruction on each other and on all of us.

Every nuclear development, whatever its strategic or tactical significance, has only one result, and that is to add to an arsenal which is already quite beyond reason.

There is an argument in defence of the possession of nuclear weapons which holds that the terror created by the existence of those weapons is in itself the fulfilment of a peaceful purpose. The argument advanced here tonight that that 50 million killed over four years by concerted war in a conventional sense in Europe and the argument that somehow the existence of this mutually assured destruction phenomenon has since that time preserved this planet from destruction.

It is, I think, probably an example of northern hemisphere or European arrogance that we overlook now the 30 million people in this world who have died in wars since then—while we are apparently beset from the two superpowers by a system designed to have people stop killing each other.

I believe that the fear they inspire is not a justification for their existence. **'**

With his booming voice and idiosyncratic, commanding phrasing David Lange was accorded a standing ovation from both sides of the house and his team went on to win the debate. But Lange and the New Zealand people won a larger moral victory on the world stage for the intractable stance against the proliferation of nuclear weapons and the banning of US warships from New Zealand waters.

Ronald Reagan

'Tear Down This Wall'

Brandenberg Gate, West Berlin, 12 June 1987.

The Berlin Wall was built by the Communists in August 1961 to keep Germans from escaping Communist-dominated East Berlin into Democratic West Berlin. The four-metre concrete wall topped by electrified fences cut a 45-kilometre scar through Berlin and was manned by armed guard posts. For the next three decades the Berlin Wall stood as a stark reminder of the Cold War that existed between the United States and Soviet Union.

Ronald Reagan (1911-2004) was the 40th President of the United States of America. A talented sportsman in his youth, Reagan took a job as a sports announcer in Illinois before moving to Hollywood where he started his film career. Self-depreciatingly describing himself as the 'Errol Flynn of the B movies' the Republican Party groomed him as Californian Governor in 1966. Despite being almost 70 when he ran for the presidency in 1980, the American people were looking for stability after a disillusioned four years under Jimmy Carter, and Reagan was swept to power—the oldest President in the history of the nation.

In March 1981, just six weeks after his inauguration, Reagan barely survived an assassin's bullet. The following year he became the first US President to be invited to speak directly to members of the British Parliament in the Royal Gallery at the Palace of Westminster in London. A master communicator, Reagan outlined his staunch opposition to Communism and encouraged the British to aid the US in the worldwide struggle for freedom. In June 1987, at a time when President Reagan was negotiating with Soviet leader Mikhail Gorbachev to scrap intermediate range nuclear missiles,

Reagan travelled to West Berlin and invoking the memory of President John Kennedy's June 1963 visit ('Ich bin ein Berliner!') issued a challenge to his Communist counterpart.

❝ Chancellor Kohl, Governing Mayor Diepgen, ladies and gentlemen:

Twenty-four years ago, President John F Kennedy visited Berlin, speaking to the people of this city and the world at the City Hall. Well, since then two other presidents have come, each in his turn, to Berlin. And today I, myself, make my second visit to your city.

We come to Berlin, we American presidents, because it's our duty to speak, in this place, of freedom. But I must confess, we're drawn here by other things as well: by the feeling of history in this city, more than 500 years older than our own nation; by the beauty of the Grunewald and the Tiergarten; most of all, by your courage and determination. Perhaps the composer Paul Lincke understood something about American presidents. You see, like so many presidents before me, I come here today because wherever I go, whatever I do: Ich hab noch einen Koffer in Berlin. [I still have a suitcase in Berlin.]

Our gathering today is being broadcast throughout Western Europe and North America. I understand that it is being seen and heard as well in the East. To those listening throughout Eastern Europe, a special word: Although I cannot be with you, I address my remarks to you just as surely as to those standing here before me. For I join you, as I join your fellow countrymen in the West, in this firm, this unalterable belief: Es gibt nur ein Berlin. [There is only one Berlin.]

Behind me stands a wall that encircles the free sectors of this city, part of a vast system of barriers that divides the entire continent of Europe. From the Baltic, south, those barriers cut across Germany in a gash of barbed wire, concrete, dog runs, and guard towers. Farther south, there may be no visible, no obvious wall. But there remain armed guards and checkpoints all the same—still a restriction on the right to travel, still an instrument to impose upon ordinary men and women the will of a totalitarian state. Yet it is here in Berlin where the wall emerges most clearly; here, cutting across your city, where the news photo and the television screen have imprinted this brutal division of a continent upon the mind of the world. Standing before the Brandenburg Gate, every man is a German, separated from his fellow men. Every man is a Berliner, forced to look upon a scar.

President von Weizsacker has said, "The German question is open as long as the Brandenburg Gate is closed." Today I say: As long as the gate is closed, as long as this scar of a wall is permitted to stand, it is not the German question alone that remains open, but the question of freedom for all mankind. Yet I do not come here to lament. For I find in Berlin a message of hope, even in the shadow of this wall, a message of triumph.

In this season of spring in 1945, the people of Berlin emerged from their air-raid shelters to find devastation. Thousands of miles away, the people of the United States reached out to help. And in 1947 Secretary of State—as you've been told—George Marshall announced the creation of what would become known as the Marshall Plan. Speaking precisely 40 years ago this month, he said: "Our policy is directed not against any country or doctrine, but against hunger, poverty, desperation, and chaos."

In the Reichstag a few moments ago, I saw a display commemorating this 40th anniversary of the Marshall Plan. I was struck by the sign on a burnt-out, gutted structure that was being rebuilt. I understand that Berliners of my own generation can remember seeing signs like it dotted throughout the western sectors of the city. The sign read simply: "The Marshall Plan is helping here to strengthen the free world." A strong, free world in the West, that dream became real. Japan rose from ruin to become an economic giant. Italy, France, Belgium—virtually every nation in Western Europe saw political and economic rebirth; the European Community was founded.

In West Germany and here in Berlin, there took place an economic miracle, the Wirtschaftswunder. Adenauer, Erhard, Reuter, and other leaders understood the practical importance of liberty—that just as truth can flourish only when the journalist is given freedom of speech, so prosperity can come about only when the farmer and businessman enjoy economic freedom. The German leaders reduced tariffs, expanded free trade, lowered taxes. From 1950 to 1960 alone, the standard of living in West Germany and Berlin doubled.

Where four decades ago there was rubble, today in West Berlin there is the greatest industrial output of any city in Germany—busy office blocks, fine homes and apartments, proud avenues, and the spreading lawns of parkland. Where a city's culture seemed to have been destroyed, today there are two great universities, orchestras and an opera, countless theaters, and museums. Where there was want, today there's abundance—food, clothing, automobiles—the wonderful goods of the Ku'damm. From devastation, from utter ruin, you Berliners have, in freedom, rebuilt a city that once again ranks as one of the greatest on earth. The Soviets may have had other plans. But my friends, there were a few things the Soviets didn't count on—Berliner Herz, Berliner Humor, ja, und Berliner Schnauze. [Berliner heart, Berliner humor, yes, and a Berliner nose.]

In the 1950s, Khrushchev predicted: "We will bury you." But in the West today, we see a free world that has achieved a level of prosperity and well-being unprecedented in all human history. In the Communist world, we see failure, technological backwardness, declining standards of health, even want of the most basic kind--too little food. Even today, the Soviet Union still cannot feed itself. After these four decades, then, there stands before the entire world one great and inescapable conclusion: Freedom leads to prosperity. Freedom replaces the ancient hatreds among the nations with comity and peace. Freedom is the victor.

And now the Soviets themselves may, in a limited way, be coming to understand the importance of freedom. We hear much from Moscow about a new policy of reform and openness. Some political prisoners have been released. Certain foreign news broadcasts are no longer being jammed. Some economic enterprises have been permitted to operate with greater freedom from state control.

Are these the beginnings of profound changes in the Soviet state? Or are they token gestures, intended to raise false hopes in the West, or to strengthen the Soviet system without changing it? We welcome change and openness; for we believe that freedom and security go together, that the advance of human liberty can only strengthen the cause of world peace. There is one sign the Soviets can make that would be unmistakable, that would advance dramatically the cause of freedom and peace.

General Secretary Gorbachev, if you seek peace, if you seek prosperity for the Soviet Union and Eastern Europe, if you seek liberalization: Come here to this gate! Mr. Gorbachev, open this gate! Mr. Gorbachev, tear down this wall!

I understand the fear of war and the pain of division that afflict this continent—and I pledge to you my country's efforts to help overcome these burdens. To be sure, we in the West must resist Soviet expansion. So we must maintain defenses of unassailable strength. Yet we seek peace; so we must strive to reduce arms on both sides.

Beginning 10 years ago, the Soviets challenged the Western alliance with a grave new threat, hundreds of new and more deadly SS-20 nuclear missiles, capable of striking every capital in Europe. The Western alliance responded by committing itself to a counter-deployment unless the Soviets agreed to negotiate a better solution; namely, the elimination of such weapons on both sides. For many months, the Soviets refused to bargain in earnestness. As the alliance, in turn, prepared to go forward with its counter-deployment, there were difficult days—days of protests like those during my 1982 visit to this city—and the Soviets later walked away from the table.

But through it all, the alliance held firm. And I invite those who protested then—I invite those who protest today—to mark this fact: Because we remained strong, the Soviets came back to the table. And because we remained strong, today we have within reach the possibility, not merely of limiting the growth of arms, but of eliminating, for the first time, an entire class of nuclear weapons from the face of the earth.

As I speak, NATO ministers are meeting in Iceland to review the progress of our proposals for eliminating these weapons. At the talks in Geneva, we have also proposed deep cuts in strategic offensive weapons. And the Western allies have likewise made far-reaching proposals to reduce the danger of conventional war and to place a total ban on chemical weapons.

While we pursue these arms reductions, I pledge to you that we will maintain the capacity to deter Soviet aggression at any level at which it might occur. And in cooperation with many of our allies, the United States is pursuing the Strategic Defense Initiative—research to base deterrence not on the threat of offensive retaliation, but on defenses that truly defend; on systems, in short, that will not target populations, but shield them. By these means we seek to increase the safety of Europe and all the world. But we must remember a crucial fact: East and West do not mistrust each other because we are armed; we are armed because we mistrust each other. And our differences are not about weapons but about liberty. When President Kennedy spoke at the City Hall those 24 years ago, freedom was encircled, Berlin was under siege. And today, despite all the pressures upon this city, Berlin stands secure in its liberty. And freedom itself is transforming the globe.

In the Philippines, in South and Central America, democracy has been given a rebirth. Throughout the Pacific, free markets are working miracle after miracle of economic growth. In the industrialized nations, a technological revolution is taking place—a revolution marked by rapid, dramatic advances in computers and telecommunications.

In Europe, only one nation and those it controls refuse to join the community of freedom. Yet in this age of redoubled economic growth, of information and innovation, the Soviet Union faces a choice: It must make fundamental changes, or it will become obsolete.

Today thus represents a moment of hope. We in the West stand ready to cooperate with the East to promote true openness, to break down barriers that separate people, to create a safe, freer world. And surely there is no better place than Berlin, the meeting place of East and West, to make a start. Free people of Berlin: Today, as in the past, the United States stands for the strict observance and full implementation of all parts of the Four Power Agreement of 1971. Let us use this occasion, the 750th anniversary of this city, to usher in a new era, to seek a still fuller, richer life for the Berlin of the future. Together, let us maintain and develop the ties between the Federal Republic and the Western sectors of Berlin, which is permitted by the 1971 agreement.

And I invite Mr. Gorbachev: Let us work to bring the Eastern and Western parts of the city closer together, so that all the inhabitants of all Berlin can enjoy the benefits that come with life in one of the great cities of the world.

To open Berlin still further to all Europe, East and West, let us expand the vital air access to this city, finding ways of making commercial air service to Berlin more convenient, more comfortable, and more economical. We look to the day when West Berlin can become one of the chief aviation hubs in all central Europe.

With our French and British partners, the United States is prepared to help bring international meetings to Berlin. It would be only fitting for Berlin to serve as the site of United Nations meetings, or world conferences on human rights and arms control or other issues that call for international cooperation.

There is no better way to establish hope for the future than to enlighten young minds, and we would be honored to sponsor summer youth exchanges, cultural events, and other programs for young Berliners from the East. Our French and British friends, I'm certain, will do the same. And it's my hope that an authority can be found in East Berlin to sponsor visits from young people of the Western sectors.

One final proposal, one close to my heart: Sport represents a source of enjoyment and ennoblement, and you may have noted that the Republic of Korea—South Korea—has offered to permit certain events of the 1988 Olympics to take place in the North.

International sports competitions of all kinds could take place in both parts of this city. And what better way to demonstrate to the world the openness of this city than to offer in some future year to hold the Olympic Games here in Berlin, East and West? In these four decades, as I have said, you Berliners have built a great city. You've done so in spite of threats—the Soviet attempts to impose the East-mark, the blockade. Today the city thrives in spite of the challenges implicit in the very presence of this wall. What keeps you here? Certainly there's a great deal to be said for your fortitude, for your defiant courage. But I believe there's something deeper, something that involves Berlin's whole look and feel and way of life—not mere sentiment. No one could live long in Berlin without being completely disabused of illusions. Something instead, that has seen the difficulties of life in Berlin but chose to accept them, that continues to build this good and proud city in contrast to a surrounding totalitarian presence that refuses to release human energies or aspirations. Something that speaks with a powerful voice of affirmation, that says yes to this city, yes to the future, yes to freedom. In a word, I would submit that what keeps you in Berlin is love—love both profound and abiding.

Perhaps this gets to the root of the matter, to the most fundamental distinction of all between East and West. The totalitarian world produces backwardness because it does such violence to the spirit, thwarting the human impulse to create, to enjoy, to worship. The totalitarian world finds even symbols of love and of worship an affront. Years ago, before the East Germans began rebuilding their churches, they erected a secular structure: the television tower at Alexander Platz. Virtually ever since, the authorities have been working to correct what they view as the tower's one major flaw, treating the glass sphere at the top with paints and chemicals of every kind. Yet even today when the sun strikes that sphere—that sphere that towers over all Berlin—the light makes the sign of the cross. There in Berlin, like the city itself, symbols of love, symbols of worship, cannot be suppressed.

As I looked out a moment ago from the Reichstag, that embodiment of German unity, I noticed words crudely spray-painted upon the wall, perhaps by a young Berliner: "This wall will fall. Beliefs become reality." Yes, across Europe, this wall will fall. For it cannot withstand faith; it cannot withstand truth. The wall cannot withstand freedom.

And I would like, before I close, to say one word. I have read, and I have been questioned since I've been here about certain demonstrations against my coming. And I would like to say just one thing, and to those who demonstrate so. I wonder if they have ever asked themselves that if they should have the kind of government they apparently seek, no one would ever be able to do what they're doing again.

Thank you and God bless you all. **"**

Ten months after Ronald Reagan left the office of President—on 10 November 1989—the Berlin Wall was torn down as a spontaneous response to East Germany's commitment to social and political reform. The wall which had symbolised the differences between East and West, and had claimed the lives of as many as 75 people during its 28 years of existence, became a gateway to freedom for thousands and hastened the reunification of Germany in October 1990.

Ronald Reagan died on June 5, 2004, aged 93, after suffering from Alzheimer's disease for the final decade of his life.

Ann Richards

'We Can Do Better'
Atlanta, Georgia, 19 July 1988

D orothy Ann Willis was born on 1 September 1933 in Lakeview, Texas. Marrying her high school boyfriend, David Richards, she won a debate scholarship to Baylor University and obtained a Bachelor's Degree.

Ann Richards taught history at Fulmore Junior High School and raised a family of four children. A committed equal rights campaigner who was instrumental in establishing The Women's History Museum in Dallas, she was elected to Travis County, Texas Commissioner Court in 1976.

Despite a bitter campaign in which much was made of the fact that she was a recovering alcoholic, Richards became the first woman in more than 50 years to be elected State Treasurer in 1982. Four years later, she was re-elected to the position unopposed. At the Democratic National Convention in 1988, Ann Richards became only the second woman in the history of the party to deliver the Keynote Address.

The day after Vice-Presidential nominee Jesse Jackson addressed the convention in Atlanta, Georgia, Ann Richards took the stage. What Jackson's speech lacked in humility, Richards more than made up for with old-fashioned common sense and a dose of good humour.

❛ Thank you. Thank you. Thank you very much.

Good evening, ladies and gentlemen. Buenas noches, mis amigos.

I'm delighted to be here with you this evening, because after listening to George Bush all these years, I figured you needed to know what a real Texas accent sounds like.

Twelve years ago, Barbara Jordan, another Texas woman, Barbara made the keynote address to this convention, and two women in a hundred and sixty years is about par for the course.

But, if you give us a chance, we can perform. After all, Ginger Rogers did everything that Fred Astaire did. She just did it backwards and in high heels.

I want to announce to this nation that in a little more than 100 days, the Reagan-Meese-Deaver-Nofziger-Poindexter-North-Weinberger-Watt-Gorsuch-Lavelle-Stockman-Haig-Bork-Noriega-George Bush [era] will be over!

You know, tonight I feel a little like I did when I played basketball in the 8th grade. I thought I looked real cute in my uniform. And then I heard a boy yell from the bleachers, "Make that basket, Birdlegs!"

And my greatest fear is that same guy is somewhere out there in the audience tonight and he's going to cut me down to size. Because where I grew up, there really wasn't much tolerance for self-importance, people who put on airs.

I was born during the Depression in a little community just outside Waco and I grew up listening to Franklin Roosevelt on the radio. Well, it was back then that I came to understand the small truths and the hardships that bind neighbors together. Those were real people with real problems and they had real dreams about getting out of the Depression. I can remember summer nights when we'd put down what we called the Baptist pallet and we listened to the grown-ups talk. I can still hear the sound of the dominoes clicking on the marble slab my daddy had found for a tabletop. I can still hear the laughter of the man telling jokes you weren't supposed to hear—talkin' about how big that old buck deer was, laughin' about mama puttin' Clorox in the well when the frog fell in.

They talked about war and Washington and what this country needed. They talked the straight talk. And it came from people who were living their lives as best they could. And that's what we're going to do tonight. We're going to tell how the cow ate the cabbage.

I got a letter last week from a young mother in Lorena, Texas, and I wanna read part of it to you. She writes,

"Our worries go from pay day to pay day, just like millions of others. And we have two fairly decent incomes, but I worry how I'm going to pay the rising car insurance and food. I pray my kids don't have a growth spurt from August to December, so I don't have to buy new jeans. We buy clothes at the budget stores and we have them fray and fade and stretch in the first wash. We ponder and try to figure out how we're gonna pay for college and braces and tennis shoes. We don't take vacations and we don't go out to eat. Please don't think me ungrateful. We have jobs and a nice place to live, and we're healthy. We're the people you see every day in the grocery stores, and we obey the laws and pay our taxes. We fly our flags on holidays and we plod along trying to make it better for ourselves and our children and our parents. We aren't vocal any more. I think maybe we're too tired. I believe that people like us are forgotten in America."

Well, of course you believe you're forgotten, because you have been.

This Republican Administration treats us as if we were pieces of a puzzle that can't fit together. They've tried to put us into compartments and separate us from each other. Their political theory is "divide and conquer." They've suggested time and time again that what is of interest to one group of Americans is not of interest to any one else. We've been isolated. We've been lumped into that sad phraseology called "special interests." They've told farmers that they were selfish, that they would drive up food prices if they asked the government to intervene on behalf of the family farm and we watched farms go on the auction block while we bought food from foreign countries. Well, that's wrong!

They told working mothers it's all their fault—their families are falling apart because they had to go to work to keep their kids in jeans and tennis shoes and college. And they're wrong!

They told American labor they were trying to ruin free enterprise by asking for 60 days' notice of plant closings, and that's wrong. And they told the auto industry and the steel industry and the timber industry and the oil industry, companies being threatened by foreign products flooding this country, that you're protectionist if you think the government should enforce our trade laws. And that is wrong!

When they belittle us for demanding clean air and clean water, for trying to save the oceans and the ozone layer, that's wrong!

No wonder we feel isolated and confused. We want answers and their answer is that "something is wrong with you." Well nothing's wrong with you. Nothing's wrong with you that you can't fix in November!

We've been told—we've been told that the interests of the South and the Southwest are not the same interests as the North and the Northeast. They pit one group against the other. They've divided this country and in our isolation we think government isn't gonna help us and we're alone in our feelings. We feel forgotten. Well, the fact is that we are not an isolated piece of their puzzle. We are one nation. We are the United States of America.

Now, we Democrats believe that America is still the country of fair play; that we can come out of a small town or a poor neighborhood and have the same chance as anyone else and it doesn't matter whether we are black or Hispanic or disabled or a women [sic]. We believe that America is a country where small business owners must succeed, because they are the bedrock, backbone of our economy.

We believe that our kids deserve good day care and public schools. We believe our kids deserve public schools where students can learn and teachers can teach. And we wanna believe that our parents will have a good retirement and that we will too. We Democrats believe that social security is a pact that cannot be broken.

We wanna believe that we can live out our lives without the terrible fear that an illness is going to bankrupt us and our children. We Democrats believe that America can overcome any problem, including the dreaded disease called AIDS. We believe that America is still a country where there is more to life than just a constant struggle for money. And we believe that America must have leaders who show us that our struggles amount to something and contribute to something larger, leaders who want us to be all that we can be. We want leaders like Jesse Jackson.

Jesse Jackson is a leader and a teacher who can open our hearts and open our minds and stir our very souls. And he has taught us that we are as good as our capacity for caring, caring about the drug problem, caring about crime, caring about education and caring about each other.

Now, in contrast, the greatest nation of the free world has had a leader for eight straight years that has pretended that he cannot hear our questions over the noise of the helicopters. And we know he doesn't wanna answer. But we have a lot of questions. And when we get our questions asked, or there is a leak, or an investigation the only answer we get is: "I don't know," or "I forgot."

But you wouldn't accept that answer from your children. I wouldn't. Don't tell me "you don't know" or "you forgot." We're not going to have the America that we want until we elect leaders who are gonna tell the truth; not most days but every day; leaders who don't forget what they don't want to remember. And for eight straight years George Bush hasn't displayed the slightest interest in anything we care about. And now that he's after a job he can't get appointed to, he's like Columbus discovering America. He's found child care. He's found education. Poor George. He can't help it. He was born with a silver foot in his mouth.

Well, no wonder, no wonder we can't figure it out. Because the leadership of this nation is telling us one thing on TV and doing something entirely different. They tell us, they tell us that they're fighting a war against terrorists. And then we find out that the White House is selling arms to the Ayatollah. They tell us that they're fighting a war on drugs and then people come on TV and testify that the CIA and the DEA and the FBI knew they were flying drugs into America all along. And they're negotiating with a dictator who is shoveling cocaine into this country like crazy. I guess that's their Central American strategy.

Now, they tell us that employment rates are great, and that they're for equal opportunity. But we know it takes two pay-checks to make ends meet today, when it used to take one. And the opportunity they're so proud of is low-wage, dead-end jobs. And there is no major city in America where you cannot see homeless men sitting in parking lots holding signs that say "I will work for food."

Now, my friends, we really are at a crucial point in American history. Under this Administration we have devoted our resources into making this country a military colossus. But we've let our economic lines of defense fall into disrepair. The debt of this nation is greater than it has ever been in our history. We fought a world war on less debt than the Republicans have built up in the last eight years. You know, it's kind of like that brother-in-law who drives a flashy new car but he's always borrowin' money from you to make the payments.

But let's take what they are most proud of. That is their stand on defense. We Democrats are committed to a strong America, and, quite frankly, when our leaders say to us: "We need a new weapons system," our inclination is to say: "Well, they must be right."

But when we pay billions for planes that won't fly, billions for tanks that won't fire and billions for systems that won't work, that old dog won't hunt. And you don't have to be from Waco to know that when the Pentagon makes crooks rich and doesn't make America strong, that it's a bum deal.

Now I'm going to tell you I'm really glad that our young people missed the Depression and missed the great big war. But I do regret that they missed the leaders that I knew, leaders who told us when things were tough and that we'd have to sacrifice and that these difficulties might last for a while. They didn't tell us things were hard for us because we were different, or isolated, or special interests. They brought us together and they gave us a sense of national purpose.

They gave us Social Security and they told us they were setting up a system where we could pay our own money in, and when the time came for our retirement we could take the money out. People in the rural areas were told that we deserved to have electric lights and they were gonna harness the energy that was necessary to give us electricity so my grandmama didn't have to carry that old coal oil lamp around.

And they told us that they were going to guarantee when we put our money in the bank, that the money was going to be there and it was going to be insured. They did not lie to us.

And I think one of the saving graces of Democrats is that we are candid. We talk straight talk. We tell people what we think. And that tradition and those values live today in Michael Dukakis from Massachusetts.

Michael Dukakis knows that this country is on the edge of a great new era, that we're not afraid of change, that we're for thoughtful, truthful, strong leadership. Behind his calm, there's an impatience to unify this country and to get on with the future. His instincts are deeply American. They're tough and they're generous. And personally, I have to tell you that I have never met a man who had a more remarkable sense about what is really important in life.

And then there's my friend and my teacher for many years, Senator Lloyd Bentsen. And I couldn't be prouder, both as a Texan and as a Democrat, because Lloyd Bentsen understands America. From the barrio to the boardroom, he knows how to bring us together, by regions, by economics and by example. And he's already beaten George Bush once. So, when it comes right down to it, this election is a contest between those who are satisfied with what they have and those who know we can do better. That's what this election is really all about. It's about the American dream—those who want to keep it for the few and those who know it must be nurtured and passed along.

I'm a grandmother now. And I have one nearly perfect granddaughter named Lily. And when I hold that grandbaby, I feel the continuity of life that unites us, that binds generation to generation, that ties us to each other. And sometimes I spread that Baptist pallet out on the floor and Lily and I roll a ball back and forth. And I think of all the families like mine, like the one in Lorena, Texas, like the ones that nurture children all across America. And as I look at Lily, I know that it is within families that we learn both the need to respect individual human dignity and to work together for our common good. Within our families, within our nation, it is the same.

And as I sit there, I wonder if she'll ever grasp the changes I've seen in my life—if she'll ever believe that there was a time when blacks could not drink from public water fountains, when Hispanic children were punished for speaking Spanish in the public schools and women couldn't vote.

I think of all the political fights I've fought and all the compromises I've had to accept as part payment. And I think of all the small victories that have added up to national triumphs; and all the things that would never have happened and all the people who would've been left behind if we had not reasoned and fought and won those battles together. And I will tell Lily that those triumphs were Democratic Party triumphs. I want so much to tell Lily how far we've come, you and I. And as the ball rolls back and forth, I want to tell her how very lucky she is that for all our difference, we are still the greatest nation on this good earth. And our strength lies in the men and women who go to work every day, who struggle to balance their family and their jobs, and who should never, ever be forgotten.

I just hope that like her grandparents and her great-grandparents before that, Lily goes on to raise her kids with the promise that echoes in homes all across America: That we can do better. And that's what this election is all about.

Thank you very much. **'**

Ann Richards' speech placed her in the national spotlight and in November 1990, she was elected Governor of Texas. A popular Governor, it was said that she 'appointed more women, African Americans and Hispanics to government positions than any of her predecessors', but she was defeated after just one term by White House-bound George W. Bush.

After her defeat, Richards continued to advocate healthier lifestyle choices for women. She was diagnosed with osteoporosis in 1996 and championed women's issues in the remaining decade of her life.

Benazir Bhutto

'Address to the US Congress'
Washington DC, 7 June 1989

Benazir Bhutto (1953–2007) was the eldest daughter of former Pakistani leader, Zulfikar Ali Bhutto, and the first woman leader of a Muslim country in modern history.

Her father served as the President of Pakistan from 1971 to 1973 and Prime Minister from 1973 to 1977.

In November 1977, General Mohammed Zia-ul-Haq seized power in a military coup and Zulfikar Bhutto was arrested, tried and executed on the trumped-up charge of having ordered a political assassination in the early 1970s.

Having suffered a series of arrests following her father's political downfall, Benazir Bhutto fled to England in 1984 where she became head of her father's political party, the Pakistan People's Party (PPP).

In 1988, after President Zia and the American Ambassador to Pakistan were killed in a plane crash, Benazir Bhutto returned to Pakistan and launched a vigorous campaign for democratic elections. On 16 November 1988, Pakistani citizens voted in their first open election in more than a decade and Bhutto's PPP won a majority in the National Assembly.

On 1 December, 1988, Benazir Bhutto took office as Prime Minister of Pakistan.

The following year, the 35-year-old Prime Minister was invited to the United States where, in a speech before both Houses of Congress and President George H. Bush, she urged America to press for a broad-based political settlement to the Soviet invasion of Afghanistan. It was reported that Ms. Bhutto, a member of Radcliffe College (Harvard) Class of 1973, 'captivated Congress with a speech portraying herself as the embodiment of democracy, a spokesman for women, youth and those in the Islamic mainstream, a fighter for freedom in Afghanistan and a political descendant of John F. Kennedy.'

❛Mr. President, distinguished Members of the Congress, As Salaam-o-Alaikum. Peace be with you.

We gather together, friends and partners, who have fought, side by side, in the cause of liberty.

We gather together to celebrate freedom, to celebrate democracy, to celebrate the three most beautiful words in the English language: 'We the People.'

I stand here conscious of the honor you bestow on my country and on me.

I am not new to America. I recall fondly my four years I spent here as a student at Harvard.

America is a land of great technology.America is a land of economic power.

Your products are sent all over the world, a tribute to the creativity and productivity of your people.

But your greatest export is not material. Your greatest export is not a product. Your greatest export is an idea.

America's greatest contribution to the world is its concept of democracy, its concept of freedom, freedom of action, freedom of speech and freedom of thought.

President Bush, in his inaugural address, spoke of a new breeze across America. In fact, this new breeze is sweeping the whole world.

In Afghanistan, the people have freed their country of foreign occupation.

In South America, the generals are returning to their barracks and the people to the halls of government.

In the Orient, the old order is changing and the demands growing.

Glasnost and Perestroika are shaking the East bloc… the ultimate tribute to the strength of freedom, to the desire of people wherever they live to control their own destiny.

And it is the words of Lincoln that are quoted… "a government of the people, by the people, for the people."

For many of us, the root of all this progress, the foundation of democracy, lies on this continent, 200 years ago, in your covenant of freedom, in words penned by Madison... "We the People."

My presence before you is a testament to the force of freedom and democracy in Pakistan.

Throughout 1988, the call for democratic change in Pakistan grew louder.

After a decade of repression, the wave of freedom surged in Pakistan.

On November 16, the people of Pakistan participated in the first party-based elections in eleven years.

The Pakistan People's Party won a convincing victory, showing wide national support all across the four provinces of our great country. Democracy had at last returned to Pakistan.

We the people had spoken.

We the people had prevailed.

In its first days, our new government released political prisoners, legalized labor and student unions and restored press freedoms.

We signaled our right of recognition to the role of the opposition in a democratic society, giving them free and regular access to the state media for the first time in our history.

We set as our focus reconciliation, not retribution.

Some claimed to fear revenge, revenge against the murderers and torturers, revenge against those who subverted constitutional law.

But, ladies and gentlemen, there was no revenge.

For them, and for dictators across the world... democracy is the greatest revenge.

For us, the election was the end to an unspeakable ordeal.

A democratic government was overthrown in a military coup and for eleven years dictatorship ruled our nation.

Political parties were banned.

Political expression prohibited.

There was no freedom of the press.

The Constitution was suspended and amended into virtual non-existence.

Women were subjugated and laws written specifically to discriminate against them.

Political opponents were imprisoned, tortured and hanged. It was the luckier ones who went into exile.

Our struggle was driven by faith…faith in our people's ability to resist—faith in our religion, Islam, which teaches us that 'tyranny cannot endure.'

It is this same faith which has fuelled the battle for freedom next door in Afghanistan.

Both our countries have stood alongside the Afghans in their struggle for more than a decade.

For ten long years the people of Pakistan have provided sanctuary to our Afghan brothers and sisters.

We have nurtured and sustained their families.

More than three million refugees are on our soil. Still more are coming, fleeing the bloodshed.

And we have welcomed them, housed them and fed them.

And for ten long years, the United States, in a united bipartisan effort of three Administrations and six Congresses, has stood side by side with Pakistan and the brave Mujahidin.

We both deserve to be proud of that effort.

But that effort did not come without a price. Our villages were strafed, our people killed.

Our peaceful country has changed. The war has brought the curse of drug addiction to Pakistan—over one million heroin addicts—to a land that never before knew it.

Our forests and natural resources have been depleted.

Yet our commitment to pay the price for freedom has not been shaken.

And now, despite the Soviet withdrawal, peace has not returned to Afghanistan.

Even now, the Soviet Government is giving full backing to the Kabul regime's efforts to cling to power.

It has left in its possession vast quantities of lethal weapons—weapons supplemented by a regular supply of hardware including Scud missiles, some of which have already hit Pakistan territory.

More threats have been received, threats to supply new weapons never before seen in the region.

The Soviets have gone. But the force of foreign arms continues to deny Afghanistan the ultimate fruit of victory…self-determination.

Those responsible for a decade of death and destruction now blame us for the continuing bloodshed.

They accuse us of interfering in Afghanistan. Nothing is farther from the truth and nothing is more unjust.

Our concerns are for a stable, independent and neutral Afghanistan, an Afghanistan where the people can choose their own system, their own government in free and fair elections.

We in Pakistan would like to see the refugees return to their homes in peace and dignity.

Unfortunately, the conflict is not over. It has entered its closing stage, a stage often the most complex and difficult.

Distinguished friends, Pakistan and the United States have traveled a long road with the Afghans in their quest for self-determination.

Let us not at this stage, out of impatience or fatigue, become indifferent. We cannot, we must not, abandon their cause.

The world community must rise to the challenge which lies ahead. The challenge of achieving a broad-based, political settlement to the war, of rebuilding a shattered country, of helping the victims of war, of developing the Afghan economy.

Mr. Speaker, now Pakistan and the United States enter a new phase of an enduring relationship. Our shared interests and common international goals have not disappeared. If anything, they have been strengthened.

Our partnership is not a friendship of convenience. For decades we have been tied together by mutual international goals and by shared interests.

But something new has entered into the equation of bilateral relations—democracy.

We are now moral as well as political partners. Two elected governments bonded together in a common respect for constitutional government, accountability and a commitment to freedom.

Because of the intensity of our struggle for freedom, we will never take it for granted in Pakistan.

Our democratic institutions are still new and need careful tending.

Democracy's doubters have never believed that it could successfully address the problems of developing countries. But democracy in Pakistan must succeed to signal nations in political transition all over the world that freedom is on the rise.

This is the time in Pakistan when democracy's friends must come forward. We need the time and the resources to build a truly strong constitutional government. If we succeed, all democracies share in that success.

Today we are on the threshold of a new democratic partnership between our two countries, addressing new priorities. A partnership which addresses both our security concerns and our social and economic needs. A partnership which will carry us into the twenty-first century—strong in mutual trust, close in common interest, constant to the values we share; working in association with democratic governments all across the world to promote the values of freedom. This is the partnership, the new democratic Pakistan we hope to build with your continuing help.

The time is right, my friends, to make miracles in Pakistan. The dictatorship of the past has given way to the forces of the future. The years of social and economic neglect beg for redress. So I come to this land of freedom to talk about the future. The future of my country and the future of freedom everywhere. The future of our children—my child—and yours.

I come before you to declare that we cannot choose between development and democracy. We must work for both. Partners in democracy must now focus attention on urgent problems which affect mankind as a whole.

The widening gap between rich and poor countries; environmental pollution; drug abuse and trafficking; the pressure of population on world resources; and full economic participation for women everywhere.

We must join together to find remedies and solutions for these problems before they overcome us.

Of all the crises facing us, my government is giving the highest priority to the problem of drug abuse.

We are determined to eradicate this plague from our country. To that end we have established a new Ministry for Narcotics Control.

We are taking vigorous action against drug offenders.

Our close cooperation—and that of other nations—must be strengthened if we are to turn back the tide of drugs sweeping your nation and mine.

So, too, must we work together, as partners, to avert the catastrophe of a nuclear arms race.

Speaking for Pakistan, I can declare that we do not possess nor do we intend to make a nuclear device.

That is our policy.

We are committed to a regional approach to the nuclear problem and we remain ready to accept any safeguards, inspections and verifications that are applied on a non-discriminatory regional basis.

Pakistan has long advocated the creation of a nuclear-weapon-free zone in the region.

A first step in that direction could be a nuclear test ban agreement between Pakistan and its neighbors in South Asia.

We are prepared for any negotiation to prevent the proliferation of nuclear weapons in our region.

We will not provoke a nuclear arms race in the subcontinent.

The United States has long held a commitment to peace in South Asia.

It is a commitment which Pakistan shares.

It is in this spirit of peace, of regional cooperation and bilateral partnership, that I come before you today.

This then must be our agenda, democracy and development, security and international cooperation.

The people of Pakistan appreciate the assistance you have given us, the assistance which you continue to give us.

Your military assistance has helped maintain a relative balance in the region. It has contributed to Pakistan's sense of security. It has strengthened the peace and stability of the South Asian region.

Mr. Speaker, everywhere the sun is setting on the day of the dictator.

In Pakistan when the moment came, the transition was peaceful.

The whole nation, farmers, workers, the soldiers and civilians, men and women, together heralded the return of democracy.

The people have taken power in their hands.

But our work has just begun.

My friends, freedom is not an end. Freedom is a beginning.

And in Pakistan, at long last, we are ready to begin.

Our two countries stood together in the last decade to support the fight of the Afghan people for freedom.

Let us stand together now as the people of Pakistan strive to give meaning to their newfound freedom.

Come with us toward a tomorrow, better than all the yesterdays we knew.

History, the rush of events, perhaps even destiny has brought me here today.

I am proud to be the elected Prime Minister of Pakistan in this critical time.

It is an awesome obligation.

But in the words of John Fitzgerald Kennedy..."I do not shrink from this responsibility—I welcome it."

As a representative of the young, let me be viewed as one of a new generation of leaders unshackled by the constraints and irrational hatreds of the past.

As a representative of women, let my message be to them, "Yes you can!"

As a believer of Islam in this august Chamber, let my message be about a compassionate and tolerant religion, teaching hard work and family values under a merciful God, for that is the Islam which we must all come to understand.

For me and the people of Pakistan, the last eleven years have encompassed a painful odyssey.

My countrymen and I did not see our loved ones killed, or tortured, or lashed, or languishing in solitary confinement, deprived of basic human rights and freedom, in order that others might again suffer such indignities.

We sacrificed a part of our lives and bore the pain of confronting tyranny to build a just society.

We believed in ourselves, in our cause, in our people and in our country.

And when you believe, then there is no mountain too high to scale.

That is my message to the youth of America, to its women, and to its people.

Thank you distinguished Members. **'**

Benazir Bhutto remained a staunch supporter of the pro-Taliban guerrillas in Afghanistan—a position enthusiastically embraced by many American politicians at the time—but this stance changed considerably on both sides of the Pacific in the 1990s.

Bhutto, however, faced more pressing domestic issues almost from the start. Her government fell in 1990, largely because of corruption charges, but she again served as Pakistani leader from 1993 to 1996.

Attempts to modernise Pakistan had made her many enemies and, in 1996, she was once again dismissed from office on charges of corruption. When Pakistan Army Chief, Pervez Musharraf, came to power after a military coup in 1999, Bhutto and her family were living in exile in Dubai and fighting charges of international money laundering.

Despite being banned by President Musharraf from serving a third term as Prime Minister, Benazir Bhutto vowed to return to her homeland. After entering into power-sharing discussions with the President—a move which alienated her from many of her supporters—Bhutto returned to Pakistan under amnesty from her corruption charges to campaign for the 2008 elections.

On her first day back in Pakistan, on 18 October 2007, 136 people were killed in an explosion near her political rally. Just two months later, after being released from house arrest during the country's state of emergency, Benazir Bhutto was assassinated on 27 December while campaigning in Rawalpindi, Punjab province.

Al-Qaeda operatives based in Afghanistan later claimed responsibility for the assassination.

Mikhail Gorbachev

'Dissolving the Soviet Union'

Televised address, 25 December 1991.

Mikhail Sergeyevich Gorbachev was born in Privolyne, Russia in 1931. A member of the Communist Party since 1952, he rose through the ranks of the Party Central Committee and upon the death of Konstantin Chernenko in 1985, became party general secretary of the Central Committee. In the 1980s Gorbachev undertook two wide-reaching programs—openness (glasnost) and reconstruction (perestroika)—to modernise the Soviet Union and its failing economy. In 1988 he became chairman of the Presidium of the Supreme Soviet and two years later was named the first—and last—executive president of the USSR.

Paradoxically, Gorbachev's reforms brought about the end of the Communist regime that he sought to maintain. Gorbachev's reforms created greater domestic freedoms, reduced military spending and promoted a healthier relationship with the West. In 1989 Soviet troops withdrew from Afghanistan, the Communist Party voted to end 'one party rule' and Soviet republics threatened to leave the Union to govern themselves.

One of the most powerful undertakings Gorbachev was involved in was to publicly 'reinstate' the reputations of thousands of citizens jailed and executed under the Stalin regime in the 1930s and 1940s. This had a strong effect on the nation's consciousness and how the country viewed itself nationally.

In August 1991 Gorbachev survived an attempted coup in Moscow—rescued by newly elected Russian Federative President Boris Yelstsin who organised the seizure of government buildings in Moscow and then banned the Communist Party. This shift in the political and social mood of the country led to the establishment of the Commonwealth of Independent States.

On (Western Christendom's) Christmas Day, 1991, Mikhail Gorbachev resigned as president of the Union of Soviet Socialist Republics. This was the final act in an ironically peaceful dissolution of a communist (socialist) nation that had been borne in so much bloodshed and maintained by fear and oppression since the October Revolution in 1917.

❛ Dear compatriots, fellow citizens, as a result of the newly formed situation, creation of the Commonwealth of Independent States, I cease my activities in the post of the USSR president. I am taking this decision out of considerations based on principle. I have firmly stood for independence, self-rule of nations, for the sovereignty of the republics, but at the same time for preservation of the union state, the unity of the country.

Events went a different way. The policy prevailed of dismembering this country and disuniting the state, with which I cannot agree. And after the Alma-Ata meeting and the decisions taken there, my position on this matter has not changed. Besides, I am convinced that decisions of such scale should have been taken on the basis of a popular expression of will.

Yet, I will continue to do everything in my power so that agreements signed there should lead to real accord in the society, (and) facilitate the escape from the crisis and the reform process. Addressing you for the last time in the capacity of president of the USSR, I consider it necessary to express my evaluation of the road we have travelled since 1985, especially as there are a lot of contradictory, superficial and subjective judgments on that matter.

Fate had it that when I found myself at the head of the state it was already clear that all was not well in the country. There is plenty of everything: land, oil and gas, other natural riches, and God gave us lots of intelligence and talent, yet we lived much worse than developed countries and keep falling behind them more and more.

The reason could already be seen: The society was suffocating in the vice of the command-bureaucratic system, doomed to serve ideology and bear the terrible burden of the arms race. It had reached the limit of its possibilities. All attempts at partial reform, and there had been many, had suffered defeat, one after another. The country was losing perspective. We could not go on living like that. Everything had to be changed radically.

The process of renovating the country and radical changes in the world turned out to be far more complicated than could be expected. However, what has been done ought to be given its due. This society acquired freedom, liberated itself politically and spiritually, and this is the foremost achievement which we have not yet understood completely, because we have not learned to use freedom.

However, work of historic significance has been accomplished. The totalitarian system which deprived the country of an opportunity to become successful and prosperous long ago has been eliminated. A breakthrough has been achieved on the way to democratic changes. Free elections, freedom of the press, religious freedoms, representative organs of power, a multiparty (system) became a reality; human rights are recognized as the supreme principle.

The movement to a diverse economy has started, equality of all forms of property is becoming established, people who work on the land are coming to life again in the framework of land reform, farmers have appeared, millions of acres of land are being given over to people who live in the countryside and in towns.

Economic freedom of the producer has been legalized, and entrepreneurship, shareholding, privatization are gaining momentum. In turning the economy toward a market, it is important to remember that all this is done for the sake of the individual. At this difficult time, all should be done for his social protection, especially for senior citizens and children.

We live in a new world. The Cold War has ended, the arms race has stopped, as has the insane militarization which mutilated our economy, public psyche and morals. The threat of a world war has been removed. Once again I want to stress that on my part everything was done during the transition period to preserve reliable control of the nuclear weapons.

We opened ourselves to the world, gave up interference into other people's affairs, the use of troops beyond the borders of the country, and trust, solidarity and respect came in response.

The nations and peoples of this country gained real freedom to choose the way of their self-determination. The search for a democratic reformation of the multinational state brought us to the threshold of concluding a new Union Treaty. All these changes demanded immense strain. They were carried out with sharp struggle, with growing resistance from the old, the obsolete forces.

The old system collapsed before the new one had time to begin working, and the crisis in the society became even more acute.

The August coup brought the general crisis to its ultimate limit. The most damaging thing about this crisis is the break-up of the statehood. And today I am worried by our people's loss of the citizenship of a great country. The consequences may turn out to be very hard for everyone.

I am leaving my post with apprehension, but also with hope, with faith in you, your wisdom and force of spirit. We are the heirs of a great civilization, and its rebirth into a new, modern and dignified life now depends on one and all.

Some mistakes could surely have been avoided, many things could have been done better, but I am convinced that sooner or later our common efforts will bear fruit, our nations will live in a prosperous and democratic society.

I wish all the best to all of you. '

The following day the Russian government took over the offices of the former USSR. Gorbachev was now politically dead—the former leader of a system of government that no longer existed. Slow to call for democratic elections, he had failed to see the threat from hardline communists within his own party and underestimated the power of the truth to erode the credibility—from both outside and within the Soviet Union—of a discredited regime.

Queen Elizabeth II

'Annus Horribilis'

The Guildhall, London, 24 November 1992.

Queen Elizabeth II of England, the eldest daughter of King George VI, was born in 1926. Elizabeth was proclaimed Queen of England upon the death of her father on 6 February 1952 and crowned the following year, on 2 June 1953, in Westminster Abbey.

The 27-year-old monarch had already married Philip Mountbatten (her fourth cousin and Prince of Greece) in 1947 and had two of her four children—Charles (in 1948), Anne (1950), Andrew (1960), and Edward (1964). Hugely popular with her post-war Commonwealth subjects, she nevertheless oversaw the decline of the British Empire as India, Pakistan, Burma (Myanmar), Malaysia, Pacific Island, West Indian and African colonies successfully sought independence.

As Elizabeth and Philip's children grew to adulthood the public behaviour of the 'royals' and their spouses exposed those human foibles common to the rest of society—jealousy, pettiness and infidelity.

Anne, the Princess Royal, divorced her husband Mark Phillips; Prince Andrew separated from his wife Sarah Ferguson, and the marriage of the British heir, Prince Charles, and his immensely popular and beautiful wife, Diana, Princess of Wales, publicly disintegrated.

On 20 November, 1992, the Queen's primary residence, Windsor Castle, was severely damaged by fire. Rather than provoking a wave of sympathy, news that the Royal Family would not have to pay for the restoration—the British taxpayer would foot the bill—drew stinging criticism.

Celebrating the fortieth year of her reign in 1992, many started to question the need for a monarchy which lived in great pomp and spectacle but paid not a shilling in tax. When Queen Elizabeth appeared at a City of London luncheon, she delivered a speech that permeated the façade of her position and touched the hearts of her subjects.

❛Nineteen ninety-two is not a year I shall look back on with undiluted pleasure. In the words of one of my more sympathetic correspondents, it has turned out to be an 'Annus Horribilis'.

I suspect that I am not alone in thinking it so. Indeed, I suspect that there are very few people or institutions unaffected by these last months of worldwide turmoil and uncertainty. This generosity and wholehearted kindness of the Corporation of the City to Prince Philip and me would be welcome at any time, but at this particular moment, in the aftermath of Friday's tragic fire at Windsor, it is especially so. And, after this last weekend, we appreciate all the more what has been set before us today. Years of experience, however, have made us a bit more canny than the lady, less well-versed than us in the splendours of City hospitality, who, when she was offered a balloon glass for her brandy, asked for "only half a glass, please". It is possible to have too much of a good thing. A well-meaning Bishop was obviously doing his best when he told Queen Victoria, "Ma'am, we cannot pray too often, nor too fervently, for the Royal Family." The Queen's reply was, "Too fervently, no; too often, yes."

I, like Queen Victoria, have always been a believer in that old maxim "moderation in all things". I sometimes wonder how future generations will judge the events of this tumultuous year. I dare say that history will take a slightly more moderate view than that of some contemporary commentators. Distance is well known to lend enchantment, even to the less attractive views. After all, it has the inestimable advantage of hindsight. But it can also lend an extra dimension to judgement, giving it a leavening of moderation and compassion—even of wisdom—that is sometimes lacking in the reactions of those whose task it is in life to offer instant opinions on all things great and small.

No section of the community has all the virtues; neither does any have all the vices. I am quite sure that most people try to do their jobs as best they can, even if the result is not always entirely successful. He who has never failed to reach perfection has a right to be the harshest critic. There can be no doubt, of course, that criticism is good for people and institutions that are part of public life.

No institution—City, Monarchy, whatever—should expect to be free from the scrutiny of those who give it their loyalty and support, not to mention those who don't. But we are all part of the same fabric of our national society and that scrutiny, by one part of another, can be just as effective if it is made with a touch of gentleness, good humour and understanding. This sort of questioning can also act, and it should do so, as an effective engine for change.

The City is a good example of the way the process of change can he incorporated into the stability and continuity of a great institution. I particularly admire, my Lord Mayor, the way in which the City has adapted to what the Prayer Book calls "the changes and chances of this mortal life." You have set an example of how it is possible to remain effective and dynamic without losing those indefinable qualities, style and character. We only have to look around this great hall to see the truth of that.

Forty years is quite a long time. I am glad to have had the chance to witness, and to take part in, many, dramatic changes in life in this country. But I am glad to say that the magnificent standard of hospitality, given on so many occasions to the Sovereign by the Lord Mayor of London has not changed at all. It is an outward symbol of one other unchanging factor which I value above all—the loyalty given to me and my family by so many people in this country, and the Commonwealth, throughout my reign.

You, my Lord Mayor and all those whose prayers—fervent, I hope, but not too frequent—have sustained me through all these years, are friends indeed. Prince Philip and I give you all, wherever you may be, our most humble thanks. '

Although 'Annus Horribilis' was a light-hearted reference to John Dryden's 1666 poem Annus Mirabilis (The Year of Wonders), Queen Elizabeth was asking for understanding from her subjects. She accepted the public criticism but reiterated her commitment to serve her people—a constant theme that she often returned to during her long reign. But the public had spoken and she had listened.

In the following weeks it was announced that the Queen would pay tax, that the restoration of Windsor Castle (which would cost over £36 million) would be funded by public ticket sales to view Buckingham Palace and that the 'fairytale' marriage between the Prince of Wales and his wife was indeed over.

However, criticism of an aloof and out-of-touch monarch would hound her throughout the 1990s, rising to a deafening crescendo with the funeral arrangements for her former daughter-in-law Diana in 1997.

Despite these concerns, Queen Elizabeth never considered stepping down in favour of her son Charles. Entering the new millennium, she revitalised her public persona and remains the most-loved and revered reigning monarch in the world. In 2002, she celebrated her golden jubilee (the same year she lost her mother and sister to illness) and her diamond jubilee in 2012 galvanised the entire Briitish Commonwealth behind her and the Royal Family.

On September 9, 2015, Queen Elizabeth II became the longest reigning British monarch in history. Having celebrated her 90th birthday in April 2016, she continues to 'do her duty'.

Nelson Mandela

'Release from Prison'

Address to a rally upon release from prison at Cape Town, 11 February 1990.

Nelson Mandela fought against the brutal apartheid regime of South Africa and became the national and international symbol of the struggle for black South Africa's self-determination.

He was born Rolihlahla Dalibhunga Mandela, the son of a Thembu tribal chieftain on 18 July 1918 in a small village in the Transkei province in South Africa. Given the English name 'Nelson' by a schoolteacher, Mandela was raised by the acting regent of the Thembu people after the death of his father in 1927. Mandela later attended Fort Hare University, became a lawyer in Johannesburg and joined the African National Congress (ANC) in 1944. With friends Oliver Tambo and Walter Sisulu, Mandela formed the Youth League of the ANC when he felt the ANC leadership was too conservative. The same year he married his first wife, Evelyn Mase, the mother of his first three children.

For the next 20 years Mandela was involved in a campaign of non-violent defiance against the South African government's apartheid policies. In 1952 he was arrested for violating the Suppression of Communism Act (which was intended to crush any mass movement against apartheid) and banned from attending meetings for the next two years. In 1955 the 'Freedom Charter' adopted at the Congress of the People called for equal rights for blacks and equal share of the country's wealth with whites.

The following year, Nelson Mandela, along with 155 other political activists, was accused of attempting to overthrow the South African government by violent means. Charged with high treason, the charges were dropped against Mandela after a four-year trial. During this time, Mandela divorced his first wife and married Winnie Madikizela in 1958.

On 21 March, 1960 South African police opened fire on unarmed anti-apartheid protestors in Sharpeville, killing 69 civilians—most of whom were shot in the back as they ran away from the police. The government declared a State of Emergency and banned the ANC and other opposition minority groups. Nelson Mandela responded to the banning of the ANC by forming the underground Umkhonto we Sizwe ('Spear of the Nation' or 'MK') movement whose policy was to target and destroy government utilities and symbols of apartheid—but not people. In 1961 Mandela 'illegally' escaped the country and studied guerrilla warfare in Africa and Europe. Returning from overseas after a year on the run, Mandela was arrested by South African security police and sentenced to five years jail on Robben Island. In 1964 the government brought further charges including sabotage, high treason and conspiracy to overthrow the government against him.

Although Nelson Mandela and the other accused escaped execution they were sentenced to life imprisonment. At Robben Island Prison, Mandela was confined to a small cell without a bed or plumbing and was forced to do hard labour in a quarry. He could write and receive a letter every six months and was allowed to meet with a visitor for thirty minutes once every year. In the late 1960s his mother and eldest son were killed in separate car accidents but Mandela was not allowed to attend either funeral. But even when confined to prison, Mandela led a protest of civil disobedience at Robben Island that effectively forced the South African government to improve prison conditions.

During the 1970s and 1980s Mandela became the symbolic leader of an international movement (led by exiled colleague Oliver Tambo) to end apartheid in South Africa. In the last nine years of his sentence, after contracting tuberculosis, Mandela was moved to Pollsmoor Prison where he effectively lived under house arrest whilst the Botha government negotiated with him. In 1989 F W de Klerk became South African president and bowing to political, social and economic pressures, immediately instigated a program to end apartheid. International sanctions had cost the country $4 billion between 1988 and 1990 and de Klerk knew that the apartheid goal of congregating blacks into separate homelands was impossible to maintain. The South African president lifted the ban on the ANC, suspended executions and released most of the prisoners from the Rivonia Trial in 1964.

Finally, in February 1990, de Klerk ordered Mandela's release. Nelson delivered this speech to acknowledge the litany of people who had been involved in the struggle to end apartheid.

‘ Friends, comrades and fellow South Africans.

I greet you all in the name of peace, democracy and freedom for all.

I stand here before you not as a prophet but as a humble servant of you, the people. Your tireless and heroic sacrifices have made it possible for me to be here today. I therefore place the remaining years of my life in your hands.

On this day of my release, I extend my sincere and warmest gratitude to the millions of my compatriots and those in every corner of the globe who have campaigned tirelessly for my release.

I send special greetings to the people of Cape Town, this city which has been my home for three decades. Your mass marches and other forms of struggle have served as a constant source of strength to all political prisoners.

I salute the African National Congress. It has fulfilled our every expectation in its role as leader of the great march to freedom. I salute our President, Comrade Oliver Tambo, for leading the ANC even under the most difficult circumstances.

I salute the rank and file members of the ANC. You have sacrificed life and limb in the pursuit of the noble cause of our struggle.

I salute combatants of Umkhonto we Sizwe, like Solomon Mahlangu and Ashley Kriel who have paid the ultimate price for the freedom of all South Africans.

I salute the South African Communist Party for its sterling contribution to the struggle for democracy. You have survived 40 years of unrelenting persecution. The memory of great communists like Moses Kotane, Yusuf Dadoo, Bram Fischer and Moses Mabhida will be cherished for generations to come.

I salute General Secretary Joe Slovo, one of our finest patriots. We are heartened by the fact that the alliance between ourselves and the Party remains as strong as it always was.

I salute the United Democratic Front, the National Education Crisis Committee, the South African Youth Congress, the Transvaal and Natal Indian Congresses and COSATU and the many other formations of the Mass Democratic Movement.

I also salute the Black Sash and the National Union of South African Students. We note with pride that you have acted as the conscience of white South Africa. Even during the darkest days in the history of our struggle you held the flag of liberty high. The large-scale mass mobilisation of the past few years is one of the key factors which led to the opening of the final chapter of our struggle.

I extend my greetings to the working class of our country. Your organised strength is the pride of our movement. You remain the most dependable force in the struggle to end exploitation and oppression.

I pay tribute to the many religious communities who carried the campaign for justice forward when the organisations for our people were silenced.

I greet the traditional leaders of our country—many of you continue to walk in the footsteps of great heroes like Hintsa and Sekhukune.

I pay tribute to the endless heroism of youth, you, the young lions. You, the young lions, have energised our entire struggle. I pay tribute to the mothers and wives and sisters of our nation. You are the rock-hard foundation of our struggle. Apartheid has inflicted more pain on you than on anyone else.

On this occasion, we thank the world community for their great contribution to the anti-apartheid struggle. Without your support our struggle would not have reached this advanced stage. The sacrifice of the frontline states will be remembered by South Africans forever.

My salutations would be incomplete without expressing my deep appreciation for the strength given to me during my long and lonely years in prison by my beloved wife and family. I am convinced that your pain and suffering was far greater than my own.

Before I go any further I wish to make the point that I intend making only a few preliminary comments at this stage. I will make a more complete statement only after I have had the opportunity to consult with my comrades.

Today the majority of South Africans, black and white, recognise that apartheid has no future. It has to be ended by our own decisive mass action in order to build peace and security. The mass campaign of defiance and other actions of our organisation and people can only culminate in the establishment of democracy. The destruction caused by apartheid on our sub-continent is incalculable. The fabric of family life of millions of my people has been shattered. Millions are homeless and unemployed. Our economy lies in ruins and our people are embroiled in political strife. Our resort to the armed struggle in 1960 with the formation of the military wing of the ANC, Umkhonto we Sizwe, was a purely defensive action against the violence of apartheid. The factors which necessitated the armed struggle still exist today. We have no option but to continue. We express the hope that a climate conducive to a negotiated settlement will be created soon so that there may no longer be the need for the armed struggle. I am a loyal and disciplined member of the African National Congress. I am therefore in full agreement with all of its objectives, strategies and tactics. The need to unite the people of our country is as important a task now as it always has been. No individual leader is able to take on this enormous task on his own. It is our task as leaders to place our views before our organisation and to allow the democratic structures to decide. On the question of democratic practice, I feel duty bound to make the point that a leader of the movement is a person who has been democratically elected at a national conference. This is a principle which must be upheld without any exceptions.

Today, I wish to report to you that my talks with the government have been aimed at normalising the political situation in the country. We have not as yet begun discussing the basic demands of the struggle. I wish to stress that I myself have at no time entered into negotiations about the future of our country except to insist on a meeting between the ANC and the government. Mr. De Klerk has gone further than any other Nationalist president in taking real steps to normalise the situation. However, there are further steps as outlined in the Harare Declaration that have to be met before negotiations on the basic demands of our people can begin. I reiterate our call for—inter alia—the immediate ending of the State of Emergency and the freeing of all, and not only some, political prisoners. Only such a normalised situation, which allows for free political activity, can allow us to consult our people in order to obtain a mandate. The people need to be consulted on who will negotiate and on the content of such negotiations. Negotiations cannot take place above the heads or behind the backs of our people. It is our belief that the future of our country can only be determined by a body which is democratically elected on a non-racial basis. Negotiations on the dismantling of apartheid will have to address the overwhelming demand of our people for a democratic, non-racial and unitary South Africa. There must be an end to white monopoly on political power and a fundamental restructuring of our political and economic systems to ensure that the inequalities of apartheid are addressed and our society thoroughly democratised.

It must be added that Mr. De Klerk himself is a man of integrity who is acutely aware of the dangers of a public figure not honouring his undertakings. But as an organisation we base our policy and strategy on the harsh reality we are faced with. And this reality is that we are still suffering under the policy of the Nationalist government.

Our struggle has reached a decisive moment. We call on our people to seize this moment so that the process towards democracy is rapid and uninterrupted. We have waited too long for our freedom. We can no longer wait. Now is the time to intensify the struggle on all fronts. To relax our efforts now would be a mistake which generations to come will not be able to forgive. The sight of freedom looming on the horizon should encourage us to redouble our efforts.

It is only through disciplined mass action that our victory can be assured. We call on our white compatriots to join us in the shaping of a new South Africa. The freedom movement is a political home for you too. We call on the international community to continue the campaign to isolate the apartheid regime. To lift sanctions now would be to run the risk of aborting the process towards the complete eradication of apartheid.

Our march to freedom is irreversible. We must not allow fear to stand in our way. Universal suffrage on a common voters' role in a united democratic and non-racial South Africa is the only way to peace and racial harmony.

In conclusion I wish to quote my own words during my trial in 1964. They are true today as they were then:

"I have fought against white domination and I have fought against black domination. I have cherished the ideal of a democratic and free society in which all persons live together in harmony and with equal opportunities. It is an ideal which I hope to live for and to achieve. But if needs be, it is an ideal for which I am prepared to die." '

After his release from prison in 1990, Nelson Mandela led the ANC in its negotiations with the minority National Party government to bring an end to apartheid, the armed struggle in the Natal province and to establish a multiracial government. But the battle was not won without bloodshed. The ANC adopted a policy of a 'rolling mass action' of protests and strikes to show the government that people supported an end to violence. In September 1992 Mandela and de Klerk signed the 'Record of Understanding' which promised to investigate the role of the police in propagating violence and established an elected constitutional assembly to develop a new South African constitution. The following year Mandela and the South African President were jointly awarded the Nobel Peace Prize for their efforts.

Nelson Mandela's achievement in leading his country to freedom did not come without personal sacrifice—even after his release. In 1992 he separated from his wife Winnie after she was convicted of kidnapping and being an accessory to assault by men acting as her bodyguards in the murder of 13-year-old Stompie Seipei. Mandela married Graca Machel, the widow of the former president of Mozambique, in 1998, a year before he retired to private life.

In 1994 the ANC won 252 of the 400 seats in the country's first free elections with Nelson Mandela elected South African President on 10 May 1994. Mandela was President for five years, and was succeeded by his deputy Thabo Mbeki in June 1999. He continued his activism and philanthropy before 'retiring from retirement' to spend his final years with his third wife Graça Machel. He died in December 2013, aged 95.

For Mandela, the 'walk to freedom' had taken an entire lifetime.

Hillary Clinton

'On Women's Rights'

UN World Conference on Women, Beijing, China, 5 September 1995

O n the inauguration of husband Bill Clinton to the US Presidency in 1993, Hillary Rodham Clinton (b. 1948) became equally well-known as America's First Lady.

Hillary Rodham had previously worked for the Children's Defense Fund and was a member of a House of Representatives Committee preparing to impeach President Nixon in 1974. She joined Bill Clinton on the faculty of the University of Arkansas Law School and the pair married in 1976.

Politically savvy, with a strong sense of justice and morality, Hillary Rodham Clinton was at her husband's side in 1991 when the Democratic nominee for the US presidency confirmed to *60 Minutes* that his dalliances with other women had 'caused pain' in their marriage. Her steadfast belief in her husband was crucial to Clinton's subsequent success and she became one of his most important advisers during his presidency—to the point of taking an office in the West Wing of the White House.

In September 1995, during the first term of her husband's presidency (1993-2001), Hillary Clinton was invited to address the Fourth Annual United Nations Conference on Women, which was held in Beijing, China.

The following speech drew widespread applause from the delegates of 180 countries for its confronting and remarkably frank addressing of issues, but also took on a special resonance because it was delivered in China, where many violations of human rights against women still occur.

❝This is truly a celebration—a celebration of the contributions women make in every aspect of life: in the home, on the job, in their communities, as mothers, wives, sisters, daughters, learners, workers, citizens and leaders.

It is also a coming together, much the way women come together every day in every country. We come together in fields and in factories. In village markets and supermarkets. In living rooms and board rooms.

Whether it is while playing with our children in the park, or washing clothes in a river, or taking a break at the office water cooler, we come together and talk about our aspirations and concerns. And time and again, our talk turns to our children and our families.

However different we may be, there is far more that unites us than divides us. We share a common future. And we are here to find common ground so that we may help bring new dignity and respect to women and girls all over the world—and in so doing, bring new strength and stability to families as well.

By gathering in Beijing, we are focusing world attention on issues that matter most in the lives of women and their families: access to education, health care, jobs, and credit, the chance to enjoy basic legal and human rights and participate fully in the political life of their countries.

There are some who question the reason for this conference. Let them listen to the voices of women in their homes, neighborhoods and workplaces.

There are some who wonder whether the lives of women and girls matter to economic and political progress around the globe. Let them look at the women gathered here and at Huairou—the homemakers, nurses, teachers, lawyers, policy makers and women who run their own businesses.

It is conferences like this that compel governments and peoples everywhere to listen, look and face the world's most pressing problems.

Wasn't it after the women's conference in Nairobi ten years ago that the world focused for the first time on the crisis of domestic violence?

Earlier today, I participated in a World Health Organization forum, where government officials, NGOs and individual citizens are working on ways to address the health problems of women and girls.

Tomorrow, I will attend a gathering of the United Nations Development Fund for Women. There, the discussion will focus on local—and highly successful—programs that give hard-working women access to credit so they can improve their lives and the lives of their families.

What we are learning around the world is that if women are healthy and educated, their families will flourish. If women are free from violence, their families will flourish. If women have a chance to work and earn as full and equal partners in society, their families will flourish.

And when families flourish, communities and nations will flourish.

That is why every woman, every man, every child, every family and every nation on our planet has a stake in the discussion that takes place here.

Over the past 25 years, I have worked persistently on issues relating to women, children and families. Over the past two and a half years, I have had the opportunity to learn more about the challenges facing women in my country and around the world. I have met new mothers in Jogjakarta, Indonesia, who come together regularly in their village to discuss nutrition, family planning and baby care. I have met working parents in Denmark who talk about the comfort they feel in knowing that their children can be cared for in creative, safe and nurturing after-school centers. I have met women in South Africa who helped lead the struggle to end apartheid and are now helping build a new democracy. I have met with the leading women of the western hemisphere who are working every day to promote literacy and better health care for the children of their countries. I have met women in India and Bangladesh who are taking out small loans to buy milk cows, rickshaws, thread and other materials to create a livelihood for themselves and their families. I have met doctors and nurses in Belarus and Ukraine who are trying to keep children alive in the aftermath of Chernobyl.

The great challenge of this conference is to give voice to women everywhere whose experiences go unnoticed, whose words go unheard.

Women comprise more than half the world's population. Women are 70 per cent of the world's poor and two-thirds of those who are not taught to read and write. Women are the primary caretakers for most of the world's children and elderly. Yet much of the work we do is not valued—not by economists, not by historians, not by popular culture and not by government leaders.

At this very moment, as we sit here, women around the world are giving birth, raising children, cooking meals, washing clothes, cleaning houses, planting crops, working on assembly lines, running companies and running countries.

Women are also dying from diseases that should have been prevented or treated. They are watching their children succumb to malnutrition caused by poverty and economic deprivation. They are being denied the right to go to school by their own fathers and brothers. They are being forced into prostitution and they are being barred from the ballot box and the bank lending office.

Those of us with the opportunity to be here have the responsibility to speak for those who could not.

As an American, I want to speak up for women in my own country—women who are raising children on the minimum wage, women who can't afford health care or child care, women whose lives are threatened by violence, including violence in their own homes.

I want to speak up for mothers who are fighting for good schools, safe neighborhoods, clean air and clean airwaves; for older women, some of them widows, who have raised their families and now find that their skills and life experiences are not valued in the workplace; for women who are working all night as nurses, hotel clerks and fast food chefs so that they can be at home during the day with their kids; and for women everywhere who simply don't have enough time to do everything they are called upon to do each day.

Speaking to you today, I speak for them, just as each of us speaks for women around the world who are denied the chance to go to school, or see a doctor, or own property, or have a say about the direction of their lives, simply because they are women.

The truth is that most women around the world work both inside and outside the home, usually by necessity.

We need to understand that there is no formula for how women should lead their lives. That is why we must respect the choices that each woman makes for herself and her family. Every woman deserves the chance to realize her God-given potential. We must also recognize that women will never gain full dignity until their human rights are respected and protected.

Our goals for this conference, to strengthen families and societies by empowering women to take greater control over their own destinies, cannot be fully achieved unless all governments—here and around the world—accept their responsibility to protect and promote internationally recognized human rights.

The international community has long acknowledged, and recently affirmed at Vienna, that both women and men are entitled to a range of protections and personal freedoms, from the right of personal security to the right to determine freely the number and spacing of the children they bear.

No one should be forced to remain silent for fear of religious or political persecution, arrest, abuse or torture.

Tragically, women are most often the ones whose human rights are violated. Even in the late twentieth century, the rape of women continues to be used as an instrument of armed conflict. Women and children make up a large majority of the world's refugees. And when women are excluded from the political process, they become even more vulnerable to abuse.

I believe that, on the eve of a new millennium, it is time to break our silence. It is time for us to say here in Beijing, and for the world to hear, that it is no longer acceptable to discuss women's rights as separate from human rights. These abuses have continued because, for too long, the history of women has been a history of silence.

Even today, there are those who are trying to silence our words. The voices of this conference and of the women at Huairou must be heard loud and clear.

It is a violation of human rights when babies are denied food, or drowned, or suffocated, or their spines broken, simply because they are girls.

It is a violation of human rights when women and girls are sold into the slavery of prostitution.

It is a violation of human rights when women are doused with gasoline, set on fire and burned to death because their marriage dowries are deemed too small.

It is a violation of human rights when individual women are raped in their own communities and when thousands of women are subjected to rape as a tactic or prize of war. It is a violation of human rights when a leading cause of death worldwide among women aged fourteen to 44 is the violence they are subjected to in their own homes.

It is a violation of human rights when young girls are brutalized by the painful and degrading practice of genital mutilation.

It is a violation of human rights when women are denied the right to plan their own families and that includes being forced to have abortions or being sterilized against their will.

If there is one message that echoes forth from this conference, it is that human rights are women's rights, and women's rights are human rights. Let us not forget that among those rights are the right to speak freely and the right to be heard.

Women must enjoy the right to participate fully in the social and political lives of their countries if we want freedom and democracy to thrive and endure.

It is indefensible that many women in non-governmental organizations who wished to participate in this conference have not been able to attend—or have been prohibited from fully taking part.

Let me be clear. Freedom means the right of people to assemble, organize and debate openly. It means respecting the views of those who may disagree with the views of their governments. It means not taking citizens away from their loved ones and jailing them, mistreating them, or denying them their freedom or dignity because of the peaceful expression of their ideas and opinions.

In my country, we recently celebrated the 75th anniversary of women's suffrage. It took 150 years after the signing of our Declaration of Independence for women to win the right to vote. It took 72 years of organized struggle on the part of many courageous women and men. It was one of America's most divisive philosophical wars. But it was also a bloodless war. Suffrage was achieved without a shot fired.

We have also have been reminded, in VJ Day observances last weekend, of the good that comes when men and women join together to combat the forces of tyranny and build a better world.

We have seen peace prevail in most places for a half century. We have avoided another world war. But we have not solved older, deeply rooted problems that continue to diminish the potential of half the world's population.

Now it is time to act on behalf of women everywhere.

If we take bold steps to better the lives of women, we will be taking bold steps to better the lives of children and families too. Families rely on mothers and wives for emotional support and care; families rely on women for labor in the home; and increasingly, families rely on women for income needed to raise healthy children and care for other relatives. As long as discrimination and inequities remain so commonplace around the world—as long as girls and women are valued less, fed less, fed last, overworked, underpaid, not schooled and subjected to violence in and out of their homes—the potential of the human family to create a peaceful, prosperous world will not be realized.

Let this conference be ours, and the world's call to action.

And let us heed the call so that we can create a world in which every woman is treated with respect and dignity, every boy and girl is loved and cared for equally and every family has the hope of a strong and stable future.

Thank you very much. ❜

The Clintons' eight years in the White House were controversial, productive and ultimately shook their marriage to its very foundation.

Hillary Rodham Clinton's sponsorship of a scheme to reform health care was a spectacular failure when brought before Congress in 1993, but her support of her husband as the Lewinsky Affair destroyed the last year of his presidency, portrayed her as strong, loyal and forgiving.

In 2000, she was elected Democratic Senator for New York but despite a tenacious struggle to the very end, she faltered in her bid to be the first woman to sit in the White House when beaten by Barack Obama in the race for the Democratic nomination in 2008.

Newly-elected US President Obama offered Clinton the key position of Secretary of State in his administration. Clinton left the post in 2013 after four years, with many predicting she would steel herself for a bid for the Democratic Presidential nomination in 2016. After declaring her candidacy in April 2015, she eventually secured the nomination after a close contest with Bernie Sanders.

Fascing a conflicted Republican Party whose candidate, billionaire Donald Trump, continues to divide the nation Hillary Rodham Clinton is poised to become the first female US President in history.

Earl Spencer

'Eulogy for Diana, Princess of Wales'

Westminster Abbey, London, 9 September 1997.

The tragic death of Princess Diana in a car accident in Paris in 1997 created an unprecedented outpouring of emotion in England and around the world.

Lady Diana Frances Spencer was born in Norfolk, England on 1 July, 1961, the third child of Earl Spencer and his first wife. On 29 July, 1981, shortly after her 20th birthday and in a frenzied atmosphere of world-wide media scrutiny, Diana married Charles, the Prince of Wales and heir to the British throne. Diana bore two sons, Princes William (b.1982) and Henry 'Harry' (b.1984) and threw her considerable position and newfound celebrity behind several charitable causes—notably children, the homeless, AIDS sufferers and a Red Cross campaign to ban land mines world-wide.

But her marriage to Prince Charles was doomed—a mismatch from the start—and the pair grew increasingly alienated before announcing their separation in 1992 and eventual divorce four years later. Diana kept her title, the Princess of Wales, and continued her charitable works. But her public comments on the failings of her marriage and her relationship with the Royal Family only increased media interest in her personal life. Hounded by Europe's voracious 'paparazzi' she was killed in a car accident on the night of 31 August, 1997, along with boyfriend Dodi Fayed, as their driver sped away from a media pack in Paris.

Diana's tragic death shocked the Royal Family into making a formal announcement of regret, which the Queen delivered at 6:00pm from Buckingham Palace on Friday, 5 September. Four days later, Diana's coffin was borne in procession from Kensington Palace to Westminster Abbey with her brother, Earl Spencer, Prince William, Prince Harry, The Prince of Wales and The Duke of Edinburgh walking behind.

At the funeral at Westminster Abbey, her brother—the ninth Earl Spencer—delivered a moving eulogy.

'I stand before you today, the representative of a family in grief, in a country in mourning, before a world in shock.

We are all united, not only in our desire to pay our respects to Diana, but rather in our need to do so, because such was her extraordinary appeal that the tens of millions of people taking part in this service all over the world via television and radio who never actually met her feel that they too lost someone close to them in the early hours of Sunday morning.

It is a more remarkable tribute to Diana then I can ever hope to offer to her today.

Diana was the very essence of compassion, of duty, of style, of beauty.

All over the world she was the symbol of selfless humanity. A standard bearer for the rights of the truly downtrodden. A very British girl who transcended nationality. Someone with a natural nobility who was classless and who proved in the last year that she needed no royal title to continue to generate her particular brand of magic.

Today is our chance to say 'thank you' for the way you brightened our lives, even though God granted you but half a life. We will all feel cheated always that you were taken from us so young and yet we must learn to be grateful that you came at all.

Only now you are gone do we truly appreciate what we are without, and we want you to know that life without you is very, very difficult.

We have all despaired for our loss over the past week and only the strength of the message you gave us through your years of giving has afforded us the strength to move forward.

There is a temptation to rush, to canonize your memory. There is no need to do so. You stand tall enough as a human being of unique qualities, and do not need to be seen as a saint.

Indeed, to sanctify your memory would be to miss out on the very core of your being— your wonderfully mischievous sense of humour with a laugh that bent you double, your joy for life transmitted wherever you took your smile and the sparkle in those unforgettable eyes, your boundless energy which you could barely contain.

But your greatest gift was your intuition and it was a gift you used wisely. This is what under pinned all your other wonderful attributes.

And if we look to analyse what it was about you that had such a wide appeal we find it in your instinctive feel for what was really important in all our lives.

Without your God-given sensitivity, we would be immersed in greater ignorance at the anguish of AIDS and HIV sufferers, the plight of the homeless, the isolation of lepers, the random destruction of land mines.

Diana explained to me once that it was her innermost feelings of suffering that made it possible for her to connect with her constituency of the rejected.

And here we come to another truth about her. For all the status, the glamour, the applause, Diana remained throughout a very insecure person at heart, almost childlike in her desire to do good for others so she could release herself from deep feelings of unworthiness of which her eating disorders were merely a symptom.

The world sensed this part of her character and cherished her vulnerability.

The last time I saw Diana was on July 1st, her birthday, in London when typically she was not taking time to celebrate her special day with friends but was guest of honour at a fund-raising charity evening. She sparkled, of course.

But I would rather cherish the days I spent with her in March when she came to visit me and my children at our home in South Africa. I am proud of the fact that, apart from when she was on public display meeting President Mandela, we managed to contrive to stop the ever-present paparazzi from getting a single picture of her. That meant a lot to her.

These are days I will always treasure. It was as if we were transported back to our childhood when we spent such an enormous amount of time together as the two youngest in the family.

Fundamentally she hadn't changed at all from the big sister who mothered me as a baby, fought with me at school, who endured those long journeys between our parents' home with me at weekends.

It is a tribute to her level-headedness and strength that despite the most bizarre life after her childhood, she remained intact, true to herself.

There is no doubt she was looking for a new direction in her life at this time.

She talked endlessly of getting away from England, mainly because of the treatment that she received at the hands of the newspapers.

I don't think she ever understood why her genuinely good intentions were sneered at by the media, why there appeared to be a permanent quest on their behalf to bring her down. It is baffling.

My own and only explanation is that genuine goodness is threatening to those at the opposite end of the moral spectrum.

It is a point to remember that of all the ironies about Diana, perhaps the greatest was this: a girl given the name of the ancient goddess of hunting was, in the end, the most hunted person of the modern age.

She would want us today to pledge ourselves to protecting her beloved boys, William and Harry, from a similar fate, and I do this here, Diana, on your behalf.

We will not allow them to suffer the anguish that used regularly to drive you to tearful despair. And beyond that, on behalf of your mother and sisters, I pledge that we, your blood family, will do all we can to continue the imaginative and loving way in which you were steering these two exceptional young men so that their souls are not simply immersed by duty and tradition but can sing openly as you planned.

We fully respect the heritage into which they have both been born and will always respect and encourage them in their royal role. But we, like you, recognize the need for them to experience as many different aspects of life as possible to arm them spiritually and emotionally for the years ahead. I know you would have expected nothing less from us.

William and Harry, we all care desperately for you today. We are all chewed up with sadness at the loss of a woman who wasn't even our mother. How great your suffering is we cannot even imagine.

I would like to end by thanking God for the small mercies he has shown us at this dreadful time, for taking Diana at her most beautiful and radiant and when she had joy in her private life.

Above all, we give thanks for the life of a woman I'm so proud to be able to call my sister the unique, the complex, the extraordinary and irreplaceable Diana whose beauty, both internal and external, will never be extinguished from our minds. '

As Earl Spencer spoke, a spontaneous wave of applause from the thousands of

mourners outside the Abbey swept over the congregation inside. While many applauded his condemnation of the role the media played in his sister's death and agreed with his stinging criticism of the conditions that had allowed Diana's life to be so publicly exposed, just as many thought the eulogy ungracious to the Royal Family.

That afternoon Diana's body was interred on the Spencer family home, Althorp, in Northamptonshire on a landscaped island known as 'The Oval'. Diana, the 'Princess of Hearts', was finally at rest away from the prying eyes of the public.

Aung San Suu Kyi

'Freedom of Thought'
American University, Washington DC, 26 January 1997

A ung San Suu Kyi was born in Burma on January 1945, the daughter of national hero, General Aung San, who founded the modern Burmese Army which liberated the country from Japanese occupation during World War II. When Aung was two years old, her father, who headed the shadow Burmese government under British rule, was assassinated by a political rival. Her mother, Khin Kyi, was later appointed Burmese ambassador to India. Aung studied politics at New Delhi University and later gained her BA at St Hugh's College, Oxford.

In 1962, democratic rule in Burma ended with a military coup headed by General Ne Win. For the next 26 years, the military enforced the 'Burmese Way to Socialism' which led to the establishment of one party rule under the Burma Socialist Programme Party (BSPP) in 1974.

In 1988, Aung San Suu Kyi, who had married British scholar Michael Aris and had given birth to two sons, returned to Burma to care for her ailing mother. This coincided with a bloody military response to peaceful student demonstrations against one party rule and the resignation of General Ne Win as head of the BSPP.

On 26 August, in Rangoon, Aung San Suu Kyi stood under a large poster of her slain father and addressed a large gathering of democratic supporters and proposed the establishment of a People's Consultative Committee to help resolve the crisis.

In October, the democratic movement was brutally crushed by another military coup headed by General Saw Maung and Burma's second struggle for independence began.

Although she had lived overseas for most of her life, Aung San Suu Kyi could not 'remain indifferent' to Burma's struggle. She became the leader of the National League of Democracy and was first placed under house arrest in Rangoon in July 1989.

Under martial law, this meant that she could be detained for three years without trial. Her husband and sons visited her for what would be the last time as a family in September 1989. The following year, the military government attempted to cut her contact with the outside world.

Separated from her family and denied her personal liberty and freedom of speech, Aung continued to speak out against Burma's military rule—a stance which saw her win the 1990 Sakharov Prize for Freedom of Thought (awarded by the European Parliament), the 1991 Nobel Peace Prize and the 1992 Nehru Peace Prize.

Although she was released from house detention in 1995 and was briefly reunited with her husband, she refused to leave Burma because she knew she would not have been allowed to re-enter her own country. As a result, all of Aung San Suu Kyi's most famous speeches have been delivered by third parties, by video or in essay form.

The commencement address at the American University, Washington DC, on 26 January, 1997, was delivered on her behalf by her husband, Dr. Michael Aris, upon her receiving an Honorary Doctor of Laws degree.

❛It is an honour to receive an honorary Doctor of Laws degree from a university known for its liberal values and international outlook. It is a privilege to deliver the commencement speech at this assembly. However, what would have been the greatest joy, that of seeing the faces of the graduating students, has been denied to me. There is little that can compare with the light of hope and anticipation that shines from those who have satisfactorily completed one phase of their lives and are about to embark on another more complete, more challenging phase.

No educational institutional can fully prepare its pupils to cope with all that they will have to face during the course of their lives. However, such values as intellectual freedom, humanitarian ideals and public service, fostered by the American University, should go a long way towards equipping young men and young women to make the best of any environment in which they may find themselves.

Beginning a new life is a challenge that will put to the test our mental, intellectual, emotional and spiritual resources. Some are destined to lead tranquil lives, safe in the security of a society that guarantees fundamental rights. Others may find themselves in situations where they have to strive incessantly for the most basic of rights, the right to life itself.

It is no simple matter to decide who are the more fortunate, those to whom life gives all or those who have to give all to life. A fulfilled life is not necessarily one constructed strictly in accordance with one's own blueprint, it can be a glorious collage of materials that have come unexpectedly to hand.

How wonderful it is that we do not know what tomorrow will bring. Of course we all hope that our tomorrow will be happy. But happiness takes on many forms. Political prisoners have known the most sublime moments of perfect communion with their highest ideals during periods when they were incarcerated in isolation, cut off from contact with all that was familiar and dear to them. From where do those resources spring, if not from an innate strength at our core, a spiritual strength that transcends material bounds? My colleagues who spent years in the harsh conditions of Burmese prisons, and I myself, have had to draw on such inner resources on many occasions.

Nobody can take away from us the essential and ultimate freedom of choosing our priorities in life.

We may not be able to control the external factors that affect our existence, but we can decide how we wish to conduct our inner lives. We may live in a society that does not grant freedom of expression, but we can decide how much value we wish to put on the duty to speak out for our rights. We may not be able to pursue our beliefs without bringing down on us the full vengeance of a cruel state mechanism, but we can decide how much we are prepared to sacrifice for our beliefs.

Those of us who decided to work for democracy in Burma made our choice in the conviction that the danger of standing up for basic human rights in a repressive society was preferable to the safety of a quiescent life in servitude. Ours is a non-violent movement that depends on faith in the human predilection for fair play and compassion. Some would insist that man is primarily an economic animal interested only in his material well being. This is too narrow a view of a species which has produced numberless brave men and women who are prepared to undergo relentless persecution for the sake of upholding deeply held beliefs and principles. It is my pride and inspiration that such men and women exist in my country today.

In Burma, it is accepted as a political tradition that revolutionary changes are brought about through the active participation of students. The independence movement of our country was carried out to a successful conclusion by young leaders, including my own father, General Aung San, who began their political careers at Rangoon University. An institution with such an outstanding reputation for spirited opposition to established authority is naturally a prime target for any authoritarian government. The military regime which assumed state power in 1962 blasted the Rangoon University Students' Union building out of existence within a few months of their rule and made it illegal for students to form a union.

In 1988, the people of Burma rose up against the rule of the Burma Socialist Programme Party, the civilian cloak of a military dictatorship. At the vanguard of the nationwide demonstrations were students who demanded, among other basic rights, the right to form a union. The response of the military junta was to shoot them down. More than eight years and much repression on, the students of Burma have still not relinquished their quest for an association which would promote their interests and articulate their aspirations and grievances.

As recently as last month, there were student demonstrations where the call for the right to form a union was reiterated. The security forces used violence to disperse the demonstrators and a number of young people from my party, the National League for Democracy, were arrested on the grounds that they had been involved in the organization of the demonstrations. I was accused of having held meetings with students and holding discussion with them. Things have indeed come to a sorry pass in a country if meetings between politicians and students are seen as acts of subversion.

My party has never made a secret of our sympathy for the aspirations of students. We work to forge close links between the different generations that a continuity of purpose and endeavour might be threaded into the fabric of our nation.

When we are struggling against overwhelming odds, when we are pitting ourselves against the combined might of the state apparatus and military power, we are sometimes subject to doubts, usually the doubts of those whose belief in the permanence of an existing order is absolute. It is amazing how many people still remain convinced that it is only wisdom to accept the status quo. We have faith in the power to change what needs to be changed, but we are under no illusion that the transition from dictatorship to liberal democracy will be easy, or that democratic government will mean the end of all our problems. We know that our greatest challenges lie ahead of us and that our struggle to establish a stable, democratic society will continue beyond our own lifespan. We are aware that much will be demanded of us and that there will be times when we are discouraged and disappointed. But we know that we are not alone.

The cause of liberty and justice finds sympathetic responses in far reaches of the globe. Thinking and feeling people everywhere, regardless of colour or creed, understand the deeply rooted human need for a meaningful existence that goes beyond the mere gratification of material desires. Those fortunate enough to live in societies where they are entitled to full political rights can reach out to help their less fortunate brethren in other parts of our troubled planet. Young women and young men setting forth to leave their mark on the world might wish to cast their eyes beyond their own frontiers towards the shadowlands of lost rights. You who are gathered here to celebrate the opening of the doors of hope and opportunity might wish to assist our fight for a Burma where young people can know the joys of hope and opportunity.

Part of our struggle is to make the international community understand that we are a poor country, not because there is an insufficiency of resources and investment, but because we are deprived of the basic institutions and practices that make for good government. There are multinational business concerns which have no inhibitions about dealing with repressive regimes. Their justification for economic involvement in Burma is that their presence will actually assist the process of democratization.

Investment that only goes to enrich an already wealthy elite bent on monopolizing both economic and political power cannot contribute towards legality and justice, the foundation stones for a sound democracy. I would therefore like to call upon those who have an interest in expanding their capacity for promoting intellectual freedom and humanitarian ideals to take a principled stand against companies which are doing business with the military regime of Burma. Please use your liberty to promote ours.

This honorary degree that you have conferred on me today constitutes a recognition of our struggle. I would like to conclude by expressing my sincere thanks to the American University and its Board of Trustees for thus supporting the cause of democracy and human rights in Burma.

Thank you. '

Although Michael Aris was stricken with prostate cancer, the Burmese government (which was renamed the Union of Myanmar by the military government in 1989) would not allow him to visit his wife.

When he passed away in 1999, Aung San Suu Kyi regarded the separation as 'one of the sacrifices she had had to make in order to work for a free Burma.' Aung was placed under house arrest again in September 2000, but although she was freed after nineteen months, she was later held in 'secret detention' for three months before being returned to house arrest.

In 2007, it was anticipated that protests from Buddhist monks in Burma and growing international pressure would lead to her release after twelve years, but despite solidarity protests held in twelve cities around the world, Aung remains still under house arrest.

Aung is often called 'Daw' Aung San Suu Kyi in her homeland, which is a maternal title of affection meaning a favourite aunt.

Boris Yeltsin

'Yekaterinburg Apology'

St Petersburg, Russia, 17 July 1998

oris Yeltsin (1931–2007) was an abrasive, erratic and unpredictable Russian President—he famously suspended parliament in 1993, sacked two prime ministers and two premiers in 18 months and fired his entire cabinet in 1999.

Boris Nikolayevich Yeltsin was born in Yekaterinburg, Ukraine, in 1931. After joining the Communist Party of the Soviet Union in 1961, he was inducted into the Central Committee of the party by newly-elected general secretary Mikhail Gorbachev in 1985.

Yeltsin served as Moscow Party Chief in 1985 and was a member of the party Politburo before being replaced for criticising the slow rate of change. He was the first popularly elected President of the Russian Federation in 1990, at a time when the Soviet Union was crumbling.

After the dissolution of the Soviet Union in 1991, he was regarded as a hero and saviour in Russia, but a buffoon and a liability internationally.

However, there were signs of a great man trying to escape mounting health problems and an alcoholic haze. Yeltsin had become a national hero in August 1991 when he led a people's protest against a coup and mobilised the Russian army to surround public buildings resulting in the surrender of the plotters.

After the break-up of the Soviet Union in 1991, Yeltsin remained Russian President and following his re-election in 1994, continued to press for reform.

In 1998, Yeltsin made an impassioned speech in the cathedral of Peter and Paul at Yekaterinburg—the place of his birth—acknowledging the previously unspoken fate of Tsar Nicholas II, his wife Alexandria and their five children. DNA and forensic technology had only recently confirmed to the world the shameful secret—covered up by the Soviet Union for decades—of the execution of the Russian Royal Family there by Red Army soldiers on 17 July 1918.

On the eightieth anniversary of their death, a noticeably ill President Yeltsin addressed millions of Russians—and the world media—and officially apologised for the atrocity via this televised speech.

‘It's an historic day for Russia. Eighty years have passed since the slaying of the last Russian emperor and his family. We have long been silent about this monstrous crime. We must say the truth: The Yekaterinburg massacre has become one of the most shameful pages of our history.

By burying the remains of innocent victims we want to expiate the sins of our ancestors. Guilty are those who committed this heinous crime and those who have been justifying it for decades—all of us.

We must not lie to ourselves, explaining this senseless cruelty with political goals. The execution of the Romanov family was the result of an irreconcilable split in Russian society. Its results are felt to this day. The burial of the victims' remains is an act of human justice, an expiation of common guilt.

We all bear responsibility for the historical memory of the nation; and that's why I could not fail to come here. I must be here as both an individual and the President.

I bow my head before the victims of the merciless slaving.

While building a new Russia we must rely on its historical experience. Many glorious pages of our history are linked with the Romanovs. But also connected with their name is one of the most bitter lessons—that attempts to change life by violence are doomed.

We must finish this century, which has become the century of blood and lawlessness for Russia, with repentance and reconciliation irrespective of political and religious views and ethnic origin. This is our historic chance. On the eve of the third millennium, we must do it for the sake of our generation and those to come. Let's remember those innocent victims who have fallen to hatred and violence.

May they rest in peace. *'*

By the end of the decade and with Russia on the brink of financial collapse (the rouble lost 75 per cent of its value during the 1990s), Yeltsin went into semi-retirement while the government was run by Prime Minister Yevgeny Primakov.

Yeltsin refused to resign as President and hand over Russia to former Communist Party interests and sacked Primakov in June 1999.

When parliamentary elections were held in December 1999 Yeltsin stood down in favour of his new Prime Minister, Alexander Putin.

On 1 January 2000, Boris Yeltsin exited the world stage when he voluntarily resigned his position of President and Putin was subsequently elected to the position in March of that year.

After Boris Yeltsin died in April 2007 of heart failure, he became the first Russian statesman in more than a century to be buried in a church ceremony. President Putin declared the day of Yeltsin's funeral a national day of mourning.

Elie Wiesel

'The Perils of Indifference'
East Room, White House, Washington DC, 12 April 1999.

An impassioned insight into the causes and nature of the Holocaust during World War II came from a scholar born in Sighet, Transylvania (now part of Romania). Eliezer Wiesel was born on 30 September 1928 in a small village, his life revolving around 'family, religious study, community and God'.

In the summer of 1944, 15-year-old Elie Wiesel, along with his father, mother and sisters, was deported by the Nazis to the Auschwitz death camp in occupied Poland. Wiesel and his father were selected for slave labour and were set to work at the nearby Buna rubber factory. Daily life was a constant struggle against overwhelming despair—starvation rations, brutal discipline and, as Wiesel later wrote, the memory of children whose bodies were 'turned into wreaths of smoke beneath a silent blue sky'.

Wiesel and his father were hurriedly evacuated from Auschwitz by a forced march to Gleiwitz in January 1945 as the Russian Army drew near, and then to Buchenwald via an open train car. There, his father, mother, and a younger sister eventually died but Elie Wiesel was liberated by American troops in April 1945. After the war, he moved to Paris and became a journalist. Originally vowing to remain silent on his Holocaust experiences, he was encouraged to write about them by French Nobel laureate Francois Mauriac. Since then, Wiesel has written over 40 books including *Night*, which was first published in 1960. Settling in New York and becoming an American citizen, he has been Andrew Mellon Professor in the Humanities at Boston University since 1976 and has received numerous awards and honours including the 1986 Nobel Peace Prize and the Presidential Medal of Freedom.

The Founding Chair of the United States Holocaust Memorial, Elie Wiesel was invited to participate in a series of Millennium Lectures hosted by President Bill Clinton and First Lady Hillary Rodham Clinton at the White House leading up to the year 2000. Here, in his speech in the East Room of the White House, Wiesel reiterated his belief that 'to remain silent and indifferent is the greatest sin of all'

❟ Mr President, Mrs Clinton, members of Congress, Ambassador Holbrooke, Excellencies, friends.

Fifty-four years ago to the day, a young Jewish boy from a small town in the Carpathian Mountains woke up, not far from Goethe's beloved Weimar, in a place of eternal infamy called Buchenwald. He was finally free, but there was no joy in his heart. He thought there never would be again.

Liberated a day earlier by American soldiers, he remembers their rage at what they saw. And even if he lives to be a very old man, he will always be grateful to them for that rage, and also for their compassion. Though he did not understand their language, their eyes told him what he needed to know—that they, too, would remember, and bear witness.

And now, I stand before you, Mr. President—Commander-in-Chief of the army that freed me, and tens of thousands of others—and I am filled with a profound and abiding gratitude to the American people.

Gratitude is a word that I cherish. Gratitude is what defines the humanity of the human being. And I am grateful to you, Hillary—or Mrs. Clinton—for what you said, and for what you are doing for children in the world, for the homeless, for the victims of injustice, the victims of destiny and society. And I thank all of you for being here.

We are on the threshold of a new century, a new millennium. What will the legacy of this vanishing century be? How will it be remembered in the new millennium? Surely it will be judged, and judged severely, in both moral and metaphysical terms. These failures have cast a dark shadow over humanity: two World Wars, countless civil wars, the senseless chain of assassinations—Gandhi, the Kennedys, Martin Luther King, Sadat, Rabin—bloodbaths in Cambodia and Nigeria, India and Pakistan, Ireland and Rwanda, Eritrea and

Ethiopia, Sarajevo and Kosovo; the inhumanity in the gulag and the tragedy of Hiroshima. And, on a different level, of course, Auschwitz and Treblinka. So much violence, so much indifference.

What is indifference? Etymologically, the word means "no difference." A strange and unnatural state in which the lines blur between light and darkness, dusk and dawn, crime and punishment, cruelty and compassion, good and evil.

What are its courses and inescapable consequences? Is it a philosophy? Is there a philosophy of indifference conceivable? Can one possibly view indifference as a virtue? Is it necessary at times to practice it simply to keep one's sanity, live normally, enjoy a fine meal and a glass of wine, as the world around us experiences harrowing upheavals?

Of course, indifference can be tempting—more than that, seductive. It is so much easier to look away from victims. It is so much easier to avoid such rude interruptions to our work, our dreams, our hopes. It is, after all, awkward, troublesome, to be involved in another person's pain and despair. Yet, for the person who is indifferent, his or her neighbor are of no consequence. And, therefore, their lives are meaningless. Their hidden or even visible anguish is of no interest. Indifference reduces the other to an abstraction.

Over there, behind the black gates of Auschwitz, the most tragic of all prisoners were the "Muselmanner," as they were called. Wrapped in their torn blankets, they would sit or lie on the ground, staring vacantly into space, unaware of who or where they were, strangers to their surroundings. They no longer felt pain, hunger, thirst. They feared nothing. They felt nothing. They were dead and did not know it.

Rooted in our tradition, some of us felt that to be abandoned by humanity then was not the ultimate. We felt that to be abandoned by God was worse than to be punished by Him. Better an unjust God than an indifferent one. For us to be ignored by God was a harsher punishment than to be a victim of His anger. Man can live far from God—not outside God. God is wherever we are. Even in suffering? Even in suffering.

In a way, to be indifferent to that suffering is what makes the human being inhuman. Indifference, after all, is more dangerous than anger and hatred. Anger can at times be creative. One writes a great poem, a great symphony, one does something special for the sake of humanity because one is angry at the injustice that one witnesses. But indifference is never creative. Even hatred at times may elicit a response. You fight it. You denounce it. You disarm it. Indifference elicits no response. Indifference is not a response.

Indifference is not a beginning, it is an end. And, therefore, indifference is always the friend of the enemy, for it benefits the aggressor—never his victim, whose pain is magnified when he or she feels forgotten. The political prisoner in his cell, the hungry children, the homeless refugees—not to respond to their plight, not to relieve their solitude by offering them a spark of hope is to exile them from human memory. And in denying their humanity we betray our own.

Indifference, then, is not only a sin, it is a punishment. And this is one of the most important lessons of this outgoing century's wide-ranging experiments in good and evil.

In the place that I come from, society was composed of three simple categories: the killers, the victims, and the bystanders. During the darkest of times, inside the ghettoes and death camps—and I'm glad that Mrs. Clinton mentioned that we are now commemorating that event, that period, that we are now in the Days of Remembrance—but then, we felt abandoned, forgotten. All of us did.

And our only miserable consolation was that we believed that Auschwitz and Treblinka were closely guarded secrets; that the leaders of the free world did not know what was going on behind those black gates and barbed wire; that they had no knowledge of the war against the Jews that Hitler's armies and their accomplices waged as part of the war against the Allies.

If they knew, we thought, surely those leaders would have moved heaven and earth to intervene. They would have spoken out with great outrage and conviction. They would have bombed the railways leading to Birkenau, just the railways, just once.

And now we knew, we learned, we discovered that the Pentagon knew, the State Department knew. And the illustrious occupant of the White House then, who was a great leader—and I say it with some anguish and pain, because, today is exactly 54 years marking his death—Franklin Delano Roosevelt died on April the 12th, 1945, so he is very much present to me and to us.

No doubt, he was a great leader. He mobilized the American people and the world, going into battle, bringing hundreds and thousands of valiant and brave soldiers in America to fight fascism, to fight dictatorship, to fight Hitler. And so many of the young people fell in battle. And, nevertheless, his image in Jewish history—I must say it—his image in Jewish history is flawed.

The depressing tale of the *St. Louis* is a case in point. Sixty years ago, its human cargo—maybe 1,000 Jews—was turned back to Nazi Germany. And that happened after the Kristallnacht, after the first state sponsored pogrom, with hundreds of Jewish shops destroyed, synagogues burned, thousands of people put in concentration camps. And that ship, which was already on the shores of the United States, was sent back.

I don't understand. Roosevelt was a good man, with a heart. He understood those who needed help. Why didn't he allow these refugees to disembark? A thousand people—in America, a great country, the greatest democracy, the most generous of all new nations in modern history. What happened? I don't understand. Why the indifference, on the highest level, to the suffering of the victims?

But then, there were human beings who were sensitive to our tragedy. Those non-Jews, those Christians, that we called the "Righteous Gentiles," whose selfless acts of heroism saved the honor of their faith. Why were they so few? Why was there a greater effort to save SS murderers after the war than to save their victims during the war?

Why did some of America's largest corporations continue to do business with Hitler's Germany until 1942? It has been suggested, and it was documented, that the Wehrmacht could not have conducted its invasion of France without oil obtained from American sources. How is one to explain their indifference?

And yet, my friends, good things have also happened in this traumatic century: the defeat of Nazism, the collapse of communism, the rebirth of Israel on its ancestral soil, the demise of apartheid, Israel's peace treaty with Egypt, the peace accord in Ireland. And let us remember the meeting, filled with drama and emotion, between Rabin and Arafat that you, Mr. President, convened in this very place. I was here and I will never forget it.

And then, of course, the joint decision of the United States and NATO to intervene in Kosovo and save those victims, those refugees, those who were uprooted by a man whom I believe that because of his crimes, should be charged with crimes against humanity. But this time, the world was not silent. This time, we do respond. This time, we intervene.

Does it mean that we have learned from the past? Does it mean that society has changed? Has the human being become less indifferent and more human? Have we really learned from our experiences? Are we less insensitive to the plight of victims of ethnic cleansing and other forms of injustices in places near and far? Is today's justified intervention in Kosovo, led by you, Mr. President, a lasting warning that never again will the deportation, the terrorization of children and their parents be allowed anywhere in the world? Will it discourage other dictators in other lands to do the same?

What about the children? Oh, we see them on television, we read about them in the papers, and we do so with a broken heart. Their fate is always the most tragic, inevitably. When adults wage war, children perish. We see their faces, their eyes. Do we hear their pleas? Do we feel their pain, their agony? Every minute one of them dies of disease, violence, famine. Some of them—so many of them—could be saved.

And so, once again, I think of the young Jewish boy from the Carpathian Mountains. He has accompanied the old man I have become throughout these years of quest and struggle. And together we walk towards the new millennium, carried by profound fear and extraordinary hope. ’

When introduced by Hillary Clinton, the First Lady stated, 'It was more than a year ago that I asked Elie if he would be willing to participate in these Millennium Lectures ... I never could have imagined that when the time finally came for him to stand in this spot and to reflect on the past century and the future to come, that we would be seeing children in Kosovo crowded into trains, separated from families, separated from their homes, robbed of their childhoods, their memories, their humanity.'

She could just as easily have commented that those who refuse to heed the lessons of history are condemned to repeat it.

George W. Bush

'A Great People Has Been Moved'
Washington, DC, 11 September, 2001

The '9/11' attacks in New York and Washington changed global politics and the position of the United States within it. On Tuesday, September 11, 2001, two fully-fuelled jumbo jets - American Airlines Flight 11 carrying 92 people and United Airlines Flight 175 carrying 65 people - departed Boston for Los Angeles. Both jets were hijacked by Mideast terrorists operating from inside the United States and were crashed into the twin towers of the World Trade Centre at 8:46 am and 9:02 am respectively. The impact and subsequent fire caused both 110-story towers to collapse, killing 2,792 people, including hundreds of New York rescue workers – police, fire and ambulance personnel – as well as people who worked in the two towers.

United Airlines Flight 93, departing Newark (New Jersey) for San Francisco, and American Airlines Flight 77, which left Dulles (Virginia) for Los Angeles, were also hijacked by two other teams of hijackers. Flight 77, with 64 people on board, was diverted to Washington, D.C., and then crashed into the Pentagon killing another 125 military personnel inside the building. Flight 93, with 44 people on board, had also been redirected toward Washington – its target unclear - but passengers were alerted by loved ones on cell phones and overpowered the terrorists and crashed the plane into a field in Pennsylvania.

President Bush was visiting a primary school in Sarasota, Florida when he was informed of the attacks. He made a brief statement at 9:15 am before leaving Florida and remaining in the air until midday, when he landed in Barksdale Air Force Base in Louisiana. That evening he returned to the White

House and addressed the American people. This speech, given on the night of the attacks by US President George W. Bush, marked the beginning of America's and its allies' 'war on terror' at the start of the new millennium.

❝Good evening.

Today, our fellow citizens, our way of life, our very freedom came under attack in a series of deliberate and deadly terrorist acts. The victims were in airplanes or in their offices: secretaries, business men and women, military and federal workers, moms and dads, friends and neighbors. Thousands of lives were suddenly ended by evil, despicable acts of terror. The pictures of airplanes flying into buildings, fires burning, huge structures collapsing have filled us with disbelief, terrible sadness, and a quiet, unyielding anger. These acts of mass murder were intended to frighten our nation into chaos and retreat. But they have failed. Our country is strong.

A great people has been moved to defend a great nation. Terrorist attacks can shake the foundations of our biggest buildings, but they cannot touch the foundation of America. These acts shatter steel, but they cannot dent the steel of American resolve. America was targeted for attack because we're the brightest beacon for freedom and opportunity in the world. And no one will keep that light from shining. Today, our nation saw evil - the very worst of human nature - and we responded with the best of America. With the daring of our rescue workers, with the caring for strangers and neighbors who came to give blood and help in any way they could.

Immediately following the first attack, I implemented our government's emergency response plans. Our military is powerful, and it's prepared. Our emergency teams are working in New York City and Washington D.C. to help with local rescue efforts. Our first priority is to get help to those who have been injured, and to take every precaution to protect our citizens at home and around the world from further attacks. The functions of our government continue without interruption. Federal agencies in Washington which had to be evacuated today are reopening for essential personnel tonight and will be open for business tomorrow. Our financial institutions remain strong, and the American economy will be open for business as well.

The search is underway for those who were behind these evil acts. I have directed the full resources of our intelligence and law enforcement communities to find those responsible and to bring them to justice. We will make no distinction between the terrorists who committed these acts and those who harbor them.

I appreciate so very much the members of Congress who have joined me in strongly condemning these attacks. And on behalf of the American people, I thank the many world leaders who have called to offer their condolences and assistance. America and our friends and allies join with all those who want peace and security in the world, and we stand together to win the war against terrorism.

Tonight, I ask for your prayers for all those who grieve, for the children whose worlds have been shattered, for all whose sense of safety and security has been threatened. And I pray they will be comforted by a Power greater than any of us, spoken through the ages in Psalm 23:

"Even though I walk through the valley of the shadow of death, I fear no evil for you are with me."

This is a day when all Americans from every walk of life unite in our resolve for justice and peace. America has stood down enemies before, and we will do so this time. None of us will ever forget this day, yet we go forward to defend freedom and all that is good and just in our world.

Thank you. Good night. And God bless America. ❜

George Walker Bush was born in New Haven, Connecticut on 6 July, 1946, the oldest son of George and Barbara Bush. The Bush family grew up in Midland and Houston, Texas, with George W. attending Yale University (his father George H. Bush's alma mater) and earned an MBA from Harvard Business School. When Bush ran for the presidency in 2000 much was made of his wild youth, his national guard service during the Vietnam War and his shift to sobriety after his marriage in 1976. The millions he made from the oil industry and his stake in the Texas Rangers baseball franchise – all while his father was President of the United States – also raised concerns but it didn't stop him from being electable in his own right.

In 1978 Bush tried to follow his father into the House of Representatives but was defeated by his Democratic rival, Kent Hance. In 1994, after his father had been voted out of the White House, George W. was elected governor of Texas and went onto become the first Texas governor to be elected to a second four-year term. In 2001 George W. (nicknamed 'Dubya' by a sceptical press) became the 42nd President of the United States after one of the closest and most controversial elections in American history. Bush defeated former Democratic vice-president Al Gore by a mere five electoral votes (despite Gore securing 500,000 more primary votes). The outcome was ultimately decided in Florida, where Bush's younger brother Jeb was the governor, but it was a result contested by the Gore camp until mid-December 2000.

In his first year as president, Bush faced the biggest test of any world leader in a generation. History now shows that the United States of America responded to the attack with all its military might. Afghanistan was 'liberated' from Taliban rule in 2002 and Iraq was invaded in 2003 on a false premise – the presence of 'weapons of mass destruction'– and against the wishes of the United Nations.

George W. Bush was elected to a second term as US President in 2004.

Steve Jobs

'Stanford University Commencement Address'
Stanford University, California – June 12, 2005

In July 2005, Apple founder and computer technology innovator Steve Jobs was invited to give the Commencement Address for the graduating year at Stanford University in his home state of California. At the time, Jobs had risen phoenix like from his sacking from the company he started some 20 years before and, while fighting pancreatic cancer, was riding the crest of a second wave of success having returned to Apple as CEO.

Jobs, who presented to the public as a confident entrepreneur when he released the iPod and iPhone to the world, was apparently nervous, his wife Lauren later observed, about giving the speech at Stanford. The invitation meant a lot to him and he practiced repeatedly, trying the speech out several times in front of his family and fine-tuning it where necessary to fit into an effective 15-18 minute time-frame. Jobs used a simple but effective technique in structuring three life lessons in three short stories, but the message was universal.

Do what you love.

Jobs' speech resonated with the students and with the wider public and has since been viewed 22 million times on YouTube.

❛I am honored to be with you today at your commencement from one of the finest universities in the world. I never graduated from college. Truth be told, this is the closest I've ever gotten to a college graduation. Today I want to tell you three stories from my life. That's it. No big deal. Just three stories.

The first story is about connecting the dots.

I dropped out of Reed College after the first six months, but then stayed around as a drop-in for another 18 months or so before I really quit. So why did I drop out?

It started before I was born. My biological mother was a young, unwed college graduate student, and she decided to put me up for adoption. She felt very strongly that I should be adopted by college graduates, so everything was all set for me to be adopted at birth by a lawyer and his wife. Except that when I popped out they decided at the last minute that they really wanted a girl. So my parents, who were on a waiting list, got a call in the middle of the night asking: "We have an unexpected baby boy; do you want him?" They said: "Of course." My biological mother later found out that my mother had never graduated from college and that my father had never graduated from high school. She refused to sign the final adoption papers. She only relented a few months later when my parents promised that I would someday go to college.

And 17 years later I did go to college. But I naively chose a college that was almost as expensive as Stanford, and all of my working-class parents' savings were being spent on my college tuition. After six months, I couldn't see the value in it. I had no idea what I wanted to do with my life and no idea how college was going to help me figure it out. And here I was spending all of the money my parents had saved their entire life. So I decided to drop out and trust that it would all work out OK. It was pretty scary at the time, but looking back it was one of the best decisions I ever made. The minute I dropped out I could stop taking the required classes that didn't interest me, and begin dropping in on the ones that looked interesting.

It wasn't all romantic. I didn't have a dorm room, so I slept on the floor in friends' rooms, I returned coke bottles for the 5¢ deposits to buy food with, and I would walk the 7 miles across town every Sunday night to get one good meal a week at the Hare Krishna temple. I loved it. And much of what I stumbled into by following my curiosity and intuition turned out to be priceless later on. Let me give you one example:

Reed College at that time offered perhaps the best calligraphy instruction in the country. Throughout the campus every poster, every label on every drawer, was beautifully hand-calligraphed. Because I had dropped out and didn't have to take the normal classes, I decided to take a calligraphy class to learn how to do this. I learned about serif and san serif typefaces, about varying the amount of space between different letter combinations, about what makes great typography great. It was beautiful, historical, artistically subtle in a way that science can't capture, and I found it fascinating.

None of this had even a hope of any practical application in my life. But 10 years later, when we were designing the first Macintosh computer, it all came back to me. And we designed it all into the Mac. It was the first computer with beautiful typography. If I had never dropped in on that single course in college, the Mac would have never had multiple typefaces or proportionally spaced fonts. And since Windows just copied the Mac, it's likely that no personal computer would have them. If I had never dropped out, I would have never dropped in on this calligraphy class, and personal computers might not have the wonderful typography that they do. Of course it was impossible to connect the dots looking forward when I was in college. But it was very, very clear looking backwards 10 years later.

Again, you can't connect the dots looking forward; you can only connect them looking backwards. So you have to trust that the dots will somehow connect in your future. You have to trust in something — your gut, destiny, life, karma, whatever. This approach has never let me down, and it has made all the difference in my life.

My second story is about love and loss.

I was lucky — I found what I loved to do early in life. Woz and I started Apple in my parents' garage when I was 20. We worked hard, and in 10 years Apple had grown from just the two of us in a garage into a $2 billion company with over 4000 employees. We had just released our finest creation — the Macintosh — a year earlier, and I had just turned 30. And then I got fired. How can you get fired from a company you started? Well, as Apple grew we hired someone who I thought was very talented to run the company with me, and for the first year or so things went well. But then our visions of the future began to diverge and eventually we had a falling out. When we did, our Board of Directors sided with him. So at 30 I was out. And very publicly out. What had been the focus of my entire adult life was gone, and it was devastating.

I really didn't know what to do for a few months. I felt that I had let the previous generation of entrepreneurs down – that I had dropped the baton as it was being passed to me. I met with David Packard and Bob Noyce and tried to apologise for screwing up so badly. I was a very public failure, and I even thought about running away from the valley. But something slowly began to dawn on me — I still loved what I did. The turn of events at Apple had not changed that one bit. I had been rejected, but I was still in love. And so I decided to start over.

I didn't see it then, but it turned out that getting fired from Apple was the best thing that could have ever happened to me. The heaviness of being successful was replaced by the lightness of being a beginner again, less sure about everything. It freed me to enter one of the most creative periods of my life.

During the next five years, I started a company named NeXT, another company named Pixar, and fell in love with an amazing woman who would become my wife. Pixar went on to create the world's first computer animated feature film, Toy Story, and is now the most successful animation studio in the world. In a remarkable turn of events, Apple bought NeXT, I returned to Apple, and the technology we developed at NeXT is at the heart of Apple's current renaissance. And Laurene and I have a wonderful family together.

I'm pretty sure none of this would have happened if I hadn't been fired from Apple. It was awful tasting medicine, but I guess the patient needed it. Sometimes life hits you in the head with a brick. Don't lose faith. I'm convinced that the only thing that kept me going was that I loved what I did. You've got to find what you love. And that is as true for your work as it is for your lovers. Your work is going to fill a large part of your life, and the only way to be truly satisfied is to do what you believe is great work. And the only way to do great work is to love what you do. If you haven't found it yet, keep looking. Don't settle. As with all matters of the heart, you'll know when you find it. And, like any great relationship, it just gets better and better as the years roll on. So keep looking until you find it. Don't settle.

My third story is about death.

When I was 17, I read a quote that went something like: "If you live each day as if it was your last, someday you'll most certainly be right." It made an impression on me, and since then, for the past 33 years, I have looked in the mirror every morning and asked myself: "If today were the last day of my life, would I want to do what I am about to do today?" And whenever the answer has been "No" for too many days in a row, I know I need to change something.

Remembering that I'll be dead soon is the most important tool I've ever encountered to help me make the big choices in life. Because almost everything — all external expect-ations, all pride, all fear of embarrassment or failure – these things just fall away in the face of death, leaving only what is truly important. Remembering that you are going to die is the best way I know to avoid the trap of thinking you have something to lose. You are already naked. There is no reason not to follow your heart.

About a year ago I was diagnosed with cancer. I had a scan at 7:30 in the morning, and it clearly showed a tumour on my pancreas. I didn't even know what a pancreas was. The doctors told me this was almost certainly a type of cancer that is incurable, and that I should expect to live no longer than three to six months. My doctor advised me to go home and get my affairs in order, which is doctor's code for prepare to die. It means to try to tell your kids everything you thought you'd have the next 10 years to tell them in just a few months. It means to make sure everything is buttoned up so that it will be as easy as possible for your family. It means to say your goodbyes.

I lived with that diagnosis all day. Later that evening I had a biopsy, where they stuck an endoscope down my throat, through my stomach and into my intestines, put a needle into my pancreas and got a few cells from the tumour. I was sedated, but my wife, who was there, told me that when they viewed the cells under a microscope the doctors started crying because it turned out to be a very rare form of pancreatic cancer that is curable with surgery. I had the surgery and I'm fine now.

This was the closest I've been to facing death, and I hope it's the closest I get for a few more decades. Having lived through it, I can now say this to you with a bit more certainty than when death was a useful but purely intellectual concept:

No one wants to die. Even people who want to go to heaven don't want to die to get there. And yet death is the destination we all share. No one has ever escaped it. And that is as it should be, because Death is very likely the single best invention of Life. It is Life's change agent. It clears out the old to make way for the new. Right now the new is you, but someday not too long from now, you will gradually become the old and be cleared away. Sorry to be so dramatic, but it is quite true.

Your time is limited, so don't waste it living someone else's life. Don't be trapped by dogma — which is living with the results of other people's thinking. Don't let the noise of others' opinions drown out your own inner voice. And most important, have the courage to follow your heart and intuition. They somehow already know what you truly want to become. Everything else is secondary.

When I was young, there was an amazing publication called The Whole Earth catalogue, which was one of the bibles of my generation. It was created by a fellow named Stewart Brand not far from here in Menlo Park, and he brought it to life with his poetic touch. This was in the late 1960's, before personal computers and desktop publishing, so it was all made with typewriters, scissors, and Polaroid cameras. It was sort of like Google in paperback form, 35 years before Google came along: it was idealistic, and overflowing with neat tools and great notions.

Stewart and his team put out several issues of The Whole Earth catalogue, and then when it had run its course, they put out a final issue. It was the mid-1970s, and I was your age. On the back cover of their final issue was a photograph of an early morning country road, the kind you might find yourself hitchhiking on if you were so adventurous. Beneath it were the words: "Stay Hungry. Stay Foolish." It was their farewell message as they signed off. Stay Hungry. Stay Foolish. And I have always wished that for myself. And now, as you graduate to begin anew, I wish that for you.

Stay Hungry. Stay Foolish.

Thank you all very much. 〟

Steven Paul Jobs was born in San Francisco, California, on February 24, 1955 to two young University of Wisconsin graduate students who made the difficult decision to give him up for adoption. His biological parents later married and had another child (a daughter, Mona Simpson), but Jobs would not find out about his real parents until he was in his 20s. Raised by Clara and Paul Jobs in Mountain View, California – an area later to be known as 'Silicon Valley'- Steve Jobs was an intelligent but unfocused school student who later dropped out of college. In the early 1970s, he started to experiment with electronic circuits and computer chips with fellow Californian Steve Wozniak, and took a job with computer games company Atari.

Jobs and Wozniak founded the Apple Computer Company in 1976 with the goal of developing an affordable home computer. Together, they revolutionized the computer industry by making machines that were smaller, cheaper and more accessible to everyday users. Company sales increased by 700% after the release of the Apple II computer and by 1980, the company was worth $1.2 billion after trading on the stock exchange. The Computer

Age had arrived.

The Apple Macintosh, however, struggled in the 1980s against the sales of IMB compatible PCs, and when Jobs forced the Board's hand for control in 1985, he was sacked by the very men he brought in to run the company. Always the innovator, Jobs started NeXT Computer Inc., which was a relative commercial failure, but then purchased the Pixar Animations Studios from filmmaker George Lucas and turned it into a juggernaut which, in turn, was later purchased by Disney. Incredibly, Jobs returned to Apple as CEO in 1997 and oversaw the development of the iMac (1998), iPod (2001), iPhone (2007) and iPad (2010), which again revolutionized computer technology in the new millennium.

In 2002, Jobs contracted pancreatic cancer which required him to have a liver transplant. He returned to public life in 2010 to launch the Apple iPad, but appeared gaunt and unwell. He died on October 5, 2011, aged 56.

Kevin Rudd

'Apology to Indigenous Australians'
Parliament House, Canberra, 13 February 2008

O n 13 February 2008, Australian Prime Minister Kevin Rudd opened the first sitting of the newly elected Labor Government by fulfilling one of his key election promises—to apologise to Indigenous Australians for the stolen generations, where thousands of children were removed from traditional communities under a government-sponsored policy.

Fifty-year-old Rudd, the son of a Queensland dairy farmer and a former State Labor Party Chief of Staff, led his party's sweep to power in the November 2007 federal elections which ended more than 11 years of conservative party rule under Liberal Prime Minister, John Howard. Bright, personable, but described as being almost 'nerdish' in his appearance and quiet manner (and perfectly fluent in the Chinese dialect of Mandarin) when he began his term as Australia's 26th Prime Minister, Rudd showed that he possessed that unique leadership quality of grasping the mood of the people with a symbolic act that had been long overdue.

At Canberra's Parliament House, Kevin Rudd became the first Australian Prime Minister since Federation in 1901 to invite the traditional owners of the area, the Ngunnawal people, to take part in a 'welcome to country' ceremony to open the 41st Australian Federal Parliament. Accompanied by Aboriginal dancers and musicians, members of the Ngambri people, who have a traditional connection to the Canberra and Yass areas, presented Mr Rudd with an Aboriginal 'message' stick.

At 9.30am in the House of Representatives, on behalf of the elected government and televised live to an audience of millions, Kevin Rudd read his own message of national reconciliation:

❛Today we honour the Indigenous peoples of this land, the oldest continuing cultures in human history.

We reflect on their past mistreatment. We reflect in particular on the mistreatment of those who were stolen generations—this blemished chapter in our nation's history.

The time has now come for the nation to turn a new page in Australia's history by righting the wrongs of the past and so moving forward with confidence to the future. We apologise for the laws and policies of successive parliaments and governments that have inflicted profound grief, suffering and loss on these our fellow Australians.

We apologise especially for the removal of Aboriginal and Torres Strait Islander children from their families, their communities and their country.

For the pain, suffering and hurt of these stolen generations, their descendants and for their families left behind, we say sorry.

To the mothers and the fathers, the brothers and the sisters, for the breaking up of families and communities, we say sorry.

And for the indignity and degradation thus inflicted on a proud people and a proud culture, we say sorry.

We the Parliament of Australia respectfully request that this apology be received in the spirit in which it is offered as part of the healing of the nation.

For the future we take heart; resolving that this new page in the history of our great continent can now be written.

We today take this first step by acknowledging the past and laying claim to a future that embraces all Australians.

A future where this parliament resolves that the injustices of the past must never, never happen again.

A future where we harness the determination of all Australians, Indigenous and non-Indigenous, to close the gap that lies between us in life expectancy, educational achievement and economic opportunity.

A future where we embrace the possibility of new solutions to enduring problems where old approaches have failed.

A future based on mutual respect, mutual resolve and mutual responsibility.

A future where all Australians, whatever their origins, are truly equal partners, with equal opportunities and with an equal stake in shaping the next chapter in the history of this great country, Australia. '

British and Australian government institutions dating back more than a hundred years before the 1970s had entered into a policy of the systematic removal of Aboriginal and Torres Strait Islander children from remote communities and suburban homes if there was a belief that children were at a social, physical or even a religious risk.

Thousands of Aboriginal children were placed into orphanages and foster homes, with parents often not informed of the reasons for the removal of their children, or the implications. Many indigenous families did not see their children again.

However well-intentioned the policy may have been as a dubious or even preventative form of child protection, there is evidence today that a primary government agenda was to breed the Aboriginal race into extinction through a program of removal from traditional communities and forced assimilation into mainstream Australia.

The practice was widely and indiscriminately applied throughout the country, often without having established cases of neglect or mistreatment and regardless of the impact on individuals, Aboriginal families or whole communities. Succeeding generations of Indigenous Australians suffered from the practice and stories from the stolen generations became an integral part of the Aboriginal experience.

The 'National Inquiry into the Separation of Aboriginal and Torres Strait Islander Children from their Families' was established by Paul Keating's Labor Government in 1995 in response to requests from key Indigenous welfare agencies and communities.

The inquiry was set up to hear submissions and personal stories to determine the extent of the stolen generations and to formally recognise the hurt caused to victims and their families by this policy.

A 700-page report entitled 'Bringing Them Home' was tabled in federal parliament in May 1997, by which time John Howard's Liberal Party had come to power.

Although individual states and territories fulfilled a key recommendation of the report and issued formal apologies to the stolen generations, Prime Minister Howard ignored an apology and issued instead a statement of 'deep and sincere regret.'

Fearing compensation claims that could have amounted to hundreds of millions of dollars and speaking, perhaps, to 'middle Australia' which had remained largely ignorant of these issues for decades, John Howard said this he was more concerned with 'practical reconciliation' than symbolic acts.

Famously, and without the slightest hint of irony, the second longest serving Prime Minister in Australian history (1996–2007) remarked that he refused to take a 'black armband view of history'… Howard's government would not apologise for past injustices.

After Kevin Rudd claimed electoral victory on 24 November 2007, he immediately indicated that Australia would ratify the Kyoto Protocol regarding limiting greenhouse emissions, wind back the previous government's controversial workplace relations legislation and inform US President George Bush that Australia would be withdrawing its troops from Iraq.

But the following February in Canberra, Prime Minister Rudd turned an important page in Australian history when he took the first step towards national reconciliation. His formal apology and the twenty-minute speech that followed were generally met with tears, joy and widespread applause.

Although Mr Rudd ruled out any retrospective compensation for the stolen generations—committing to improve the living conditions and health of today's Indigenous communities—in just 361 words he did more for healing past injustices for all Australians than a century of government policies.

Kevin Rudd did not serve a full term as Prime Minister, after his Liberal Party replaced him with his deputy Julia Gillard in 2010 following disastrous poll feedback from the Australian electorate leading up to the August election. When Gillard's minority government struggled to win over the public and the conservative Australian media Rudd, 'Lazarus-like', was reinstated as Prime Minister in June 2013 and led the Labor Party to defeat later that year.

Dr Stephen Hawking

'Questioning the Universe'

TED (Technology, Entertainment and Design) Talk, Vancouver, Canada
April 4, 2008

Theoretical physicist Stephen Hawking was born on January 8, 1942 in Oxford, England. The son of Oxford graduates, Hawking was not an exceptional student but showed an interest in physics and cosmology at an early age. At age 21, he was diagnosed with the debilitating motor neurone illness amyotrophic lateral sclerosis – also known as Lou Gehrig's disease, or ALS – a progressive neurodegenerative disease that affects nerve cells in the brain and the spinal cord.

Hawking was determined to do as much as he could in his projected short lifespan, realising he may not live long enough to even achieve his PhD. He married girlfriend Jane Wilde in 1965 and fathered a son, Robert, but by 1969 he was already confined to a wheelchair and was losing the use of speech. Despite his diminishing physical abilities, he fathered a daughter (Lucy), wrote his first book and expanded upon the work of close friend Roger Penrose to ponder the birth of the universe, investigate the fate of stars and propose the existence of black holes. By the mid-1970s, he was already a major celebrity within the scientific community.

Hawking's proposal that matter, in the form of radiation, could escape the gravitational force of a collapsed star was a ground-breaking discovery and earned him the prestigious Albert Einstein Award in 1978. The following year, he was named Lucasian Professor of Mathematics at Cambridge University. In 1985, he lost his voice following a tracheotomy and required around the clock nurse care. Hawking learned to communicate through the use of a computer speaking program that could be directed by his head or eye movement and converted into electronic speech. The innovation would be him an icon.

In 1988, the publication of A Brief History of Time brought Hawking to international mainstream prominence. Since then he has sought to discover and articulate the origins of the universe, propose theories about space travel and the existence of intelligent life in the universe and even contemplate mankind's ultimate fate.

In April 2008, Stephen Hawking answered questions about the origins of the universe in a talk sponsored by the TED (Technology, Entertainment, Design) organisation, which regularly organises global conferences on behalf of the privately run, non-profit Sapling Foundation. Speakers are allowed a maximum of 18 minutes to present their talk in the most engaging manner they can. Hawking delivered the following talk via video link from London in his now familiar, synthesized voice. Each paragraph is indented in real time:

0:12

There is nothing bigger or older than the universe. The questions I would like to talk about are: one, where did we come from? How did the universe come into being? Are we alone in the universe? Is there alien life out there? What is the future of the human race?

0:42

Up until the 1920s, everyone thought the universe was essentially static and unchanging in time. Then it was discovered that the universe was expanding. Distant galaxies were moving away from us. This meant they must have been closer together in the past. If we extrapolate back, we find we must have all been on top of each other about 15 billion years ago. This was the Big Bang, the beginning of the universe.

1:19

But was there anything before the Big Bang? If not, what created the universe? Why did the universe emerge from the Big Bang the way it did? We used to think that the theory of the universe could be divided into two parts. First, there were the laws like Maxwell's equations and general relativity that determined the evolution of the universe, given its state over all of space at one time. And second, there was no question of the initial state of the universe.

1:58

We have made good progress on the first part, and now have the knowledge of the laws of evolution in all but the most extreme conditions. But until recently, we have had little idea about the initial conditions for the universe. However, this division into laws of evolution and initial conditions depends on time and space being separate and distinct. Under extreme conditions, general relativity and quantum theory allow time to behave like another dimension of space. This removes the distinction between time and space, and means the laws of evolution can also determine the initial state. The universe can spontaneously create itself out of nothing.

2:57

Moreover, we can calculate a probability that the universe was created in different states. These predictions are in excellent agreement with observations by the WMAP satellite of the cosmic microwave background, which is an imprint of the very early universe. We think we have solved the mystery of creation. Maybe we should patent the universe and charge everyone royalties for their existence.

3:32

I now turn to the second big question: are we alone, or is there other life in the universe? We believe that life arose spontaneously on the Earth, so it must be possible for life to appear on other suitable planets, of which there seem to be a large number in the galaxy.

3:57

But we don't know how life first appeared. We have two pieces of observational evidence on the probability of life appearing. The first is that we have fossils of algae from 3.5 billion years ago. The Earth was formed 4.6 billion years ago and was probably too hot for about the first half billion years. So life appeared on Earth within half a billion years of it being possible, which is short compared to the 10-billion-year lifetime of a planet of Earth type. This suggests that the probability of life appearing is reasonably high. If it was very low, one would have expected it to take most of the ten billion years available.

4:58

On the other hand, we don't seem to have been visited by aliens. I am discounting the reports of UFOs. Why would they appear only to cranks and weirdos? If there is a government conspiracy to suppress the reports and keep for itself the scientific knowledge the aliens bring, it seems to have been a singularly ineffective policy so far. Furthermore, despite an extensive search by the SETI project, we haven't heard any alien television quiz shows. This probably indicates that there are no alien civilizations at our stage of development within a radius of a few hundred light years. Issuing an insurance policy against abduction by aliens seems a pretty safe bet.

6:01

This brings me to the last of the big questions: the future of the human race. If we are the only intelligent beings in the galaxy, we should make sure we survive and continue. But we are entering an increasingly dangerous period of our history. Our population and our use of the finite resources of planet Earth are growing exponentially, along with our technical ability to change the environment for good or ill. But our genetic code still carries the selfish and aggressive instincts that were of survival advantage in the past. It will be difficult enough to avoid disaster in the next hundred years, let alone the next thousand or million.

7:07

Our only chance of long-term survival is not to remain inward-looking on planet Earth, but to spread out into space. The answers to these big questions show that we have made remarkable progress in the last hundred years. But if we want to continue beyond the next hundred years, our future is in space. That is why I am in favor of manned -or should I say, personned - space flight.

7:46

All of my life I have sought to understand the universe and find answers to these questions. I have been very lucky that my disability has not been a serious handicap. Indeed, it has probably given me more time than most people to pursue the quest for knowledge. The ultimate goal is a complete theory of the universe, and we are making good progress.

Thank you for listening.

8:25
Curator Chris Anderson then asked: Professor, if you had to guess either way, do you now believe that it is more likely than not that we are alone in the Milky Way, as a civilization of our level of intelligence or higher? (This answer took seven minutes for Hawking to respond) ...

16:17
Stephen Hawking: I think it quite likely that we are the only civilization within several hundred light years; otherwise we would have heard radio waves. The alternative is that civilizations don't last very long, but destroy themselves.

16:39
Chris Anderson: Professor Hawking, thank you for that answer. We will take it as a salutary warning, I think, for the rest of our conference this week. Professor, we really thank you for the extraordinary effort you made to share your questions with us today. Thank you very much indeed.
16:57 (Applause)

In 1990, Stephen and Jane Hawking divorced and he married Elaine Mason, one of his nurses. After that marriage ended in 2006, Hawking reconciled with his children (a third child had been born in 1979) and his ex-wife, who had remarried, and continued to probe the origins of the universe. As his health slowly deteriorates, he continues to reconcile his discovery that the Big Bang may have occurred through spontaneous creation rather than on the command of a deity. Hawking was the source of an Oscar-winning biopic (The Theory of Everything, 2014), spoke out about the potential dangers of artificial intelligence (AI) and become a pop culture favourite.

Hawking remains that rarest of world celebrities — one whose prominence and fame is a result of his intellect rather than the limitations of his own physical body.

Julia Gillard

'Misogyny Speech'
Australian House of Representatives, Canberra, October 9, 2012

On June 24, 2010, Julia Gillard – the then Deputy Prime Minister of Australia – toppled sitting Labor Prime Minister Kevin Rudd in a party room ballot and became the first female Prime Minister in Australian history. A popular figure when he was elected in 2007, the scholarly Rudd had alienated the rank and file of his own Party and was on the nose with the often fickle Australian public in news polls leading up to the 2010 election. As is the wont of political parties that operate under the Westminster System, the leader of the government is not popularly elected but is chosen by the party rom members. Rudd was out and Gillard was in.

Gillard, a former lawyer and union official, had just two months to sell her vision for the future to the Australian public and a veracious media after calling the election for August 21. Rather than celebrate the fact that Australia had finally joined many other nations in having a female prime minister, the Rupert Murdoch-run media and the Liberal Opposition under conservative Tony Abbott tried to characterise Gillard as personally disloyal, a union 'hack' and a political opportunist. On many levels, it worked.

The August 2010 Federal election finished in a tied parliament, with neither of the two major political parties winning an absolute majority of seats to form government. It was Gillard's ability as a negotiator and her party's progressive political platform that led her to make a deal with the fledgling Greens Party and two independents to form a minority government. This also meant, as newly elected Prime Minister in her own right, her Labor-Greens-Independent coalition had to modify many of her election policies – most notably, her party's promise not to implement an emissions trading scheme but to seek a 'national consensus' on the issue. The Greens forced her hand, and the carbon trading scheme was back on the agenda.

There was the public perception that there was a double lack of legitimacy to Gillard's Prime Ministership – she had 'knifed' her leader in the back, the media railed; she had lied to the Australian public about the carbon tax, the Opposition postured; she was at the beckon call of minority parties, the public was told. In 2011 and for much of 2012, Gillard was struggled to articulate her party's compromised policies and was pilloried for her government's inability to handle the growing refugee crisis with thousands arriving by boat from war-torn Middle East. Despite her government having the highest legislation rate (0.495 passing rate of bills) of any post-war Prime Minister, things only got worse for her.

Julia Gillard was criticised for the way she talked (she was born in Wales), the way she dressed, her hairstyle and the fact that she was, among other things, an unmarried, childless atheist living in The Lodge (the Prime Minister's official residence in Canberra). Her integrity was questioned, her name was mocked ('Ju-liar') and even the death of her father in 2012 misrepresented ('the old man died of shame' one radio commentator observed). Federal Opposition leader Tony Abbott, a conservative Catholic and the father of three adult daughters, led the charge against her, both inside and outside of parliament.

On October 9, 2012, during debate over a scandal in which the Speaker of the House Peter Slipper was accused of sending 'lewd' texts to a young male staffer, the Prime Minister of Australia stood to her feet in Federal Parliament and called out Tony Abbott in a speech that reverberated around the world:

❦ Thank you very much Deputy Speaker and I rise to oppose the motion moved by the Leader of the Opposition. And in so doing I say to the Leader of the Opposition I will not be lectured about sexism and misogyny by this man. I will not. And the Government will not be lectured about sexism and misogyny by this man. Not now, not ever.

The Leader of the Opposition says that people who hold sexist views and who are misogynists are not appropriate for high office. Well I hope the Leader of the Opposition has got a piece of paper and he is writing out his resignation. Because if he wants to know what misogyny looks like in modern Australia, he doesn't need a motion in the House of Representatives, he needs a mirror. That's what he needs.

Let's go through the Opposition Leader's repulsive double standards, repulsive double standards when it comes to misogyny and sexism. We are now supposed to take seriously that the Leader of the Opposition is offended by Mr Slipper's text messages, when this is the Leader of the Opposition who has said, and this was when he was a minister under the last government – not when he was a student, not when he was in high school – when he was a minister under the last government.

He has said, and I quote, in a discussion about women being under-represented in institutions of power in Australia, the interviewer was a man called Stavros. The Leader of the Opposition says "If it's true, Stavros, that men have more power generally speaking than women, is that a bad thing?"

And then a discussion ensues, and another person says "I want my daughter to have as much opportunity as my son." To which the Leader of the Opposition says "Yeah, I completely agree, but what if men are by physiology or temperament, more adapted to exercise authority or to issue command?"

Then ensues another discussion about women's role in modern society, and the other person participating in the discussion says "I think it's very hard to deny that there is an underrepresentation of women," to which the Leader of the Opposition says, "But now, there's an assumption that this is a bad thing."

This is the man from whom we're supposed to take lectures about sexism. And then of course it goes on. I was very offended personally when the Leader of the Opposition, as Minister of Health, said, and I quote, "Abortion is the easy way out." I was very personally offended by those comments. You said that in March 2004, I suggest you check the records.

I was also very offended on behalf of the women of Australia when in the course of this carbon pricing campaign, the Leader of the Opposition said "What the housewives of Australia need to understand as they do the ironing…" Thank you for that painting of women's roles in modern Australia.

And then of course, I was offended too by the sexism, by the misogyny of the Leader of the Opposition catcalling across this table at me as I sit here as Prime Minister, "If the Prime Minister wants to, politically speaking, make an honest woman of herself...", something that would never have been said to any man sitting in this chair. I was offended when the Leader of the Opposition went outside in the front of Parliament and stood next to a sign that said "Ditch the witch."

I was offended when the Leader of the Opposition stood next to a sign that described me as a man's bitch. I was offended by those things. Misogyny, sexism, every day from this Leader of the Opposition. Every day in every way, across the time the Leader of the Opposition has sat in that chair and I've sat in this chair, that is all we have heard from him.

And now, the Leader of the Opposition wants to be taken seriously, apparently he's woken up after this track record and all of these statements, and he's woken up and he's gone "Oh dear, there's this thing called sexism, oh my lords, there's this thing called misogyny. Now who's one of them? Oh, the Speaker must be because that suits my political purpose."

Doesn't turn a hair about any of his past statements, doesn't walk into this Parliament and apologise to the women of Australia. Doesn't walk into this Parliament and apologise to me for the things that have come out of his mouth. But now seeks to use this as a battering ram against someone else.

Well this kind of hypocrisy must not be tolerated, which is why this motion from the Leader of the Opposition should not be taken seriously.

And then second, the Leader of the Opposition is always wonderful about walking into this Parliament and giving me and others a lecture about what they should take responsibility for.

Always wonderful about that — everything that I should take responsibility for, now apparently including the text messages of the Member for Fisher. Always keen to say how others should assume responsibility, particularly me.

Well can anybody remind me if the Leader of the Opposition has taken any responsibility for the conduct of the Sydney Young Liberals and the attendance at this event of members of his frontbench?

Has he taken any responsibility for the conduct of members of his political party and members of his frontbench who apparently when the most vile things were being said about my family, raised no voice of objection? Nobody walked out of the room; no-one walked up to Mr Jones and said that this was not acceptable.

Instead of course, it was all viewed as good fun until it was run in a Sunday newspaper and then the Leader of the Opposition and others started ducking for cover.

Big on lectures of responsibility, very light on accepting responsibility himself for the vile conduct of members of his political party.

Third, Deputy Speaker, why the Leader of the Opposition should not be taken seriously on this motion.

The Leader of the Opposition and the Deputy Leader of the Opposition have come into this place and have talked about the Member for Fisher. Well, let me remind the Opposition and the Leader of the opposition party about their track record and association with the Member for Fisher.

I remind them that the National Party preselected the Member for Fisher for the 1984 election, that the National Party preselected the Member for Fisher for the 1987 election, that the Liberals preselected Mr Slipper for the 1993 election, then the 1996 election, then the 1998 election, then for the 2001 election, then for the 2004 election, then for the 2007 election and then for the 2010 election.

And across these elections, Mr Slipper enjoyed the personal support of the Leader of the Opposition. I remind the Leader of the Opposition that on 28 September 2010, following the last election campaign, when Mr Slipper was elected as Deputy Speaker, the Leader of the Opposition at that stage said this, and I quote.

He referred to the Member for Maranoa, who was also elected to a position at the same time, and then went on as follows: "And the Member for Fisher will serve as a fine complement to the Member for Scullin in the chair. I believe that the Parliament will be well-served by the team which will occupy the chair in this chamber. I congratulate the Member for Fisher, who has been a friend of mine for a very long time, who has served this Parliament in many capacities with distinction."

The words of the Leader of the Opposition on record, about his personal friendship with Mr [Slipper], and on record about his view about Mr Slipper's qualities and attributes to be the Speaker.

No walking away from those words, they were the statement of the Leader of the

Opposition then. I remind the Leader of the Opposition, who now comes in here and speaks about apparently his inability to work with or talk to Mr Slipper. I remind the Leader of the Opposition he attended Mr Slipper's wedding.

Did he walk up to Mr Slipper in the middle of the service and say he was disgusted to be there? Was that the attitude he took? No, he attended that wedding as a friend.

The Leader of the Opposition keen to lecture others about what they ought to know or did know about Mr Slipper. Well with respect, I'd say to the Leader of the Opposition after a long personal association including attending Mr Slipper's wedding, it would be interesting to know whether the Leader of the Opposition was surprised by these text messages.

He's certainly in a position to speak more intimately about Mr Slipper than I am, and many other people in this Parliament, given this long personal association.

Then of course the Leader of the Opposition comes into this place and says, and I quote, "Every day the Prime Minister stands in this Parliament to defend this Speaker will be another day of shame for this Parliament, another day of shame for a government which should already have died of shame."

Well can I indicate to the Leader of the Opposition the Government is not dying of shame, my father did not die of shame, what the Leader of the Opposition should be ashamed of is his performance in this Parliament and the sexism he brings with it. Now about the text messages that are on the public record or reported in the – that's a direct quote from the Leader of the Opposition so I suggest those groaning have a word with him.

On the conduct of Mr Slipper, and on the text messages that are in the public domain, I have seen the press reports of those text messages. I am offended by their content. I am offended by their content because I am always offended by sexism. I am offended by their content because I am always offended by statements that are anti-women.

I am offended by those things in the same way that I have been offended by things that the Leader of the Opposition has said, and no doubt will continue to say in the future. Because if this today was an exhibition of his new feminine side, well I don't think we've got much to look forward to in terms of changed conduct.

I am offended by those text messages. But I also believe, in terms of this Parliament making a decision about the speakership, that this Parliament should recognise that there is a court case in progress. That the judge has reserved his decision, that having waited for a number of months for the legal matters surrounding Mr Slipper to come to a conclusion, that this Parliament should see that conclusion.

I believe that is the appropriate path forward, and that people will then have an opportunity to make up their minds with the fullest information available to them.

But whenever people make up their minds about those questions, what I won't stand for, what I will never stand for is the Leader of the Opposition coming into this place and peddling a double standard. Peddling a standard for Mr Slipper he would not set for himself. Peddling a standard for Mr Slipper he has not set for other members of his frontbench.

Peddling a standard for Mr Slipper that has not been acquitted by the people who have been sent out to say the vilest and most revolting things like his former Shadow Parliamentary Secretary Senator Bernardi.

I will not ever see the Leader of the Opposition seek to impose his double standard on this Parliament. Sexism should always be unacceptable. We should conduct ourselves as it should always be unacceptable. The Leader of the Opposition says do something; well he could do something himself if he wants to deal with sexism in this Parliament.

He could change his behaviour, he could apologise for all his past statements, he could apologise for standing next to signs describing me as a witch and a bitch, terminology that is now objected to by the frontbench of the Opposition.

He could change a standard himself if he sought to do so. But we will see none of that from the Leader of the Opposition because on these questions he is incapable of change. Capable of double standards, but incapable of change. His double standards should not rule this Parliament.

Good sense, common sense, proper process is what should rule this Parliament. That's what I believe is the path forward for this Parliament, not the kind of double standards and political game-playing imposed by the Leader of the Opposition now looking at his watch because apparently a woman's spoken too long.

I've had him yell at me to shut up in the past, but I will take the remaining seconds of my speaking time to say to the Leader of the Opposition I think the best course for him is to reflect on the standards he's exhibited in public life, on the responsibility he should take for his public statements; on his close personal connection with Peter Slipper, on the hypocrisy he has displayed in this House today.

And on that basis, because of the Leader of the Opposition's motivations, this Parliament today should reject this motion and the Leader of the Opposition should think seriously about the role of women in public life and in Australian society because we are entitled to a better standard than this. '

Julia Gillard was born on 29 September 1961 in Barry, Wales, and immigrated to Australia with her family when she was five years old. Growing up in South Australia, she attended the University of Adelaide and graduated with a law degree in 1986. Specialising in industrial law, she was the successful Labor candidate for the Melbourne seat of Lalor in 1998, and was elected unopposed as Deputy Opposition Leader to Kevin Rudd in 2006.

In June 2013, two years and three days after she succeeded Kevin Rudd as Prime Minister, Gillard was replaced by Rudd in another party room ballot. With plunging opinion polls and an election looming, the Labor Party had lost its way and its nerve. Gillard was out and Rudd was back in. Julia Gillard immediately announced her retirement from politics and Federal Labor was easily defeated by the Tony Abbott-led Liberal party at the September elections.

While Kevin Rudd was later suspected as the source of much of the white-anting Julia Gillard experienced by her own party, and Tony Abbott suffered a similar fate and was dumped as Prime Minister by his own party in 2015, history will look favourably on the role Gillard played in Australian politics. As Australia's first female Prime Minister, she suffered much more political scrutiny and personal barbs than her male colleagues have ever encountered, but she still managed to pave the way for Australia's next female Prime Minister.

Malala Yousafzai

'A World at School Speech'

UN General Assembly, New York, July 12, 2013

On the afternoon of October 9, 2012, schoolgirl Malala Yousafzai boarded a school bus in the northwest Pakistani district of Swat. A gunman on the bus asked for her by name and then fired three shots at her. One hit her on the left side of her forehead at an angle, travelled under her skin and lodged in her shoulder. Two other girls on the bus were also injured. Malala's condition was critical, and she was repatriated to Germany in a medically induced coma for emergency treatment. Offers came in from around the world to help her and she continued on to Queen Elizabeth Hospital in Birmingham, England for surgery and extensive rehabilitation.

In surviving this assassination attempt, Malala became 'the most famous teenager in the world'. Her 'crime' was in promoting education for girls in the Swat Valley, an area under the control of fundamental Muslims the Taliban, on a BBC Urdu website. In January 2009 the Taliban proclaimed that girls could not attend school in the area and began a program of destroying school buildings. Although this edict was later relaxed as the Taliban struggled to maintain a hold on the area, Malala's family ran a number of local schools and were vocal opponents of the Taliban.

Nominated for the International Children's Peace Prize in 2011, she was awarded Pakistan's National Youth peace prize the same year. The New York Times featured her life in a documentary in 2012, which brought her greater international acclaim, but also to the attention of local Taliban leaders. The young girl who spoke out would have to be silenced.

On July 12 2013, the first ever 'Youth Takeover' movement took place in organizations all over the world, including at the United Nations in New

York. The 'A World at School' organization and their partners brought together hundreds of young education advocates from around the world, including Malala Yousafzai. It was the 16-year old's birthday, and her first public speech since being attacked by the Taliban. The UN named July 12, 2013 'Malala Day'.

❟ In the name of God, The Most Beneficent, The Most Merciful.

Honourable UN Secretary General Mr Ban Ki-moon,

Respected President General Assembly Vuk Jeremic

Honourable UN envoy for Global education Mr Gordon Brown,

Respected elders and my dear brothers and sisters;

Today, it is an honour for me to be speaking again after a long time. Being here with such honourable people is a great moment in my life.

I don't know where to begin my speech. I don't know what people would be expecting me to say. But first of all, thank you to God for whom we all are equal and thank you to every person who has prayed for my fast recovery and a new life. I cannot believe how much love people have shown me. I have received thousands of good wish cards and gifts from all over the world. Thank you to all of them. Thank you to the children whose innocent words encouraged me. Thank you to my elders whose prayers strengthened me.

I would like to thank my nurses, doctors and all of the staff of the hospitals in Pakistan and the UK and the UAE government who have helped me get better and recover my strength. I fully support Mr Ban Ki-moon the Secretary-General in his Global Education First Initiative and the work of the UN Special Envoy Mr Gordon Brown. And I thank them both for the leadership they continue to give. They continue to inspire all of us to action.

Dear brothers and sisters, do remember one thing. Malala day is not my day. Today is the day of every woman, every boy and every girl who have raised their voice for their rights. There are hundreds of Human rights activists and social workers who are not only speaking for human rights, but who are struggling to achieve their goals of education, peace and equality. Thousands of people have been killed by the terrorists and millions have been injured. I am just one of them.

So here I stand ... one girl among many.

I speak – not for myself, but for all girls and boys.

I raise up my voice – not so that I can shout, but so that those without a voice can be heard.

Those who have fought for their rights:

Their right to live in peace.

Their right to be treated with dignity.

Their right to equality of opportunity.

Their right to be educated.

Dear Friends, on the 9th of October 2012, the Taliban shot me on the left side of my forehead. They shot my friends too. They thought that the bullets would silence us. But they failed. And then, out of that silence came, thousands of voices. The terrorists thought that they would change our aims and stop our ambitions but nothing changed in my life except this: Weakness, fear and hopelessness died. Strength, power and courage was born. I am the same Malala. My ambitions are the same. My hopes are the same. My dreams are the same.

Dear sisters and brothers, I am not against anyone. Neither am I here to speak in terms of personal revenge against the Taliban or any other terrorists group. I am here to speak up for the right of education of every child. I want education for the sons and the daughters of all the extremists especially the Taliban.

I do not even hate the Talib who shot me. Even if there is a gun in my hand and he stands in front of me. I would not shoot him. This is the compassion that I have learnt from Muhammad-the prophet of mercy, Jesus Christ and Lord Buddha. This is the legacy of change that I have inherited from Martin Luther King, Nelson Mandela and Muhammad Ali Jinnah. This is the philosophy of non-violence that I have learnt from Gandhi Jee, Bacha Khan and Mother Teresa. And this is the forgiveness that I have learnt from my mother and father. This is what my soul is telling me, be peaceful and love everyone.

Dear sisters and brothers, we realise the importance of light when we see darkness. We realise the importance of our voice when we are silenced. In the same way, when we were in Swat, the north of Pakistan, we realised the importance of pens and books when we saw the guns.

282

The wise saying, "The pen is mightier than sword" was true. The extremists are afraid of books and pens. The power of education frightens them. They are afraid of women. The power of the voice of women frightens them. And that is why they killed 14 innocent medical students in the recent attack in Quetta. And that is why they killed many female teachers and polio workers in Khyber Pukhtoon Khwa and FATA. That is why they are blasting schools every day. Because they were and they are afraid of change, afraid of the equality that we will bring into our society.

I remember that there was a boy in our school who was asked by a journalist, "Why are the Taliban against education?" He answered very simply. By pointing to his book he said, "A Talib doesn't know what is written inside this book." They think that God is a tiny, little conservative being who would send girls to the hell just because of going to school. The terrorists are misusing the name of Islam and Pashtun society for their own personal benefits. Pakistan is peace-loving democratic country. Pashtuns want education for their daughters and sons. And Islam is a religion of peace, humanity and brotherhood. Islam says that it is not only each child's right to get education, rather it is their duty and responsibility.

Honourable Secretary General, peace is necessary for education. In many parts of the world especially Pakistan and Afghanistan; terrorism, wars and conflicts stop children to go to their schools. We are really tired of these wars. Women and children are suffering in many parts of the world in many ways. In India, innocent and poor children are victims of child labour. Many schools have been destroyed in Nigeria. People in Afghanistan have been affected by the hurdles of extremism for decades. Young girls have to do domestic child labour and are forced to get married at early age. Poverty, ignorance, injustice, racism and the deprivation of basic rights are the main problems faced by both men and women.

Dear fellows, today I am focusing on women's rights and girls' education because they are suffering the most. There was a time when women social activists asked men to stand up for their rights. But, this time, we will do it by ourselves. I am not telling men to step away from speaking for women's rights rather I am focusing on women to be independent to fight for themselves.

Dear sisters and brothers, now it's time to speak up.

So today, we call upon the world leaders to change their strategic policies in favour of peace and prosperity.

We call upon the world leaders that all the peace deals must protect women and children's rights. A deal that goes against the dignity of women and their rights is unacceptable.

We call upon all governments to ensure free compulsory education for every child all over the world.

We call upon all governments to fight against terrorism and violence, to protect children from brutality and harm.

We call upon the developed nations to support the expansion of educational opportunities for girls in the developing world.

We call upon all communities to be tolerant – to reject prejudice based on cast, creed, sect, religion or gender. To ensure freedom and equality for women so that they can flourish. We cannot all succeed when half of us are held back.

We call upon our sisters around the world to be brave – to embrace the strength within themselves and realise their full potential.

Dear brothers and sisters, we want schools and education for every child's bright future. We will continue our journey to our destination of peace and education for everyone. No one can stop us. We will speak for our rights and we will bring change through our voice. We must believe in the power and the strength of our words. Our words can change the world.

Because we are all together, united for the cause of education. And if we want to achieve our goal, then let us empower ourselves with the weapon of knowledge and let us shield ourselves with unity and togetherness.

Dear brothers and sisters, we must not forget that millions of people are suffering from poverty, injustice and ignorance. We must not forget that millions of children are out of schools. We must not forget that our sisters and brothers are waiting for a bright peaceful future.

So let us wage a global struggle against illiteracy, poverty and terrorism and let us pick up our books and pens. They are our most powerful weapons.

One child, one teacher, one pen and one book can change the world.

Education is the only solution. Education First. '

Malala Yousafzai was born on 12 July 1997 in Mingora, in the Sway Valley in Pakistan's northwest Khyber Pakhtunkhwa province. On 15 October 2012, the former British Prime Minister Gordon Brown, the then UN Special Envoy for Global Education, visited her in the hospital and launched a petition in her name. Using the slogan 'I am Malala', the petition called on international organisations to end discrimination against girls and to ensure the world's 61 million out-of-school children were in education by the end of 2015.

After her shooting, Malala attended the all-girls' Edgbaston High School in Birmingham and published a best-selling memoir (I am Malala: The Story of the Girl Who Stood Up for Education and was Shot by the Taliban, co-written with British journalist Christina Lamb). The non for profit Malala Fund was established to offer education and training to girls aged 14 to 18, with Malala stating that leaders around the world needed to invest in 'books not bullets'.

On October 10, 2014, at age 17, Malala Yousafzai became the world's youngest Nobel laureate when she was named co-recipient of the 2014 Nobel Peace Prize.

Pope Francis

'Apology to Church Victims of Sexual Abuse'

St. Charles Borromeo Seminary, Montgomery County, Pennsylvania, 2015

O n March 13, 2013, Cardinal Jorge Bergoglio of Argentina was elected the 266th Pope of the Catholic Church upon the resignation of Pope Benedict XVI due to ill health. The first non-European pontiff as well as being the first Jesuit Pope Francis, as he became known, also inherited a firestorm that had quickly engulfed the Catholic Church in the new millennium.

Between 2001 and 2010, the Vatican requested that Dioceses from around the world send their sexual abuse files to Rome to be centrally administered. The historic and systematic failure, however, of those in Church power to report criminal sexual abuse to law enforcement agencies had a far-reaching effect on support for religious institutions especially in traditional Catholic heartlands such as Ireland, Belgium, Spain, Australia and the United States of America.

In the US alone, more than 6,500 clergy were accused of abuse dating back to 1950 – about 6% of all clergy who served in the Catholic Church – with hundreds removed from contact with children or from the priesthood altogether. More than 17,000 victims were identified or came forward, with more than $3 billion paid out in compensation by the 195 US dioceses. Many of the Bishops in charge of those dioceses, men who routinely covered up the abuse over the years and merely transferred paedophile priests to other parishes, escaped scrutiny for their failure to notify police authorities. When newly elected Pope Francis visited the US in 2015, he tackled the problem head on.

On Sunday, September 27, 2015 at St. Charles Borromeo Seminary,

Montgomery County, Pennsylvania, Pope Francis spoke to five victims—three women, two men — of sexual abuse at the hands of clergy members, family or teachers. The group and their families were accompanied by Cardinal Seán Patrick O'Malley, Archbishop of Boston and chairman of the commission set up by the Pope for the protection of minors, Archbishop Charles Chaput and Bishop Michael Fitzgerald. The Pope greeted the victims individually, listened to their stories and prayed with them.

Pope Francis renewed the Church's commitment that 'all victims are heard and treated with justice, that the guilty be punished and that the crimes of abuse be combated with an effective prevention activity in the Church and in society.' The meeting lasted about half an hour and ended with a blessing from the Holy Father. The Pope then addressed the congregation of 300 US Bishops, and the media:

❛ I carry in my heart the stories, the suffering and the pain of the minors that have been sexually abused by priests. I'm overwhelmed by the shame that people who were in charge of caring for those young ones raped them and caused them great damages. I regret this profoundly. God cries! The crimes and sins of the sexual abuse to minors can't be kept a secret anymore. I commit to the zealous oversight of the Church to protect minors, and I promise that everyone responsible will be held accountable. You, they, the survivors of abuse have become real heralds of hope and ministers of mercy. Humbly we owe each one of them and their families our gratitude for their immense courage for making the light of Christ shine over the evil of minor sexual abuse. I say this because I have just met by a group of people who were abused when they were children that are helped and accompanied here in Philadelphia …

My dearest brothers and sisters in Christ, I am grateful for this opportunity to meet you. I am blessed by your presence. Thank you for coming here today.

Words cannot fully express my sorrow for the abuse you suffered. You are precious children of God who should always expect our protection, our care and our love. I am profoundly sorry that your innocence was violated by those who you trusted. In some cases the trust was betrayed by members of your own family, in other cases by priests who carry a sacred responsibility for the care of soul. In all circumstances, the betrayal was a terrible violation of human dignity.

For those who were abused by a member of the clergy, I am deeply sorry for the times when you or your family spoke out, to report the abuse, but you were not heard or believed. Please know that the Holy Father hears you and believes you. I deeply regret that some bishops failed in their responsibility to protect children. It is very disturbing to know that in some cases bishops even were abusers. I pledge to you that we will follow the path of truth wherever it may lead. Clergy and bishops will be held accountable when they abuse or fail to protect children.

We are gathered here in Philadelphia to celebrate God's gift of family life. Within our family of faith and our human families, the sins and crimes of sexual abuse of children must no longer be held in secret and in shame. As we anticipate the Jubilee Year of Mercy, your presence, so generously given despite the anger and pain you have experienced, reveals the merciful heart of Christ. Your stories of survival, each unique and compelling, are powerful signs of the hope that comes from the Lord's promise to be with us always.

It is good to know that you have brought family members and friends with you today. I am grateful for their compassionate support and pray that many people of the church will respond to the call to accompany those who have suffered abuse. May the Door of Mercy be opened wide in our dioceses, our parishes, our homes and our hearts, to receive those who were abused and to seek the path to forgiveness by trusting in the Lord. We promise to support your continued healing and to always be vigilant to protect the children of today and tomorrow.

When the disciples who walked with Jesus on the road to Emmaus recognized that He was the Risen Lord, they asked Jesus to stay with them. Like those disciples, I humbly beg you and all survivors of abuse to stay with us, to stay with the Church, and that together, as pilgrims on the journey of faith, we might find our way to the Father. **'**

Jorge Mario Bergoglio was born on December 17, 1936, in Buenos Aires Argentina. Entering the priesthood in 1969 after studying at a Jesuit seminary, Bergoglio served as archbishop of Buenos Aires from 1998 to 2013 as well as becoming a cardinal in 2001. When he was elected to the papacy in 2013, at age 76, he took the papal name in honour of St Francis of Assis.

Having not been part of the insular, political atmosphere of the Vatican enclave of Bishops, Pope Francis brought a refreshing humility and open-mindedness to the papacy. Opting to live modestly in a two-room apartment rather than following the tradition of his predecessors in remaining in the luxurious Apostolic Palace in The Vatican, Pope Francis spoke compassionately of the need for environmental stewardship, of the importance of finding peace in the world, of the reconciliation of the abused to the church and the acceptance of gay and divorced people searching 'for the Lord and are of good will.'

In December 2013, Pope Francis was named Person of the Year by *Time* magazine.

Barack Obama

Common-Sense Gun Safety Reform
White House, Washington D.C., January 5, 2016

J ust over 45 years after Rev. Martin Luther King Jnr declared 'I have a dream ...' Democratic presidential nominee Barack Obama became the first black US President in history. A popular figure when he took office in January 2009, he easily won a second term four years later despite being stymied by a Republican-dominated Congress and Senate. Conservative America continued to oppose his measures and categorised his presidency as 'a failure'. For a man who had not brought the hint of a scandal to his eight years as president, this view is not only unjustified but also unfair. Conservatives focused on peripheral issues – was Obama born in the US, they asked; was he even a Christian? – and highlighted his inability to bring about real change in that most vexatious of American issues, gun control.

After numerous mass shootings that occurred during his presidency – the death of 12 cinema goers in Colorado by gunman James Holmes in July 2011; the Sandy Hook school massacre in December 2012 that claimed the lives of 20 infant school children and seven adults; and the South Carolina Church killings, in which a white supremacist shot dead nine black people as they prayed together – Barack Obama, in the final year of his presidency, bypassed a do-nothing Congress and rolled out his own 'common sense gun safety' measures.

An often emotional President Obama delivered the following speech at the White House on 5 January, 2016, in the presence of many of the families of victims of America's gun violence:

Five years ago this week, a sitting member of Congress and 18 others were shot at, at a supermarket in Tucson, Arizona. It wasn't the first time I had to talk to the nation in response to a mass shooting, nor would it be the last. Fort Hood. Binghamton. Aurora. Oak Creek. Newtown. The Navy Yard. Santa Barbara. Charleston. San Bernardino. Too many.

Thanks to a great medical team and the love of her husband, Mark, my dear friend and colleague, Gabby Giffords, survived. She's here with us today, with her wonderful mom. Thanks to a great medical team, her wonderful husband, Mark - who, by the way, the last time I met with Mark – this is just a small aside – you may know Mark's twin brother is in outer space. He came to the office, and I said, how often are you talking to him? And he says, well, I usually talk to him every day, but the call was coming in right before the meeting so I think I may have not answered his call – which made me feel kind of bad. That's a long-distance call. So I told him if his brother, Scott, is calling today, that he should take it. Turn the ringer on.

I was there with Gabby when she was still in the hospital, and we didn't think necessarily at that point that she was going to survive. And that visit right before a memorial - about an hour later Gabby first opened her eyes. And I remember talking to mom about that. But I know the pain that she and her family have endured these past five years, and the rehabilitation and the work and the effort to recover from shattering injuries.

And then I think of all the Americans who aren't as fortunate. Every single year, more than 30,000 Americans have their lives cut short by guns - 30,000. Suicides. Domestic violence. Gang shootouts. Accidents. Hundreds of thousands of Americans have lost brothers and sisters, or buried their own children. Many have had to learn to live with a disability, or learned to live without the love of their life.

A number of those people are here today. They can tell you some stories. In this room right here, there are a lot of stories. There's a lot of heartache. There's a lot of resilience, there's a lot of strength, but there's also a lot of pain. And this is just a small sample.

The United States of America is not the only country on Earth with violent or dangerous people. We are not inherently more prone to violence. But we are the only advanced country on Earth that sees this kind of mass violence erupt with this kind of frequency. It doesn't happen in other advanced countries. It's not even close. And as I've said before, somehow we've become numb to it and we start thinking that this is normal.

And instead of thinking about how to solve the problem, this has become one of our most polarized, partisan debates - despite the fact that there's a general consensus in America about what needs to be done. That's part of the reason why, on Thursday, I'm going to hold a town hall meeting in Virginia on gun violence. Because my goal here is to bring good people on both sides of this issue together for an open discussion.

I'm not on the ballot again. I'm not looking to score some points. I think we can disagree without impugning other people's motives or without being disagreeable. We don't need to be talking past one another. But we do have to feel a sense of urgency about it. In Dr. King's words, we need to feel the "fierce urgency of now." Because people are dying. And the constant excuses for inaction no longer do, no longer suffice.

That's why we're here today. Not to debate the last mass shooting, but to do something to try to prevent the next one. To prove that the vast majority of Americans, even if our voices aren't always the loudest or most extreme, care enough about a little boy like Daniel to come together and take common-sense steps to save lives and protect more of our children.

Now, I want to be absolutely clear at the start — and I've said this over and over again, this also becomes routine, there is a ritual about this whole thing that I have to do — I believe in the Second Amendment. It's there written on the paper. It guarantees a right to bear arms. No matter how many times people try to twist my words around - I taught constitutional law, I know a little about this — I get it. But I also believe that we can find ways to reduce gun violence consistent with the Second Amendment.

I mean, think about it. We all believe in the First Amendment, the guarantee of free speech, but we accept that you can't yell "fire" in a theater. We understand there are some constraints on our freedom in order to protect innocent people. We cherish our right to privacy, but we accept that you have to go through metal detectors before being allowed to board a plane. It's not because people like doing that, but we understand that that's part of the price of living in a civilized society.

And what's often ignored in this debate is that a majority of gun owners actually agree. A majority of gun owners agree that we can respect the Second Amendment while keeping an irresponsible, law-breaking feud from inflicting harm on a massive scale.

Today, background checks are required at gun stores. If a father wants to teach his daughter how to hunt, he can walk into a gun store, get a background check, purchase his weapon safely and responsibly. This is not seen as an infringement on the Second Amendment. Contrary to the claims of what some gun rights proponents have suggested, this hasn't been the first step in some slippery slope to mass confiscation. Contrary to claims of some presidential candidates, apparently, before this meeting, this is not a plot to take away everybody's guns. You pass a background check; you purchase a firearm.

The problem is some gun sellers have been operating under a different set of rules. A violent felon can buy the exact same weapon over the Internet with no background check, no questions asked. A recent study found that about one in 30 people looking to buy guns on one website had criminal records - one out of 30 had a criminal record. We're talking about individuals convicted of serious crimes - aggravated assault, domestic violence, robbery, illegal gun possession. People with lengthy criminal histories buying deadly weapons all too easily. And this was just one website within the span of a few months.

So we've created a system in which dangerous people are allowed to play by a different set of rules than a responsible gun owner who buys his or her gun the right way and subjects themselves to a background check. That doesn't make sense. Everybody should have to abide by the same rules. Most Americans and gun owners agree. And that's what we tried to change three years ago, after 26 Americans — including 20 children — were murdered at Sandy Hook Elementary.

Two United States Senators — Joe Manchin, a Democrat from West Virginia, and Pat Toomey, a Republican from Pennsylvania, both gun owners, both strong defenders of our Second Amendment rights, both with "A" grades from the NRA — that's hard to get - worked together in good faith, consulting with folks like our Vice President, who has been a champion on this for a long time, to write a common-sense compromise bill that would have required virtually everyone who buys a gun to get a background check. That was it. Pretty common-sense stuff. Ninety percent of Americans supported that idea. Ninety percent of Democrats in the Senate voted for that idea. But it failed because 90 percent of Republicans in the Senate voted against that idea.

How did this become such a partisan issue? Republican President George W. Bush once said, "I believe in background checks at gun shows or anywhere to make sure that guns don't get into the hands of people that shouldn't have them." Senator John McCain introduced a bipartisan measure to address the gun show loophole, saying, "We need this amendment because criminals and terrorists have exploited and are exploiting this very obvious loophole in our gun safety laws." Even the NRA used to support expanded background checks. And by the way, most of its members still do. Most Republican voters still do.

How did we get here? How did we get to the place where people think requiring a comprehensive background check means taking away people's guns?

Each time this comes up, we are fed the excuse that common-sense reforms like background checks might not have stopped the last massacre, or the one before that, or the one before that, so why bother trying. I reject that thinking. We know we can't stop every act of violence, every act of evil in the world. But maybe we could try to stop one act of evil, one act of violence.

Some of you may recall, at the same time that Sandy Hook happened, a disturbed person in China took a knife and tried to kill - with a knife - a bunch of children in China. But most of them survived because he didn't have access to a powerful weapon. We maybe can't save everybody, but we could save some. Just as we don't prevent all traffic accidents but we take steps to try to reduce traffic accidents.

As Ronald Reagan once said, if mandatory background checks could save more lives, "it would be well worth making it the law of the land." The bill before Congress three years ago met that test. Unfortunately, too many senators failed theirs.

In fact, we know that background checks make a difference. After Connecticut passed a law requiring background checks and gun safety courses, gun deaths decreased by 40 percent - 40 percent. Meanwhile, since Missouri repealed a law requiring comprehensive background checks and purchase permits, gun deaths have increased to almost 50 percent higher than the national average. One study found, unsurprisingly, that criminals in Missouri now have easier access to guns.

And the evidence tells us that in states that require background checks, law-abiding Americans don't find it any harder to purchase guns whatsoever. Their guns have not been confiscated. Their rights have not been infringed.

And that's just the information we have access to. With more research, we could further improve gun safety. Just as with more research, we've reduced traffic fatalities enormously over the last 30 years. We do research when cars, food, medicine, even toys harm people so that we make them safer. And you know what - research, science - those are good things.

They work. (Laughter and applause.) They do.

But think about this. When it comes to an inherently deadly weapon - nobody argues that guns are potentially deadly - weapons that kill tens of thousands of Americans every year, Congress actually voted to make it harder for public health experts to conduct research into gun violence; made it harder to collect data and facts and develop strategies to reduce gun violence. Even after San Bernardino, they've refused to make it harder for terror suspects who can't get on a plane to buy semi-automatic weapons. That's not right. That can't be right.

So the gun lobby may be holding Congress hostage right now, but they cannot hold America hostage. We do not have to accept this carnage as the price of freedom.

Now, I want to be clear. Congress still needs to act. The folks in this room will not rest until Congress does. Because once Congress gets on board with common-sense gun safety measures we can reduce gun violence a whole lot more. But we also can't wait. Until we have a Congress that's in line with the majority of Americans, there are actions within my legal authority that we can take to help reduce gun violence and save more lives -- actions that protect our rights and our kids.

After Sandy Hook, Joe and I worked together with our teams and we put forward a whole series of executive actions to try to tighten up the existing rules and systems that we had in place. But today, we want to take it a step further. So let me outline what we're going to be doing.

Number one, anybody in the business of selling firearms must get a license and conduct background checks, or be subject to criminal prosecutions. It doesn't matter whether you're doing it over the Internet or at a gun show. It's not where you do it, but what you do.

We're also expanding background checks to cover violent criminals who try to buy some of the most dangerous firearms by hiding behind trusts and corporations and various cut-outs.

We're also taking steps to make the background check system more efficient. Under the guidance of Jim Comey and the FBI, our Deputy Director Tom Brandon at ATF, we're going to hire more folks to process applications faster, and we're going to bring an outdated background check system into the 21st century.

And these steps will actually lead to a smoother process for law-abiding gun owners, a smoother process for responsible gun dealers, a stronger process for protecting the people from - the public from dangerous people. So that's number one.

Number two, we're going to do everything we can to ensure the smart and effective enforcement of gun safety laws that are already on the books, which means we're going to add 200 more ATF agents and investigators. We're going to require firearms dealers to report more lost or stolen guns on a timely basis. We're working with advocates to protect victims of domestic abuse from gun violence, where too often - where too often, people are not getting the protection that they need.

Number three, we're going to do more to help those suffering from mental illness get the help that they need. High-profile mass shootings tend to shine a light on those few mentally unstable people who inflict harm on others. But the truth is, is that nearly two in three gun deaths are from suicides. So a lot of our work is to prevent people from hurting themselves.

That's why we made sure that the Affordable Care Act - also known as Obamacare - (laughter and applause) - that law made sure that treatment for mental health was covered the same as treatment for any other illness. And that's why we're going to invest $500 million to expand access to treatment across the country.

It's also why we're going to ensure that federal mental health records are submitted to the background check system, and remove barriers that prevent states from reporting relevant information. If we can continue to de-stigmatize mental health issues, get folks proper care, and fill gaps in the background check system, then we can spare more families the pain of losing a loved one to suicide.

And for those in Congress who so often rush to blame mental illness for mass shootings as a way of avoiding action on guns, here's your chance to support these efforts. Put your money where your mouth is.

Number four, we're going to boost gun safety technology. Today, many gun injuries and deaths are the result of legal guns that were stolen or misused or discharged accidentally. In 2013 alone, more than 500 people lost their lives to gun accidents – and that includes 30 children younger than five years old. In the greatest, most technologically advanced nation on Earth, there is no reason for this. We need to develop new technologies that make guns safer. If we can set it up so you can't unlock your phone unless you've got the right fingerprint, why can't we do the same thing for our guns? If there's an app that can help us find a missing tablet - which happens to me often the older I get - if we can do it for your iPad, there's no reason we can't do it with a stolen gun. If a child can't open a bottle of aspirin, we should make sure that they can't pull a trigger on a gun. Right?

So we're going to advance research. We're going to work with the private sector to update firearms technology.

And some gun retailers are already stepping up by refusing to finalize a purchase without a complete background check, or by refraining from selling semi-automatic weapons or high-capacity magazines. And I hope that more retailers and more manufacturers join them - because they should care as much as anybody about a product that now kills almost as many Americans as car accidents.

I make this point because none of us can do this alone. I think Mark made that point earlier. All of us should be able to work together to find a balance that declares the rest of our rights are also important — Second Amendment rights are important, but there are other rights that we care about as well. And we have to be able to balance them. Because our right to worship freely and safely —that right was denied to Christians in Charleston, South Carolina. And that was denied Jews in Kansas City. And that was denied Muslims in Chapel Hill, and Sikhs in Oak Creek. They had rights, too.

Our right to peaceful assembly — that right was robbed from moviegoers in Aurora and Lafayette. Our unalienable right to life, and liberty, and the pursuit of happiness — those rights were stripped from college students in Blacksburg and Santa Barbara, and from high schoolers at Columbine, and from first-graders in Newtown. First-graders. And from every family who never imagined that their loved one would be taken from our lives by a bullet from a gun.

Every time I think about those kids it gets me mad. And by the way, it happens on the streets of Chicago every day.

So all of us need to demand a Congress brave enough to stand up to the gun lobby's lies. All of us need to stand up and protect its citizens. All of us need to demand governors and legislatures and businesses do their part to make our communities safer. We need the wide majority of responsible gun owners who grieve with us every time this happens and feel like your views are not being properly represented to join with us to demand something better.

And we need voters who want safer gun laws, and who are disappointed in leaders who stand in their way, to remember come election time.

I mean, some of this is just simple math. Yes, the gun lobby is loud and it is organized in defense of making it effortless for guns to be available for anybody, any time. Well, you know what, the rest of us, we all have to be just as passionate. We have to be just as organized in defense of our kids. This is not that complicated. The reason Congress blocks laws is because they want to win elections. And if you make it hard for them to win an election if they block those laws, they'll change course, I promise you.

And, yes, it will be hard, and it won't happen overnight. It won't happen during this Congress. It won't happen during my presidency. But a lot of things don't happen overnight. A woman's right to vote didn't happen overnight. The liberation of African Americans didn't happen overnight. LGBT rights - that was decades' worth of work. So just because it's hard, that's no excuse not to try.

And if you have any doubt as to why you should feel that "fierce urgency of now," think about what happened three weeks ago. Zaevion Dobson was a sophomore at Fulton High School in Knoxville, Tennessee. He played football; beloved by his classmates and his teachers. His own mayor called him one of their city's success stories. The week before Christmas, he headed to a friend's house to play video games. He wasn't in the wrong place at the wrong time. He hadn't made a bad decision. He was exactly where any other kid would be. Your kid. My kids. And then gunmen started firing. And Zaevion - who was in high school, hadn't even gotten started in life - dove on top of three girls to shield them from the bullets. And he was shot in the head. And the girls were spared. He gave his life to save theirs –- an act of heroism a lot bigger than anything we should ever expect from a 15-year-old. "Greater love hath no man than this that a man lay down his life for his friends."

We are not asked to do what Zaevion Dobson did. We're not asked to have shoulders that big; a heart that strong; reactions that quick. I'm not asking people to have that same level of courage, or sacrifice, or love. But if we love our kids and care about their prospects, and if we love this country and care about its future, then we can find the courage to vote. We can find the courage to get mobilized and organized. We can find the courage to cut through all the noise and do what a sensible country would do.

That's what we're doing today. And tomorrow, we should do more. And we should do more the day after that. And if we do, we'll leave behind a nation that's stronger than the one we inherited and worthy of the sacrifice of a young man like Zaevion.

Thank you very much, everybody. God bless you. Thank you. God bless America. ❜

The son of a Kenyan father and teenage anthropology student Anne Dunham, Barack Hussein Obama Jnr was born in Honolulu, Hawaii, in 1961. Obama's parents met at the University of Hawaii, but separated when Barack was just two years old. His mother later married Lolo Soetoro, an Indonesian national, and had another child (a daughter, Maya). Barack Obama attended school in Jakarta until the age of ten before returning to Honolulu to live with his maternal grandparents. His mother returned to Hawaii in 1977 after her second marriage ended, but Obama only met his Kenyan father on one other occasion before Obama Snr was killed in a car accident in 1982. Obama's mother died of ovarian cancer in 1995, at the age of 53.

Barack Obama attended Columbia College in New York City where he majored in political science, before going on to Harvard Law School. He later worked as a civil rights attorney in Chicago before being elected to Illinois State Senate in 1996. After a failed bid for selection as the Democratic nominee for the US House of Representatives in 2000, Obama successfully ran for the US Senate, his profile boosted by his selection to deliver the keynote address to the Democratic National Convention in Boston in 2004. Only the third African American to be popularly elected to Congress, he was elected to the US Senate with a staggering 70% of the vote in his favour.

Obama announced his candidacy for President of the United States on February 10, 2007. After a bitter and hard-fought battle against party favourite, former first lady Hillary Clinton, Obama secured the Democratic nomination in June 2008 and overcame issues of race, religion and his relative youth to secure the US Presidency in November 2008. Among his many achievements in office, Obama saw the US through the 2008 world economic crisis, brought the Iraq war to an end, passed health care reform that resulted in almost universal coverage and steered the country away from an over-reliance on fossil fuels. Throw in America's nuclear agreement with Iran, the normalization of relations with Cuba and the push towards the legalization of same-sex marriage, and even the most casual observer could be forgiven for thinking Obama was the most successful president since Franklin D. Roosevelt.

Although his 2016 goal was to curb gun violence, and was not a government plot to 'take people's guns away' as claimed by Republican presidential candidate Donald Trump and sections of America's conservative media, President Obama's common sense reforms were derided and his tears mocked.

On the night of June 11, 2016, gunman Omar Lateen entered a gay nightclub in Orlando Florida and shot dead 49 patrons, and wounding another 53, using a military-style assault rifle. It was the worst mass shooting ever in US history.

The question haunting America about gun control remains unanswered. If not now, then when?

Sources

Mary Church Terrell–What It Means to Be Colored www.americanrhetoric.com
Theodore Roosevelt–The Man with the Muck-rake http://voicesofdemocracy.umd.edu
Emmeline Pankhurst–Freedom or Death www.thelizlibrary.org
Helen Keller–Against the War http://gos.sbc.edu
Woodrow Wilson–Fourteen Point Peace Plan www.u-s-history.com
Margaret Sanger–The Children's Era www.edchange.org
Mustafa Kemal Atatürk–Message to the Gallipoli Fallen https://www.awm.gov.au
King Edward VIII–Abdication Speech www.historyplace.com
Adolf Hitler–The Jewish Question www.adolfhitler.ws/lib/speeches
Edouard Daladier–The Nazis Aim is Slavery www.curriculumsupport.education.nsw.gov.au
Winston Churchill–We Shall Fight Them on the Beaches www.raf.mod.uk
Franklin D. Roosevelt–A Day That will Live in Infamy www.americanrhetoric.com
M. K. Ghandi–Quit India www.mkgandhi.org
Golda Meir–The Struggle for a Jewish State www.localvoter.com/speech
Margaret Chase Smith–Declaration of Conscience www.senate.gov
Harry S. Truman–MacArthur and Korea http://teachingamericanhistory.org
Douglas MacArthur–Old Soldiers Never Die www.hundredpercenter.com
Dwight D. Eisenhower–Cross of Iron www.ideotrope.org
Fidel Castro–History will Absolve Me www.lanic.utexas
Harold MacMillan–The Winds of Change www.africanhistory.about.com
John F. Kennedy–Cuban Missile Crisis http://legacy.fordham.edu
Martin Luther King Jr–I Have a Dream www.analytictech.com
Lyndon B. Johnson–Let Us Continue http://voicesofdemocracy.umd.edu
Malcolm X–The Bullet or the Ballot www.edchange.org
Robert Kennedy–Announcement of King's Death www.usconstitution.com
Edward Kennedy–Eulogy for Robert Kennedy www.tungate.com
John Kerry–Against the War in Vietnam www.thinkingpeace.com
Richard M. Nixon–Farewell to the White House www.nixonfoundation.org
Gough Whitlam–God Save the Queen www.pandora.nla.gov.au
Anwar El Sadat–Peace with Justice www.ibiblio.org
Indira Ghandi–The Liberation of Women www.international.activism.uts.edu.au
Archbishop Oscar Romero–Stop the Repression www.democraticunderground.com
Margaret Thatcher–The Falklands War www.aphids.com
David Lange–Nuclear Weapons are Indefensible www.cs.auckland.ac.nz
Ronald Reagan–Tear Down This Wall www.reaganfoundation.org

Ann Richards–We Can Do Better www.nytimes.com

Benazir Bhutto–Address to the US Congress http://americansforpakistan.com

Mikhail Gorbachev–The Collapse of the Soviet Union www.publicpurpose.com

Queen Elizabeth II–Annus Horribilis www.worldhistory.com

Nelson Mandela–Release from Prison www.anc.org.za

Hilary Clinton–On Women's Rights www.theremnant.com

Earl Spencer–Eulogy for Diana, Princess of Wales www.ex.ac.uk

Aung San Suu Kyi–Freedom of Thought www.c-span.org

Boris Yeltsin–Yekaterinburg Apology http://news.bbc.co.uk

Elie Weisel–The Perils of Indifference www.pbs.org

George W. Bush–A Great People Has Been Moved http://library.cqpress.com

Steve Jobs–Stanford University Commencement Speech http://news.stanford.edu

Kevin Rudd–Apology to Indigenous Australians http://parlinfo.aph.gov.au

Stephen Hawking–Questioning the Universe https://www.ted.com

Julia Gillard–Misogyny Speech www.smh.com.au

Malala Yousafzai–Worldwide Access to Education https://secure.aworldatschool.org

Pope Francis–Sexual Abuse by the Catholic Church https://ncronline.org

Barack Obama–Gun Control in the USA https://www.whitehouse.gov

This edition published in 2016 by New Holland Publishers Pty Ltd
London • Sydney • Auckland

The Chandlery Unit 704 50 Westminster Bridge Road London SE1 7QY United Kingdom
1/66 Gibbes Street Chatswood NSW 2067 Australia
5/39 Woodside Ave Northcote, Auckland 0627 New Zealand

www.newhollandpublishers.com

A record of this book is held at the British Library and the National Library of Australia.

ISBN: 9781742578880

Managing Director: Fiona Schultz
Designer: Lorena Susak
Production Director: James Mills-Hicks
Printer: Toppan Leefung Printing Ltd

10 9 8 7 6 5 4 3 2 1

Keep up with New Holland Publishers on Facebook
www.facebook.com/NewHollandPublishers